The Internet Publishing Handbook

For World-Wide Web, Gopher, and WAIS

Mike Franks

AF677412

Addison-Wesley Publishing Company
Reading, Massachusetts • Menlo Park, California • New York
Don Mills, Ontario • Wokingham, England • Amsterdam
Bonn • Sydney • Singapore • Tokyo • Madrid • San Juan
Paris • Seoul • Milan • Mexico City • Taipei

Many of the designations used by manufacturers and sellers to distinguish their products are claimed as trademarks. Where those designations appear in this book, and Addison-Wesley was aware of a trademark claim, the designations have been printed in initial capital letters or all capital letters.

The author and publisher have taken care in preparation of this book, but make no expressed or implied warranty of any kind and assume no responsibility for errors or omissions. No liability is assumed for incidental or consequential damages in connection with or arising out of the use of the information or programs contained herein.

Library of Congress Cataloging-in-Publication Data

Franks, Mike.

The Internet publishing handbook : for World-Wide Web, Gopher, and WAIS / Mike Franks.

p. cm.

Includes bibliographical reference (p.349) and index.

ISBN 0-201-48317-3 (pbk.)

1. Internet (Computer network) 2. Gopher servers. 3. World-Wide Web (Information retrieval system) 4. WAIS (Information retrieval system) I. Title.

TK5105.875. I57F769 1995

025.04—dc20 95-30895

CIP

Copyright © 1995 by Mike Franks

All rights reserved. No part of this publication may be reproduced, stored in a retrieval system, or transmitted, in any form or by any means, electronic, mechanical, photocopying, recording, or otherwise, without the prior written permission of the publisher. Printed in the United States of America. Published simultaneously in Canada.

Sponsoring Editor: Claire Horne
Project Editor: Sarah Weaver
Production Coordinator: Erin Sweeney
Cover design: Robert Sweeney
Text design: Greg Johnson, Art Directions
Set in 11.5 point Minion by Greg Johnson, Art Directions

1 2 3 4 5 6 7 8 9 -MA- 9998979695
First printing, October 1995

Addison-Wesley books are available for bulk purchases by corporations, institutions, and other organizations. For more information please contact the Corporate, Government, and Special Sales Department at (800) 238-9682.

Find us on the World-Wide Web at: http://www.aw.com/devpress/

To Riley, Nicholas, and Naomi. I'm a lucky guy.

Courtesy of Mino
Fortaleza, Ceará, BRASIL

Acknowledgments

I'd like to thank Richard Chabran, Phil McAbee, and John Powell for their constant support and encouragement. In addition, I wouldn't have been able to write this book if it wasn't for the advice, assistance, and interesting environment created by my coworkers at UCLA's Social Sciences Computing: G.J. Chen, Mary Johnson, Carlos Tobar, Lily Sun, Eleanor Chan, Michael Hwa, Julie Chen, Wendy Wright, and our past and present directors, Barry Gerber, Professor William Mason, and Tom Phelan. I'd also like to thank Gary Bolles for indirectly getting me started on this project. And, of course, I'd like to thank my parents whose lifelong support and sense of humor made this all possible.

Although any errorz are mine, there would have been a great many more without the help of many people. I'd like to thank Dave Brooks, William Zhang, Michelle Lew, Andy Pho, Karie Masterson, Wayne Miller, George Bing, Gloria Werner, Don Worth, Pieter Lechner, Kent Wada, and Kelly Stack for their assistance and advice. I'd also like to thank all the patient souls who allowed me to interview them by phone, via e-mail, or at crowded conferences. Clifford Lynch contributed greatly to my understanding of Z39.50. Claire Horne, my editor, was always a pleasure to work with. And copy editor Polly Kummel added a great deal of professionalism to my writing and toned down my excesses. I'd also like to thank the production crew: Sarah Weaver, Erin Sweeney, John Webber, and Greg Johnson. Finally, I'd like to thank all those on the Internet who made it possible to learn so much online.

Contents

Introduction

In America, freedom of the press is largely reserved for those who own one.

—A. J. Liebling

This book is for those of you who want to publish on the Internet. I assume that you have browsed the Internet (at least a little) and are now ready to put information of your own on the Internet. This book will provide you with the information you need to set up shop, and it will enable you to reach millions of users who connect to the Internet looking for information, services, and products.

This book will take you through the process of Internet publishing from beginning to end, using examples and advice gathered from Internet publishers around the world. It will bring you up to speed on the issues, techniques, and problems that you will encounter when you join the growing legions of educational institutions, government organizations, manufacturers and retailers, service organizations, large corporations and small businesses, those in the arts and sciences, and others who are tapping in to the Internet to publish information and quickly reach an expanding, worldwide audience, thanks to tools such as Gopher, the World-Wide Web, and the Wide Area Information Server.

As of May 1995 there were more than 30,000 Internet publishing sites: more than 7,000 Gopher servers in at least 47 countries, at least 23,000 World-Wide Web (WWW) servers in 60 countries, and about 137 Wide Area Information Service (WAIS) hosts serving 420 databases (although this ignores the role that WAIS plays behind the scenes at many Gopher and WWW sites). The beauty of publishing on the Internet is that it is just as simple for the user or viewer (the person who reads what you publish) to get information from a site in Hong Kong as it is from the computer down the hall. The computer down the hall may respond faster, but the server in Hong Kong, Rio de Janeiro, or Finland may have special information that you want. And whether you're dealing with customers around the world or around the corner, you can use this system to provide your clients with up-to-date information that can be accessed with only a few keystrokes.

Commercial Services versus the Internet

Are America Online, CompuServe, and Prodigy the same as the Internet?

No, they are commercial online services (or bulletin boards) that charge their users for access by the hour. Large as they are, they are much, much smaller than the Internet. In many ways they are the opposite of the Internet:

INTERNET

- An international collection of interconnected computers and networks
- Independent control of the equipment at each site (be it university, organization, or company)
- A tradition of academic and research activities (noncommercial), with commercial activities in the early stages
- User access to other computers and their services, largely for free, although some commercial databases are becoming available
- A strong tradition of free speech and cooperation between sites
- Access problems, although these are diminishing because of Gopher, WWW, and WAIS
- An audience of 13.5 million users (those who can browse Internet), a figure that has doubled every year for the last six years (according to an October 1994 estimate by Matrix Information and Directory Services of Austin, Texas, online at <*http://www.tic.com/mids/midshome.html*>).

COMMERCIAL ONLINE SERVICES

- Centralized computers limited to the United States (except for CompuServe)
- Central control by each online service

- Fee structures, usually with per minute charges (in addition to the basic monthly fee) for access to popular features
- Competition for users
- Some censorship
- Relative ease of use
- 2.8 million CompuServe subscribers
- 2 million America Online members
- 1 million Prodigy members

The real story is that all three of these commercial online services have begun to connect their users to the Internet, first by allowing e-mail to cross over, next by providing Gopher access, and now by providing their users with access to the Web.

What Is Internet Publishing?

Internet publishing is making material available for viewing on a computer connected to the Internet, so that others on the Internet can browse or search the information at will. It is not restricted to those who publish magazines, newspapers, or books. Information published on the Internet comes in many forms: plain text, formatted text, hypertext (links to other files), pictures, sounds, video, databases, interactive maps, and anything else you can store on a computer. The variety of content and purposes of Gopher, WWW, and WAIS servers demonstrates clearly the diversity of interests and philosophies on the Internet. Until now it was impossible for individuals and organizations to inexpensively and easily publish information all over the world. This new capability has even led some to see the vast expansion of Gopher and Web servers on the Internet as a rebirth of democracy. Although it has not reached the state envisioned by WWW creator Tim Berners-Lee, who believes publishing information should be as easy as browsing it, publishing has become much less expensive and more open to more people and therefore much more democratic.

Internet "publishers" range from the mighty to the small, from IBM to the florist down the street. Many individuals are leaving their mark on the Internet with "home pages" that might give a brief personal description of themselves and even include their children's baby pictures.

The wide variety of methods of publishing on the Internet include FTP servers, **finger daemons** (or programs), Hyper-G, Usenet News, e-mail mailing lists (list servers) and a variety of telephone and e-mail address directory services (see the glossary for definitions of these terms). But Gopher, WWW, and WAIS are our models, because they provide the easiest methods for getting your information on the Net. They are also frequently used in combination with each other. IBM, for example, has both a Gopher and a WWW server to display product information. And a WAIS server often provides the searching mechanism, hidden behind Gopher and WWW.

What You Should Get from This Book

I want you to come away from this book with three things:

- Excitement about the possibilities and prospects of publishing on the Internet
- Familiarity with the issues and choices involved
- Knowledge of where to go on the Internet to continue your education

Connecting to the Internet

This book assumes that you have already browsed the Internet to a certain extent. But if you haven't, here are some ways to start. In Chapter 2 I'll talk more about the kind of Internet access you'll need for running Gopher, WWW, and WAIS servers and Internet publishing.

Your Internet access options will vary considerably depending on whether you are affiliated with a college or university, or whether your company or organization pays for Internet access or you have to pay for it entirely on your own. Generally, universities and colleges offer greatly subsidized Internet access to their students and faculty, because the Internet has long been primarily a research resource.

There are two kinds of home access, which can be simplified as text-only and graphical. Text-only can be accomplished with old PCs and 2,400-baud (slow) modems and a dial-up connection to an Internet service provider (ISP). Graphical Internet access usually requires a Macintosh or Windows-capable PC, a 14,400-baud modem, and either a SLIP or PPP connection to an Internet service provider. This usually costs more but can still be found in metropolitan areas for $20 to $30 per month. Where possible you'll want graphical access, but don't despair if that's out of your reach for now. Gopher, WWW, and WAIS are almost completely accessible via text-only browsers.

Finding an Internet Service Provider

To figure out what your options are for gaining access to the Internet:

- Check with any educational institution with which you are affiliated. This includes elementary and high schools. In the United States more and more schools are starting to offer at least limited Internet access, sometimes through special machines in libraries or computer labs. Ask if it is possible to dial in from home.
- Check with your employer. Be sure you are aware of any restrictions the business may place on that access. Check for dial-in access as well.
- Ask friends and acquaintances if they know anyone who has Internet access and get information from them.
- Check for the existence of a FreeNet in your area. This is the movement to offer free Internet access by geographical area.
- Look in the Yellow Pages for Internet service providers and be sure to call all of them because rates and services vary widely. Where possible you want to avoid paying by the hour.
- Read the ads in local computer magazines (the kind that are given away at computer stores) for local and national ISPs.
- Check for local computer bulletin boards that also offer Internet access. This is a growing field.
- Check out such products as Internet-in-a-Box, OS/2, and others that offer the software to automatically connect you to national ISPs.

- Check with commercial online services to see what Internet access they offer. In this case you're paying for much more than just the Internet access, but you may find you enjoy those aspects as well. Prodigy, America Online, CompuServe, and others all offer some form of Internet access and plan to expand this service.

Remember that these methods are designed to get you inexpensive Internet access for browsing the Internet. That is a much less expensive option than the 24-hour dedicated connection you will require when you start publishing on the Internet.

How Best to Read This Book

All the fun stuff is in Chapter 10. That is where you'll find example after example of different kinds of publishing on the Internet. Look there for ideas, but remember it is only a small sampling of what is on the Internet. Whenever you get bored or confused, go to Chapter 10 or browse the Internet some more to renew your enthusiasm.

Second, this book is written for several types of readers. If you find material that you think is too technical, skip it and move ahead. Look for a key sentence or two in those sections so you can see what the important point is. Later, after you have read and browsed the Internet some more and have begun to actually set up your server, review these sections because they are likely to make more sense to you. If they don't, write and tell me what you didn't understand so I can make the next edition better.

Third, *follow the links.* This book is not a step-by-step guide. In almost every section I refer you to sites on the Internet, known as links or URLs (Uniform Resource Locators), for more detailed information. The URLs are scattered throughout this book like footnotes out to the Internet. You can follow these links and see what they have to say if you have a program for browsing the World-Wide Web (such as Mosaic, Netscape, or Lynx). They appear in italics at the ends of sentences and paragraphs, and look like this: <***http://sunsite.unc.edu/usenet-b/home.html***>. Things are changing so fast that you should get in the habit of checking the Internet regularly.

Pay particular attention to the resource tables in most chapters. They include books, magazines, Internet sites, mailing lists, and Usenet newsgroups (described in Chapter 2) that are particularly useful in keeping up to date. Prices are given in U.S. dollars.

What If a Link Doesn't Work?

Although I've done the best I can to make sure that all the links are correct and in working order, the Internet is constantly changing, so you may find that some links don't work. If that happens, try again later to make sure that it wasn't just busy when you tried it. Then try shortening the link, removing words one by one from the right end to get somewhere on the site. Once you've made some connection, look around for links that will get you what you want. Finally, if it's been changed completely, do a search on that subject through one of the Internet indexers listed in Table 2-1. You will almost always find related information that way, even if you don't find the original site, which may have gone out of existence.

Quick Vocabulary Lesson

Several words and concepts with which you may already be familiar are basic to understanding the Web and the Internet, so let's review them briefly:

Client/servers are tools, such as **Gopher**, **WWW**, and **WAIS** (pronounced *ways*), for accessing the Internet through one computer. A **server** offers information or a connection to other computers, called **clients** (or browsers). The program that you run on your computer to do the searching and browsing is the client program; the computers with the information (Gopher, WWW, and WAIS) are the servers. The client and server can also be separate programs running on the same machine.

Browsers are the client half of the client/server relationship on the Internet. Browsers are programs that people run to search out information on the Internet. Browsers enable you to explore the Internet, because they know how to "talk" to computers that act as information servers on the Internet. Browsers should not be confused with the servers to which they connect you. For example, NCSA Mosaic is a well-known WWW browser. Other WWW browsers include Lynx, Arena, Netscape, and many more. Gopher browsers include TurboGopher, WSGopher, HGopher, and Minuet. Browsers are only half of the Internet equation.

Servers are the other half of the Internet equation. They provide the information that client programs read. Servers come in different types: Gopher, WWW, WAIS, and many others. Basically, servers wait for clients to request information. Then they send the information if they have it.

Organization of the Book

Chapter 1, Overview of Internet Publishing, WWW, Gopher, and WAIS, takes you through the last few years on the Internet and shows how Gopher, WWW, and WAIS were developed (and what problems they solved).

Chapter 2, Groundwork, gets down to business; it deals with all the steps that you must take, no matter which system or systems you decide to use. It will make you start to think about the issues and decisions you will have to face, as well as the planning, administration, and resources that publishing on the Internet requires.

Chapter 3, Gopher and Gopher+, describes exactly what these servers allow you to do. Among the advantages detailed in this chapter is the relative simplicity of using Gopher.

Chapter 4, World-Wide Web (more properly known as the HyperText Transfer Protocol or HTTP), describes the servers that are among the fastest-growing on the Internet. This chapter describes different versions and their relative advantages. The chapter also reviews the steps involved in setting up a server, learning to write and design HyperText Markup Language (HTML) documents (the basic text of WWW servers), and announcing, advertising, and indexing your server. The chapter describes text conversion utilities and HTML editors, as well as approaches to hypertext layout and maintenance.

Chapter 5, WAIS and Indexing Alternatives, describes the extremely powerful searching capabilities behind many Gopher and WWW servers. This chapter describes various implementations (for example, FreeWAIS and WAIS Inc.) and techniques for data filtering (identifying the parts of your data files so that WAIS can index them correctly).

Chapter 6, Other Tools of the Trade, describes the use of Finger, CSOs, White Pages, Usenet News, MOOs, and Hyper-G for publishing on the Internet. These tools, often used in conjunction with Gopher, WWW, and WAIS, can provide exactly the right mix of service and flexibility.

Chapter 7, Internet Commerce, explores the developing security and charging techniques used today or in development, and Chapter 8, Hiring Out the Work, offers options if you don't have the appropriate Internet connection or computer equipment or just don't want to manage a Gopher, WWW, or WAIS information server yourself.

Chapter 9, Copyright, addresses some different aspects of publishing in this new medium including copyright and legal issues.

Chapter 10, Putting It All Together, offers case histories and interviews that show some of the creative ways people are putting information on the Internet.

The final chapter, Chapter 11, The Future of Internet Publishing, looks to the future of Gopher, WWW, and WAIS and discusses the likely resolutions of such Internet issues as network overloading, electronic money and digital signatures, document authentication, and implications for political and social issues.

The appendixes include a bibliography and a glossary, which you should check out sooner rather than later. Links to every example site or resource mentioned in the book can be found on the Internet in the Addison-Wesley Web Server, <***http://www.aw.com/devpress/***>.

Notes on Writing This Book

As you may already know from browsing the Internet, it is a constantly changing landscape that is growing at a breakneck pace. For me the excitement has been in finding that everything has changed since the last time I checked. Happily, it's now possible to surf the Internet while I'm composing this literary masterpiece. Unhappily, it is far too easy to get distracted by new sites or by new information at old ones. So although I've done my best to capture the essence of what Internet publishing is all about, I'm afraid that some material may seem dated because the details change so quickly. I've tried to give you information and perspective that will be useful no matter what software or hardware you use.

Wherever possible throughout the book I included the names of the individuals who have written programs, run sites, or have contributed to the Internet in some way. I did this for two reasons. First, because the Internet is a community of sorts, it is helpful to know the people who make up the community. You'll see their names in e-mail and on newsgroups as you wander about the Internet. It is truly possible to make your reputation on the Internet in this way (for good or ill). Second, I wanted to include names as a way to thank those who've contributed so much to the Internet. Often their contribution is entirely voluntary, and it is this spirit—more than cables or wiring—that truly makes the Internet the fascinating entity that it is.

The Internet is an unusually chaotic, active area with hundreds, if not thousands, of communities springing up around an idea, program, or controversy. Like any community, it has its rules or accepted ways of doing things, but unlike many communities the Internet is extremely open to change. New information servers are greeted with delight and a great deal of interest, and you may find unexpected rewards once you start publishing on the Internet. I'd like to take this opportunity to encourage you to be as creative as you can and not to hesitate to put your, or your organization's, personality into your work. Above all, the Internet is about the exchange of ideas, so don't hide yours.

CHAPTER 1

Overview of Internet Publishing, WWW, Gopher, and WAIS

Imagine you are a florist and you can ship anywhere in the world. Why not advertise your flowers on the Internet? This is what Jennings Florists in Victoria, British Columbia is doing, with full-color pictures of its most popular gift baskets and flower arrangements. The only link you need to reach the Jennings Florists catalog on the World-Wide Web (see Figure 1–1) is called a **URL**, or **Uniform Resource Locator** <*http://www.islandnet.com/Jennings Florists/*>. Links such as this one appear throughout the book. They'll appear in italics after I've mentioned a particular site or resource. You'll learn how to read them later in this chapter.

Or suppose you love tennis, and you want to collect and make available tennis news, equipment tips, and player information and set up an Internet tennis specialty shop. This is exactly what Tenagra Corporation decided to do; their WWW Tennis Server includes articles and links to tennis information throughout the Internet. <*http://www.tennisserver.com/*>

Or suppose your company sells computer software or hardware, and your phone lines are constantly busy with help questions and requests for the latest updates or pricing schedules. Many top high-tech companies, including Sun Microsystems, IBM, Microsoft, and Novell, post technical notes, price lists, and even software upgrades on the Internet that their users can download immediately (see Figures 1–2 and 1–3). Imagine the public relations benefit, if nothing else.

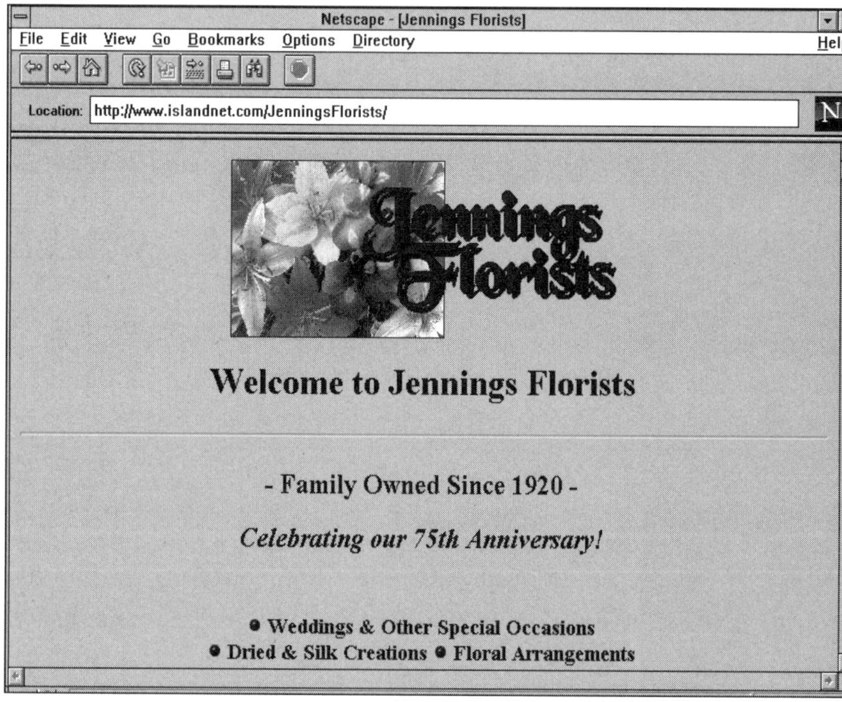

FIGURE 1–1 Jennings Florists Web Site (Reprinted with permission.)

<***http://www.sun.com/***>

<***http://www.ibm.com/***>

<***http://www.microsoft.com/***>

<***http://www.novell.com/***>

Or say you're a real estate broker, and you'd like to advertise your properties more widely. A company called Coolware has set up a site at which it is soliciting realtors and home owners to list real estate for sale. See Figure 1–4 for the sample of listings it has posted for the City of Palo Alto, California. <***http://none.coolware.com/real/realestate.html***>

And the *Encyclopaedia Britannica* is starting to provide the full text of all its volumes across the Internet (see Figure 1–5) for a fee. The company is marketing the service to colleges and universities but

FIGURE 1–2 Sun Microsystems Web Site (Reprinted with permission.)

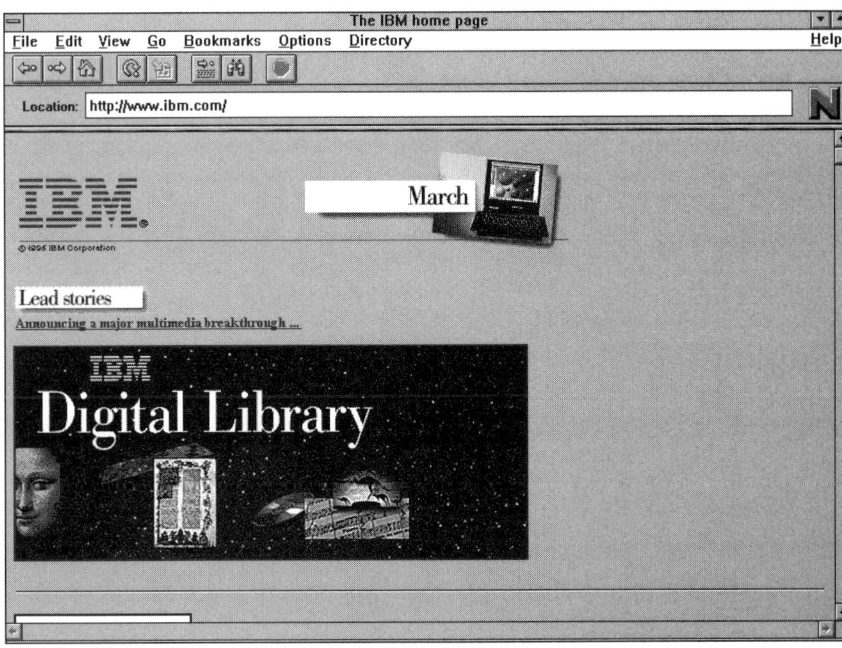

FIGURE 1–3 IBM Web Site (Reprinted with permission from International Business Machines Corporation.)

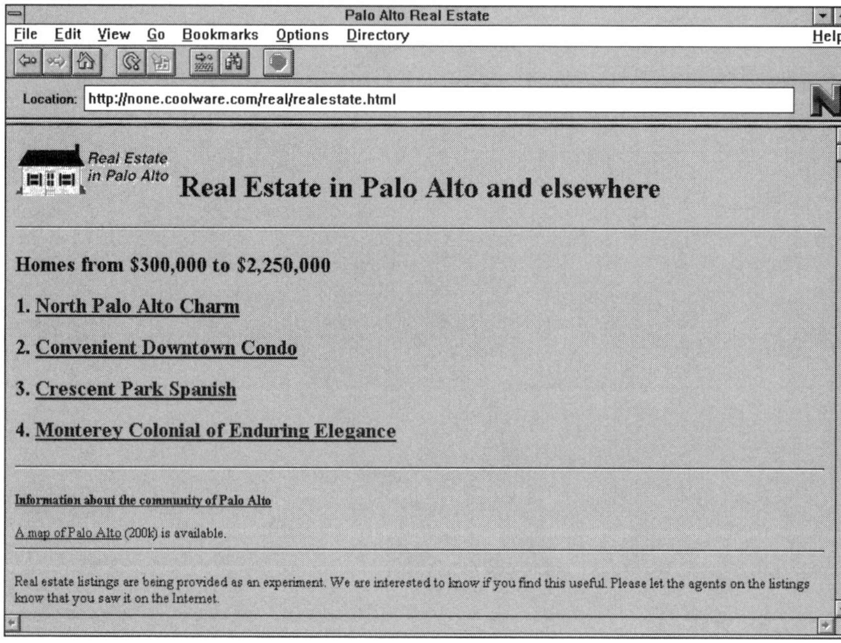

FIGURE 1–4 Palo Alto Real Estate Web Site (Reprinted with permission.)

plans to make it inexpensive enough that individuals will subscribe. *<http://www.eb.com/>*

As you can see, it's a new world in publishing. *Publishing* is defined here as making information publicly available for personal, educational, organizational, or commercial purposes. No longer do you have to spend millions of dollars to reach millions of people. You don't even have to have a computer if you want to hire someone to publish on the Internet for you. And many services offer space for WWW pages for as little as $15 per month.

Publishing on the Internet simply means putting information on one computer where it can be seen by others on the Internet. You might put stories, articles, poems, pictures, or music on the Internet. You can sell what you publish or give it away. Although the commercial and marketing possibilities are creating enormous interest, the bulk of what is published today on the Internet is available for free. Companies are finding that traditional advertising techniques don't

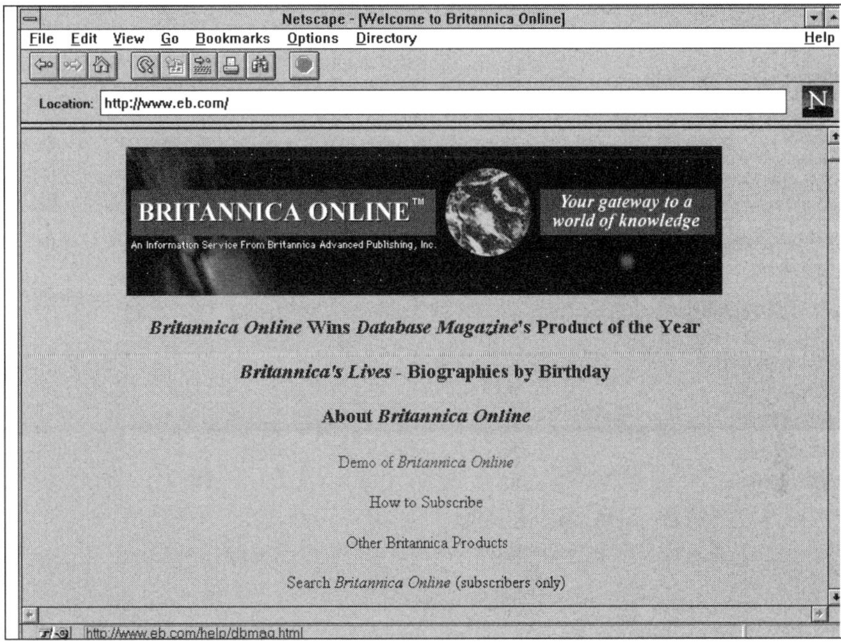

FIGURE 1–5 Britannica Online Web Site (Reprinted with permission.)

transfer well to the Internet; instead they are supplying detailed information and participating in technical forums in which their products are discussed.

A Quick History of Internet Publishing Techniques

Publishing on the Internet basically consists of making computer files available on one computer, usually called a server, and allowing others to view or download them via other computers, usually called clients. Finding and looking at these files always involves several steps:

1. Find the computer site with the file(s) you want.
2. Login to that computer.
3. Find the file(s).
4. Transfer the file(s).

5. Disconnect.
6. Look at the file(s) on your own system.

Programmers and computer technical administrators have used this procedure for many years. Now Gopher, WWW, and WAIS make this process incredibly easy and much more efficient for everyone else. In fact, Gopher, WWW, and WAIS take very similar steps behind the scenes as you browse the Internet, blissfully oblivious to the details.

File Transfer Protocol (FTP)

File Transfer Protocol, or **FTP**, is the original method of using the Internet to transfer files between different computer systems. FTP is available on many systems and allows you to reach out from one computer to another and retrieve files. FTP requires that you know the name of the computer to which you wish to connect and have a login ID and password for that computer. Friends or colleagues who have the passwords to each other's accounts can use FTP. Or you can set a computer up for anonymous use.

For years **anonymous FTP** was the method of choice for publishing on the Internet. Anonymous FTP (a term that's used as a noun and a verb on the Internet) does not require the client to have an ID for the publishing computer in order to connect and download files. Users login with the ID *anonymous* and usually are asked to give their e-mail address as a password. Even this is sometimes not required. Figure 1–6 is a sample FTP session that shows how complicated it can get.

Anonymous FTP allowed true publishing to occur on the Internet, because once you made your information available via anonymous FTP, anyone on the Internet could download it. This method proved so popular among the programmers and technical people (most Internet users in those days) that thousands of FTP sites (computers with files available for anonymous FTP downloads) sprang up over the years. A wealth of software, text files, and other information was scattered among thousands of computers. The problem was finding

FIGURE 1–6 Sample FTP Session

```
ftp somewhere.com
Connected to somewhere.com.
220 somewhere.com FTP server (Sun Aug 14 14:49:48 EDT 1994)
ready.
Name (somewhere.com:franks): anonymous
331 Guest login ok, send your e-mail address as password.
Password:
230 Guest login ok, access restrictions apply.
ftp> cd directory/that/has/your/file
250 CWD command successful.
ftp> binary
200 Type set to I.
ftp> get filename.zip
200 PORT command successful.
150 Opening BINARY mode data connection for filename.zip.
226 Transfer complete.
local: filename.zip remote: filename.zip
140398 bytes received in 7 seconds (20 Kbytes/s)
ftp>
ftp> quit
221 Goodbye.
```

User types what is in **bold text**.

The password doesn't show up when typed. For **anonymous FTP**, your e-mail address is the password.

Users have to change to the directory that contains the file they want.

Binary means transfer file as is. ASCII is the alternative, but it is for text files only.

The transfer rate will vary considerably depending on the links between you and the FTP site.

the site that had what you wanted and then locating the information in the thousands of files that might be stored on that same computer.

Archie—Indexing FTP Sites

In 1990 Peter Deutsch and Alan Emtage, grad students at McGill University in Canada, came up with **Archie**, an interesting approach to solving this problem. (The name *Archie* actually derives from the word *archives*. When similar programs were created later, their authors used characters in the Archie comic books to name them. Veronica is actually an acronym for Very Easy Rodent-Oriented

Net-wide Index to Computer Archives, *rodent* being a reference to the Gopher servers for Veronica indexes. Jughead, another character, is short for Jonzy's Universal Gopher Hierarchy Excavation and Display.) Deutsch and Emtage set up one computer to connect automatically to a certain number of FTP servers every night and download their directory structures and indexes. They added these indexes to a database and then would allow anyone on the Internet to connect to their machine and run a search program. The search program allowed the user to search by file name and would return all the occurrences of a particular file name, complete with date, directory path, and FTP site address. The Archie program could also e-mail the results to you. Clearly, this was a tremendous service to the Internet community and, as great ideas often do, it spread quickly. Refer to Figure 1–7 for a sample Archie search for the file list.com (an excellent DOS file lister from shareware author Vernon Buerg).

Although Archie allowed users to quickly find the FTP sites with the most recent copies of particular files, it wasn't especially user

FIGURE 1–7 Results of Archie Search for *list.com*

Note that the directories often tell you something about the program. For example, this one looks like it runs on a DEC VMS operating system.

```
Host nic.switch.ch
    Location: /mirror/vms/DECUS/vms92b/analy/pccsmg
          FILE -rw-rw-r–      3993  Mar 12 1991  list.com
Host nisca.acs.ohio-state.edu
    Location: /pub/training
          FILE -rw-r–r–       18355  Jan 10 1991  list.com
Host nic.switch.ch
    Location: /mirror/vms/DECUS/vms92b/juicer
          FILE -rw-rw-r–      206  Feb 18 1988  list.com
Host oak.oakland.edu
    Location: /pub2/sigm/vol228
          FILE -rw-r–r–       2816  Feb 10 1986  list.com
    Location: /pub2/cpm/list
          FILE -rw-r–r–       1024  Feb  9 1985  list.com
```

FTP sites that show **list.com**.

Different dates may signal the existence of a more recent version of the file.

friendly. While connected to an FTP site, you could make your way through the various directories by typing in the appropriate change directory (or cd) command, but you couldn't view a file to determine whether it contained what you were looking for. For that, you first needed to use the FTP get command, download it, and then look at it on your own machine. <***http://services.bunyip.com:8000/products/archie/archie.html***>

Gopher and Gopher+

In 1991 the University of Minnesota made all this easier. In attempting to make information available campuswide, a small team of programmers led by Mark McCahill designed the Gopher protocol. This major innovation in Internet usability embodied several simple ideas:

- A simple interface that novice users could use without training
- Minimal bandwidth requirements so the network wouldn't be overloaded
- Short connections between the client and server programs so the server could quickly handle a client's request and move on to the next
- "Stateless" connections (no memory of previous contacts) between client and server, so the server wouldn't have to remember what stage each client was at
- Access to such popular Internet services as FTP, Usenet News, and telnet

This approach resulted in a menulike system that allows users either to see the contents of a file or to follow a link to other menus or files on another system. Thus was born the ability to "browse" the Internet, because Gopher allows you to read the text files you come across and, depending on your computer, to view pictures or hear sound embedded in the files you select. Gopher makes moving through directories and downloading programs much simpler than they are through FTP. See Figure 1–8 for a sample Gopher screen.

FIGURE 1–8 Sample Gopher Menu Screen

```
Internet Gopher Information Client v2.0.16
                     Home Gopher server: gopher.sscnet.ucla.edu

       1. Welcome to the UCLA Social Sciences Computing (SSCnet) Gopher
       2. Employment Listings/
       3. Info UCLA - UCLA's Gopher Server/
       4. Internet: Learning About/
       5. Internet: Notable Sites and Resources/
       6. Internet: Searching/
       7. SSCnet/
       8. Social Science Resources/
       9. UCLA Anthropology Department/
       10. UCLA Chicano Studies Research Center/
       11. UCLA Economics Department/
       12. UCLA Geography Department/
       13. UCLA History Department/
       14. UCLA ISSR Data Archives/
       15. UCLA Political Science Department/
       16. UCLA Sociology Department/
       17. WWW Browser for VT100 terminals (via Lynx) <TEL>

Press ? for Help, q to Quit                                Page: 1/1
```

Each line shows a different menu item available on this Gopher server.

Note that this is a text mode Gopher client. Graphical mode Gopher clients see the same Gopher menu.

The success of Gopher's simple interface led to explosive growth in the number of Gopher servers in the United States and then around the world. And it led to extensions of the original Gopher protocol to allow for such things as electronic forms, abstracts, alternate data formats, or views, and the ability to store **meta-information** (or behind-the-scenes information) about the files (such as modification date, file size, language, and administrator of the file). These changes are incorporated in the Gopher+ protocol, which has increased the capabilities of the Gopher system. Unfortunately, not all Gopher client programs have been updated to work with Gopher+. See Chapter 2 for more information on Gopher and Gopher+.

A Word About Protocols

Protocols underlie everything done on the Internet, so it's worth taking a moment to be sure you understand them. A **protocol** is basically an agreement that certain parts of a system, usually different computers, will behave in certain ways in order to exchange information. A common protocol would be a **client/server** model, by which the **client** computer sends requests formatted in certain ways to a **server** computer, which then responds with the answer, also formatted in a specified way.

Generally, the user has no need to know the details of the protocol, but it's often useful to understand what's going on behind the scenes.

In addition to Gopher and Gopher+, common protocols on the Internet include

- **SMTP**—Simple Mail Transfer Protocol for exchanging e-mail among different systems
- **NNTP**—Network News Transport Protocol, which enables megabytes of Usenet News to be distributed around the Internet every day
- **HTTP**—HyperText Transfer Protocol, the basis for World-Wide Web communications between Web (HTTP) servers and Web browsers (or viewing programs)
- **HTML**—HyperText Markup Language, which is a simple set of codes for creating hypertext documents with embedded images and links to other documents

Veronica—Indexing Gopher Sites

The hundreds, then thousands, of Gopher servers springing up created the need to be able to find specific items among all the Gopher sites. Now the University of Nevada at Reno (UNR) got its chance to contribute to the quest for easy Net access. There, Steven Foster of UNR applied the Archie model to **Gopherspace**, the collection of all items in all Gopher servers in the world, and called it **Veronica**. That is, he set up a computer to connect to all the registered Gopher servers and directed it to follow their menus, collecting menu and file names as it went. The compilation was searchable, and what was especially nice was that the results showed up as one or more Gopher menus, which the user could follow directly to the files or Gopher servers themselves. As the obvious utility of this system became known, universities around the world began running Veronica servers, which soon forced each to introduce its offerings with an opening screen that allows the user to select a server and type of search to use. See Figure 1–9 for an example of the selection screen and Figure 1–10 for the results of a search on the word *Gambia.*

FIGURE 1–9 Veronica Search—Selecting Servers

```
Internet Gopher Information Client v2.0.16
      Veronica search (UNR) of much of GopherSpace
--> 1. How to Compose Veronica Queries - June 23, 1994
    2. Frequently-Asked Questions (FAQ) about Veronica - July 29, 1994
    3. About Veronica:  Documents, Software, Index-Control Protocol/
    4. Experimental Veronica Query Interface:  Chooses Server for You!/
    5. Search GopherSpace by Title word(s) (via NYSERNet) <?>
    6. Search GopherSpace by Title word(s) (via University of Pisa) <?>
    7. Search GopherSpace by Title word(s) (via U. of Manitoba) <?>
    8. Search GopherSpace by Title word(s) (via SUNET) <?>
    9. Search GopherSpace by Title word(s) (via University of Koeln) <?>
    10. Search GopherSpace by Title word(s) (via UNINETT/U. of Bergen) <?>
    11. Find ONLY DIRECTORIES by Title word(s) (via NYSERNet) <?>
    12. Find ONLY DIRECTORIES by Title word(s) (via University of Pisa) <?>
    13. Find ONLY DIRECTORIES by Title word(s) (via U. of Manitoba) <?>
    14. Find ONLY DIRECTORIES by Title word(s) (via SUNET) <?>
    15. Find ONLY DIRECTORIES by Title word(s)(via University of Koeln) <?>
    16. Find ONLY DIRECTORIES by Title word(s)(via UNINETT... of Bergen) <?>

Press ? for Help, q to Quit, u to go up a menu                Page: 1/1
```

FIGURE 1–10 Results of Veronica Search for *Gambia*

```
Veronica: Search ALL GopherSpace by specifying word(s) in Titles: gambia
--> 1. *** Results provided by Veronica server at University of Koeln:
    2. Radio Gambia newsman at WBFO for training program
    3. ALL:  NEW TRAVEL INFO — Gambia
    4. GAMBIA SITUATION (L ONLY) By KIRK TROY/ABIDJAN
    5. The Gambia
    6. gambia
    7. Gambia
    8. GAMBIA and Intl. Marine Science
    9. the_gambia_communications.01
    10. Rosevear, D.R. (1937)  "Forest Conditions of the Gambia." Empire
    11. Background Notes - GAMBIA
    12. Gambia.GIF <Picture>
    13. GAMBIA / COUP / SUNDAY (L-ONLY) By KIRK TROY/ABIDJAN
    14. Key Officers for GAMBIA
    15. IFAD_loan_to_Gambia
    16. Fin.&Sub-sect. Framewk. Gambia
    17. NEW TRAVEL INFO — Gambia
    18. the_gambia_people.01

Press ? for Help, q to Quit, u to go up a menu                Page: 1/8
```

Note that this is only one of eight screens of search results.

The dynamic nature of this database meant that you could do a Veronica search one day and find three matches and then the next day do the same search and find 10 or 12 more, depending on what had been added. Suddenly, Gopher became much more powerful—instead of working your way through menu after menu, you could connect to a Veronica server and search all the menus and files with a specific word or phrase that might appear in their titles. Searching their contents was another matter. For that you needed something like WAIS.

Wide Area Information Server (WAIS)

WAIS (pronounced *ways*), started in 1988, was an experimental project designed to come up with easier ways to search Internet files for content. The team was headed by Brewster Kahle, then of Thinking Machines Corporation (a producer of parallel-processing computers), in cooperation with Apple Computer, Dow Jones, and KPMG Peat Marwick. The goal was to create a way to easily search large amounts of text, images, or other files scattered among different computers.

Based on the ANSI standard search-and-retrieval protocol **Z39.50**, then under development, WAIS allows users to type in a question in their natural language—it does not force the user to learn and use a particular computer language or syntax. The WAIS protocol then does the dirty work of translating the query into a WAIS computer language query format and sends it off to various WAIS servers on the Internet. The servers in turn search their full-text indexes and return to the user a list of hits, or matches, ranked by how well they match the original query. When the user selects a hit, the WAIS server retrieves the document that matches.

The companies that had formed the development team made the details and program source code for WAIS publicly available because they realized that WAIS would be much more useful—and have a shot at becoming an industry standard—if it were commonly accepted and used by others across the Internet.

Although WAIS as a front end, or client, hasn't caught on nearly as well as Gopher or WWW, it has become the search mechanism of choice, running in the background of other front-end systems.

World-Wide Web (WWW)

The World-Wide Web was invented by Tim Berners-Lee in 1989 in an attempt to efficiently store research data at CERN, the European Particle Physics Laboratory in Geneva, Switzerland. Berners-Lee, a consultant with a background in text-processing software development, wanted a system that would make it easy for various researchers to build up separate bodies of information and then link them electronically by matching the real links in the information (such as going from a file about horses to more specific files about thoroughbreds, quarter horses, or Olympic three-day eventing). He based the system on the concept of **hypertext**, or text with links that can be followed electronically to other documents, files, sounds, images, or even programs. The WWW system allows hypertext to link files on different computer systems. The main advantages, or power, of hypertext lie in its ability to link different pieces of information in simple ways, at exactly the spot at which you thought of the connection. In a way, hypertext links are like footnotes, except that they are easier to follow and can be of any length. For example, if this page were hypertext, it could have links to the history of hypertext, examples of hypertext, and even a video of someone discussing hypertext. This can be distracting if you want to just read from beginning to end with no detours. But the beauty of hypertext is that no one forces you to follow all the links. You follow what interests you and ignore the rest.

The World-Wide Web system is known by various names. WWW, W3, and Web are intuitive, but because it uses the HyperText Transfer Protocol (HTTP) and HyperText Markup Language (HTML), the servers are technically called *HTTP servers.* Although we'll refer to them as Web or *WWW servers,* you will often see *HTTP servers* used in technical documentation.

One important contribution of WWW was the **Uniform Resource Locator (URL)**. This address system allows you to declare the name and port number (a **port** is like a doorway, or loading dock, of a computer) of the host computer, the protocol (type of connection, such as FTP, Gopher, and so on), and the directory path and file name, all on one line. URLs have become a convenient method of passing a link on to some data source on the Internet. Net users made it common practice to include a URL for their **home page** (a personal spot on the Web) at the end of their e-mail messages. In fact, the URL system has been incorporated in the Gopher server software put out by the University of Minnesota.

The other main innovation of WWW was **HTML**, or **HyperText Markup Language**. Briefly (Chapter 4 goes into more depth), HTML is a relatively simple set of codes that turns ordinary text into hypertext when viewed by a WWW browser. The beauty of the system is that it need not be viewed on the same system that created it. In other words, an HTML file created on a Macintosh will look pretty much the same when viewed on a PC or a UNIX workstation. And what is more important, all the links function in exactly the same way. The ability to move a single file between different types of computer systems and have it work the same way in all of them is called **portability**, an essential ingredient when you want the whole world to use something.

Although WWW was seeing some success—the number of servers was increasing steadily—the creation of a WWW browser called Mosaic by the National Center for Supercomputing Applications (NCSA) in Champaign-Urbana, Illinois, led to an explosion of interest in WWW. This program, which was being given away free, was created first for X-Windows on UNIX and soon after for Macintosh and PCs running Microsoft Windows. Often called the killer application of the Internet, Mosaic made the Internet sexy by adding support for graphics. Gopher was nice and easy to use, but Mosaic was fun and much more impressive in what it could display, mostly because publishers could interweave text and images in documents to create the equivalent of a glossy brochure distributed on the Internet. Among the more popular early demonstrations of WWW was a tour of the Krannert Art Museum at the University of Illinois. Gopher could provide the same information but as menus, and the user could look at one element at a time but not the whole thing. That is, with Gopher you keep coming back to a menu from which you choose a text file, an image file, or a sound file. With WWW you can look at text and images together—perhaps several images side by side and surrounded by text.

This difference has a big effect on the visual effects of a document browsed on the Internet. Imagine being able to use buttons or links from the colorful WWW page that activate sound files or run movie files that start as soon as you select that button. This capability wows the user but puts a different load on the network and requires more sophisticated equipment. Gopher was designed for use by slow, relatively old computers, with no large drain on network resources. But WWW and Mosaic were designed in high-intensity computing environments, in which all participants had fast Internet connections and sophisticated workstations (although they will work on a 386 PC running Windows with a 14,400-baud modem).

When you start publishing on the Internet, it is good to remember that many people who want access to your information may in fact have slow Internet connections and not very powerful computers. If your company's home page takes 10 minutes to download and can only be appreciated on a top-of-the-line workstation, you may not get the audience you want. The reality of WWW is that graphic presentations are more attractive and exciting than plain text, but people won't see them if it takes five minutes or more for those images to appear on their screens. Your images won't slow down text-only Web browsers like Lynx (because Lynx simply ignores them), but those using text-mode browsers won't see and enjoy your images.

Summary

Internet publishing consists of posting or putting material on the Internet where it can be viewed or downloaded from other computers. This process has evolved both in the user interface and in the tools that have been built to enable people to find them.

We've covered a lot of ground in this chapter, so let's review the terms—you're going to need them to understand the rest of this book:

- **FTP** (File Transfer Protocol) is a tried-and-true method for transferring files, but users have to know which computer has the directory and file they want, and the process is confusing to the novice.

- **Archie** is a program that actively goes out and indexes all the known anonymous FTP servers and makes that information freely available via the Archie client program.
- **Gopher** presents menus that lead to files that you can view easily, as well as **links** to other servers. The links are easy for the novice to follow, but with thousands of Gopher servers all over the world, finding what you want is often a problem.
- **Veronica** does for Gopher servers what Archie did for FTP sites. It goes out and indexes all the known Gopher servers and provides a simple method for searching that index. The results then appear as more Gopher menus.
- **WAIS** creates indexes of the full text of files, which it then allows you to search by writing a simple query in natural language. It then applies that query to a collection of full-text indexes, supplying you with a list of those documents that most closely match. You can narrow your search by repeating the process. For example, a search on *wine* might list hundreds of documents that you can then narrow down to those wines from California or Chile or France.
- **WWW** presents hypertext, with links and images embedded in the text. This creates a powerful visual effect. Unfortunately, it does not lend itself to Veronica or Archie searches, although new indexing methods are being developed with a great deal of success. It is usually best to use a computer with fast Internet connections to browse WWW servers.

Three of the most popular publishing protocols are Gopher, World-Wide Web (WWW), and Wide Area Information Server (WAIS). They are three different protocols, or techniques for doing basically the same thing—locating a computer that has something you want, connecting to it, finding the file you're interested in, and then downloading or viewing it. Each consists of computers that act as **servers**, which wait for requests from other computers (**clients**), and then send the files you request back over the Internet. Internet publishers build servers. Internet browsers and surfers use clients.

CHAPTER 2

Groundwork

This chapter discusses the groundwork you'll need to do and some of the steps involved in publishing on the Internet. Take a look at the list in the sidebar on page 20, and then we'll go through the steps one by one. Later, in Chapters 3, 4, and 5 on Gopher, WWW, and WAIS, we'll go through these steps in detail for each type of Internet server and use examples. You need not go through all these steps now, and they are not meant to scare you off or make the process seem intimidating. Instead, they are meant as a guideline or sort of check list for you to use to keep track of all the various elements involved.

Joining the Internet Community

Think of the Internet as a place to which you are moving and that you want to fit into. It is a community with its own set of traditions and values. And as in any community (in this case a tremendously large community), smaller groups gather to discuss different issues. Your first job is to join the Internet community in the sense of learning how to make your way around and how to fit in. On the Internet you'll find a community of individuals, companies, and organizations that are discussing issues, modifying software, and creating new tools and techniques for publishing on the Internet, as well as publishing the most amazing variety of information. Keeping abreast of their activities through Usenet newsgroups and e-mail mailing lists and tracking the relevant subjects through Gopher and WWW

Steps in Internet Publishing

EXPLORATION

- Join the Internet community.
- Identify your competition.

PRODUCT PLANNING

- Define your goals.
- Identify your audience.
- Identify your data.

ANALYSIS

- Identify your needs (hardware, network connection, software, and staff).
- Identify the resources available.
- Determine how to make up the difference in resource needs and availability.
- Identify charging mechanisms, if any.
- Identify the security risks.
- Estimate your costs.

MECHANICS

- Plan your presentation.
- Prepare your data.
- Index your data and server.

IMPLEMENTATION

- Register or publicize your server with appropriate indexes or online catalogs.
- Maintain reliability of server, links, and data.
- Evaluate your server's performance and your audience's response.
- Use what you've learned.

indexes are essential parts of your publishing process because, like it or not, you are joining a community, and you need to be aware of what's going on out there.

The first step is to start getting to know the people, organizations, and issues that shape what you do on the Internet. You can simply watch and read without posting messages, if you want. *Lurking,* the Net term for *eavesdropping,* is an accepted and common practice on the Internet. When you feel more comfortable, you can start to offer your experiences, opinions, and questions.

Now we'll go through the kinds of resources you'll come across and explain them in a little more detail. The resources mentioned here have to do with the Internet or Internet publishing in general. Later on, in Chapters 3, 4, and 5 on Gopher, WWW, and WAIS, you'll find tables of resources for each kind of server. Chapters 7 and 9, on Internet commerce and copyright issues, also offer resource tables.

Usenet Newsgroups

Usenet News is an extremely large, international, cooperatively run system for exchanging messages. Usenet News is not the same as newspaper news, although there's a company called Clarinet <*http://www.clarinet.com*> that provides Associated Press and Reuters newsfeeds through Usenet News for a fee. Most of Usenet News consists of messages from individuals, which are like e-mail, except that they are divided by topics. Usenet News is organized into thousands of hierarchically arranged newsgroups, each of which focuses on a specific subject. Anyone can send and receive these messages. Depending on your site, you may get a full newsfeed or only partial information—certain newsgroups might not be carried. Disk space often is the limiting factor because a full Usenet newsfeed, consisting of all messages from all newsgroups all over the Internet, generates more than 5,400 megabytes per month.

A newsgroup is basically a subject area that is created so that those who are interested in that subject may exchange messages. They are hierarchically arranged, starting from some major categories:

- *comp*—computer science and computer-related topics.
- *news*—Usenet News network information. Check out news.newusers.questions and news.announce.newusers.
- *rec*—recreational or hobby activities.

- *sci*—hard sciences (except computer science).
- *soc*—social issues.
- *alt*—alternative newsgroups, which vary widely in subject matter and are less concerned with rules.
- *clari*—the commercial news service called Clarinet.

Other categories are often specific to a country or a university. And by no means are all newsgroups in English. New newsgroups are created by vote, except in the alt newsgroups, where the process is less formal.

News-reading programs exist for almost any computer platform conceivable—from mainframes to plain vanilla DOS PCs. Usually, the first step is to verify that you have access to a newsfeed. Then download or buy news-reading software and point it at the Usenet News server you'll be using. You'll soon see a long list of newsgroups. (I saw more than 8,000 newsgroups when I did this last at the University of California at Los Angeles, but UCLA has a Clarinet feed, which adds several thousand newsgroups.) You then select those newsgroups to which you wish to "subscribe." (There's no charge unless you license a commercial service such as Clarinet.) This isn't a permanent decision—it just helps narrow the focus a little.

Once you've subscribed to some newsgroups, you'll see (depending on your news reader) a number of "threads" or discussion chains. Reading the messages is very much like reading e-mail. An excellent starting point is Usenet Info Center, run by Kevin Atkinson, a 17-year-old student from Maryland. <***http://sunsite.unc.edu/usenet-b/home.html***>

Usenet newsgroups are an extremely dynamic source of information on the Internet. The messages look like e-mail but won't pile up in your mailbox. People pick the newsgroups that interest them and periodically monitor their threads (discussions) to see what is happening. Asking questions is fine after you've monitored the group for a little while and looked at any **FAQ** (Frequently Asked Questions) files available.

Alternative newsgroups are the easiest to create, and they are often formed as an immediate reaction to something, either a new piece of software or a new protocol or just an idea. Later, if a subject gains wider interest, it might be voted in as an official newsgroup in comp or one of the other domains. The new newsgroup might even split off into subgroups, focusing on specific aspects of a subject. This usually happens because the experts don't want to be bothered by lots of beginner questions.

Here are some newsgroups to check out. More are listed in each chapter's resource table:

- *comp.infosystems* discusses various types of information servers, past, present, and future.
- *comp.infosystems.announce* lists new information servers. It's one place that new WWW, Gopher, and WAIS sites are announced.
- *alt.answers* is where many newsgroups post their FAQs and other documentation files. Monitoring alt.answers is a good way to keep track of at least some ways in which the Internet is growing.

FAQ (Frequently Asked Questions) Files

FAQ files are often extremely useful repositories of beginner and intermediate questions in different areas. They are usually composed by the regular readers of a newsgroup, so that habitués aren't constantly distracted by questions from newcomers. By making all the usual questions and answers available, the newsgroup can concentrate on newer, more interesting issues.

FAQs pop up on the most amazing subjects, and they are periodically reposted to the Usenet newsgroup alt.answers. Check out Figure 2–1 for the first of 28 screens of the FAQ archive at the Massachusetts Institute of Technology (MIT). This directory of FAQs is located at <*ftp://rtfm.mit.edu/pub/usenet/news.answers/*>.

FIGURE 2–1 FAQ (Frequently Asked Questions) Archive

Unofficial Frequently Asked Questions list for the 1996 Centennial Olympics in Atlanta, Ga. (→ 2.)

A description of Arabic software and other resources on the Internet concerning the Arabic language and the Arabic world. (→ 7.)

More than you want to know about LEGO™, DUPLO™, and compatible construction toys. (→ 16.)

```
FAQ (Frequently Asked Questions) Archive
- ->  1.   .#index
      2.   1996-olympics-faq
      3.   386bsd-faq/
      4.   3b1-faq/
      5.   3b2-faq/
      6.   3d-programmer-info
      7.   Arabic-software-map
      8.   AudioFAQ/
      9.   Brazil-faq
      10.  C++-faq/
      11.  C-faq/
      12.  CPM-faq
      13.  ForthFaq/
      14.  GNU-Emacs-FAQ/
      15.  LANs/
      16.  LEGO-faq
      17.  Modula-2-faq
      18.  Modula-3-faq
Press ? for Help, q to Quit, u to go up a menu     Page: 1/28
```

RFCs

RFCs (Requests for Comment) are a valuable resource for the more technically inclined; I mention them here because they demonstrate an important part of Internet culture: the development of new technology through open and widespread discussion. The RFC process works as follows. First, someone develops an idea (which could be a new protocol, standard, or even a new type of service or specific tool); when they start to get serious about it, they write up an RFC document, which describes the idea in detail. At that point people start using the material and suggest changes, improvements, and alternatives. This discussion can result in amendments to the original RFCs or new RFCs of their own. The titles may sound computer nerdish, but there's nothing like source documents. And that's what RFCs are.

Eventually, either the idea dies because of lack of interest, or it becomes a recognized guidepost (*standard* has a more official meaning) for Internet programmers, developers, and users. In this way the Internet grows in sophistication by encouraging the open development and sharing of ideas. See Figure 2–2 for a short list of recent RFCs.

FIGURE 2–2 Sample RFC Titles

RFC number, which is used much more often than the RFC title. →

```
1766  PS   H. Alvestrand, "Tags for the Identification of
           Languages," 03/02/1995. (Pages=9) (Format=.txt)

1752  PS   S. Bradner, A. Mankin, "The Recommendation for
           the IP Next Generation Protocol," 01/18/1995.
           (Pages=52) (Format=.txt)

1750  I    D. Eastlake, S. Crocker, J. Schiller, "Randomness
           Recommendation for Security," 12/29/1994.
           (Pages=25) (Format=.txt)

1740  PS   P. Faltstrom, D. Crocker, E. Fair, "MIME
           Encapsulation of Macintosh files - MacMIME,"
           12/22/1994. (Pages=16) (Format=.txt)

1739  I    G. Kessler, S. Shepard, "A Primer On Internet and
           TCP/IP Tools," 12/22/1994. (Pages=32)
           (Format=.txt)
```

Both the WWW designer (Tim Berners-Lee) and the leader of the Gopher project (Mark McCahill) helped edit this RFC. →

```
1738  PS   T. Berners-Lee, L. Masinter, M. McCahill,
           "Uniform Resource Locators (URL)," 12/20/1994.
           (Pages=25) (Format=.txt)

1737  I    K. Sollins, L. Masinter, "Functional Requirements
           for Uniform Resource Names," 12/20/1994.
           (Pages=7) (Format=.txt)

1709  I    J. Gargano, D. Wasley, "K-12 Internetworking
           Guidelines," 12/23/1994. (Pages=26) (Format=.txt,
           .ps) (FYI 26)
```

RFCs are available online via Gopher, FTP, and e-mail. For retrieval information see <*gopher://ds1.internic.net:70/00/rfc/rfc-retrieval.txt*> or <*ftp://ds.internic.net/rfc/*>. Paper copies of all RFCs are available from InterNIC Information Services. For more information send e-mail to info@is.internic.net or call 800-444-4345 (choose prompt 3 from the InterNIC voicemail menu).

Mailing Lists

Mailing lists are e-mail–based systems for carrying on discussion groups. (*Note:* You'll hear these referred to as **list servers** or **listservs** as well, but list servers are actually the hardware/software for mailing list administration.) Basically, a computer is set up to accept mail at a certain address and redirect it to all members of the list. The list members do not even need to know each other, so long as they have "subscribed" to the list. Although many mailing lists are **mirrored**, or duplicated on Usenet newsgroups, many are available only as mailing lists. One advantage of mailing lists is that you will get the messages whether you look for them or not, usually within a few hours of when they are sent. So if you're the type who needs reminding, you'll like them. Mailing lists are also easy to create and so are useful for timely or focused topics with a limited audience. One-way mailing lists are often used for announcements of product upgrades.

Additionally, most mailing lists have archives, in which all their correspondence is saved. You should learn how to search these archives; they are an excellent resource. When you join a mailing list, you usually will receive a message that describes all the commands available for that list. If the list offers search features, they'll be mentioned there. If it doesn't, or if you don't want to subscribe to the list, try searching some Internet indexers to see if someone has put together an archive for that particular mailing list. I've found several this way. Mailing list archives can be a useful source of information and a record of discussions of issues of interest. Knowing how to retrieve all messages containing specific key words can be quite helpful. The following are some mailing lists that focus on Internet issues:

- *announce@is.internic.net*—This announcements-only mailing list is for anyone interested in getting current information about InterNIC and the services it provides. Send e-mail to listserv@is.internic.net, and in the body of the message type Subscribe announce [your name].
- *nics@is.internic.net*—This moderated list (each message is approved or controlled by the moderator) is intended for staff at midlevel, campus, and discipline-specific network information centers (NICs). Content includes InterNIC services aimed specifically at NICs, and mail sent to this list will be oriented to providing services, including new training resources and documentation, to end users. Send e-mail to listserv@is.internic.net in the body of the message type Subscribe nics [your name].
- *net-resources@is.internic.net*—This announcements-only list is a group effort of people all over the Internet to concentrate announcements of new resources on one list. It contains only announcements of new tools and resources available over the Internet. If you would like more information about participating in the Net resources list by becoming a monitor, send a note to scout@internic.net. Send e-mail to listserv@is.internic.net; in the body of the message type Subscribe net-resources [your name].
- RFC announcements are distributed via two mailing lists: the IETF-Announce list (IETF stands for Internet Engineering Task Force), and the RFC-DIST list. You don't want to be on both lists. To join (or quit) the IETF-Announce list, send a message to IETF-Request@cnri.reston.va.us. To join (or quit) the RFC-DIST list, send a message to RFC-Request@NIC.DDN.MIL.

Magazines and Journals (Print)

Newsstand and postal subscription magazines and journals that focus entirely on the Internet are starting to arrive on the scene, and established magazines are paying more attention to the Internet and the subject of **cyberspace**. Even *Newsweek* has a regular section called Cyberscope, which often includes URLs for interesting sites. Here are some examples of print magazines, available by subscription or at the newsstand, about the Internet:

Internet Business Advantage—$99/year (12 issues). This magazine is published by Wentworth Worldwide Media. 800-638-1639; fax 717-393-5752; e-mail success@wentworth.com.

Internet Business Journal—$149/year (12 issues). This journal offers Internet business advice and includes a column called Internet Advertising Review <***http://www.phoenix.ca/sie/iar-home.html***>. It is published by Michael Strangelove, author of *How to Advertise on the Internet.* <***http://www.phoenix.ca/ sie/ibj-home.html***>; 613-565-0982; fax 613-565-4433; e-mail @strangelove.comsubscriptions.

Internet World—$29/year (12 issues). This magazine is put out by MecklerMedia and offers interviews, columns, and advice for both new and experienced Internet users. It is available at newsstands. 815-734-1261; 800-573-3062; fax 800-896-1666; e-mail info@mecklermedia.com; <***http://www.mecklerweb.com/***>

NetGuide—$23/year (12 issues). This magazine, published by CMP Publishing, Inc., bills itself as the "Guide to Online Services and the Internet." It is available at newsstands. 800-829-0421; fax 516-562-7406; e-mail netmail@netguide.cmp.com; <***http://techweb.cmp.com/net***>.

Wired—$40/year (12 issues). This magazine has good interviews and prides itself on reporting on the latest and boldest in computer technology. It is available at newsstands. Back issues are available through its e-mail mailing list. Send e-mail to info@wired.com for details. An online version called HotWired is available at <***http://www.hotwired.com/***>. 800-SOWIRED; 415-222-6200 outside U.S.; fax 415-222-6399; e-mail talkzsubs@wired.com.

Online Magazines and Journals

Online magazines are growing rapidly. In the list that follows I've included both print magazines that are starting to offer some or all of their text online, as well as true online magazines and journals that are published entirely on the Internet. You should check them out for both content and style. Some are specifically oriented to Internet publishing issues, whereas others are computer magazines that talk about Internet issues, among other things. As with any online service you come across, elements of their layout style and design may be worth emulating. Hundreds of other online journals and "zines" focus on noncomputer topics. Following are just a few of the magazines and journals available online.

Computer-Mediated Communications Magazine—*CMC Magazine* is a free, entirely online publication that does not accept advertising. It is edited by John December, co-author of *World Wide Web Unleashed,* and reports on people, events, technology, public policy, culture, practices, research, and applications of computer-mediated communication. *Computer-mediated communication* is the academic term for what goes on when people communicate with each other via computer. WWW, Gopher, and Internet servers are a subset of computer-mediated communication. E-mail, Usenet News, and mailing lists are other examples of computer-mediated communication. *CMC Magazine* also publishes opinions and essays about issues related to computer-mediated communication. <***http://sunsite.unc.edu/cmc/mag/current/toc.html***>

GNN (Global Network Navigator)—This WWW site developed by O'Reilly and Associates (publishers of Ed Krol's *Whole Internet User's Guide and Catalog*) is one of the best and most popular examples of Internet publishing. It combines an online journal with links to Internet services and the O'Reilly book catalog. A sign of their success and the importance of the Internet: America Online purchased *GNN* in June 1995. <***http://www.digital.com/gnn/GNNhome.html***>

HotWired—This is the online version of *Wired* magazine, and it is considerably different from the print version. *HotWired* has five channels that the editors call "doorways into the digital revolution." These include technology, "way new" journalism, the arts, commerce, and electronic conversation. Unfortunately, using them requires registration, which is free so far. Be aware that you have to remember your member name and password to get back in. I wonder how many people end up re-registering because they forget their password. <***http://www.wired.com/***>

Public-Access Computer Systems Review—This free journal published by the University of Houston is primarily aimed at librarians and others who maintain publicly accessible computers. <***gopher://info.lib.uh.edu:70/11/articles/e-journals/uhlibrary/pacsreview***>

San Jose Mercury News—This daily newspaper in California's Silicon Valley has tons of computer industry and Internet news and is available by online subscription. The stories online are updated hourly. <***http://www.sjmercury.com/***>

St. Petersburg Times Interactive Media—This is an experimental site for the Interactive Media Department of the *St. Petersburg Times* in Florida. <***http://www.times.stpete.fl.us/default.html***>

TechWeb—This site by CMP Publications, Inc., offers links to many of the CMP magazines, including *Communications Week, Comm Week International, Computer Reseller News, Computer Retail Week, Electronic Buyers News, Electronic Engineering Times, Home PC, Information Week , Interactive Age, Internet Business Report, Netguide, Network Computing, OEM Magazine, Open Systems Today, VAR Business,* and *Windows Magazine*. As of May 1995 access to the last three months of its articles was free and entirely searchable. The search feature is WAIS based, and you can choose all magazines or just specific ones and then perform the search. <***http://www.techweb.com***>

Ziff-Davis Publishing—This site offers links to many of the Ziff-Davis magazines, including *PC Magazine, PCWeek, PC/Computing, MacWeek, MacUser, Computer Shopper,* and *Windows Sources.* Unfortunately, it does not provide full text, but only a sampling of what's in the print version. One convenience is the ability to download shareware mentioned in the magazines. <*http://www.ziff.com/*>

Also see this index of online journals: <*http://www.w3.org/hypertext/DataSources/bySubject/Electronic_Journals.html*>.

Internet Sites and Services of Interest to Internet Publishers

Look around the Internet for relevant standards and operating procedures. Sometimes these will come out in FAQ files or in comments on mailing lists or in newsgroups. Again, the point here is to know what the boundaries are, whether they are legal, institutional, or just "good taste." The point is to be a good Internet citizen. To do that you need to know the rules, written as well as unwritten.

The following sites offer Internet guidelines and reference information that you might find useful:

InterNIC—This site offers detailed information on the operation and resources of the Internet itself. The InterNIC is really three different services, maintained by separate companies under contract with the National Science Foundation. The service areas are Information Services (run by General Atomics), Directory and Database Services (run by AT&T), and Registration Services by Network Solutions, Inc. (NSI). <*gopher://gopher.internic.net*> or <*http://www.internic. net*> One particularly useful site provided by InterNIC is its archive, Internet Documentation (RFCs, FYIs [For Your Information files], and so on). <*gopher://ds1.internic.net:70/11/.ds/.internetdocs*>

Quality, Guidelines, and Standards for Internet Information Resources—This is a collaborative gathering of thoughts and ideas on the subject of improving information servers of all kinds. Among other lists and documents to which it provides links is "Top Ten Things Not to Do on a Web Page." <***http://coombs.anu.edu.au/SpecialProj/QLTY/ QltyHome.html***>

The Directory of Electronic Journals, Newsletters, and Academic Discussion Lists—The Association of Research Libraries helps to maintain this site, which gathers links to online publications. <***gopher://arl.cni.org:70/11/scomm/edir/***>

Organizations and Associations

You may not be a joiner, but you should be aware of these organizations, because they will be helping to shape the Internet in the years to come:

The Internet Society—This international nonprofit society's principal purpose is to "maintain and extend the development and availability of the Internet and its associated technologies and applications—both as an end in itself, and as a means of enabling organizations, professions, and individuals worldwide to more effectively collaborate, cooperate, and innovate in their respective fields and interests." It offers both individual and organization memberships. Voice: 800-468-9507 (United States only) or 703-648-9888. <***http://info.isoc.org/***> <***gopher://gopher.isoc.org/***> <***ftp://ftp.isoc.org/isoc***>

The Electronic Frontier Foundation (EFF)—The EFF is a nonprofit civil liberties organization working to protect freedom of expression, privacy, and access to online resources and information. It was founded in July 1990 by John Barlow, Mitch Kapor (founder of Lotus), Steve Wozniak (cofounder of Apple), and others to ensure that the principles embodied in the U.S. Constitution and the U.S. Bill of Rights are protected as new communications technologies emerge. The Web site includes archives of articles and court cases pertaining to most major social, political, and legal online issues.

<***http://www.eff.org/***>. 202-861-7700; fax 202-861-1258; e-mail ask@eff.org.

Internet Engineering Task Force (IETF)—The IETF is a large open international community of network designers, operators, vendors, and researchers concerned with the evolution of Internet architecture and the smooth operation of the Internet. It is open to any interested individual. The IETF organizes working groups for the technical work of designing and developing Internet protocols. <***http://www.ietf.cnri.reston.va.us/***>

The World-Wide Web Consortium (W3C)—W3C operates under the leadership of Tim Berners-Lee, the author of WWW, and was formed to document and encourage the development of a common set of tools and basic programs for continued WWW development. It is the closest thing to the "owner" of the Web. <***http://www.w3.org/***>

Electronic Privacy Information Center (EPIC)—EPIC, based in Washington, D.C., is a public interest organization established in 1994 to focus public attention on emerging privacy issues relating to the National Information Infrastructure (better known as the Information Superhighway), such as the Clipper Chip, the Digital Telephony proposal, medical records privacy, national identification systems, and the sale of consumer data. EPIC is sponsored by the Fund for Constitutional Government and Computer Professionals for Social Responsibility. EPIC publishes online newsletters and reports, pursues litigation under the Freedom of Information Act, and conducts policy research on emerging privacy issues. <***http://epic.digicash.com/epic/***> or send e-mail to info@epic.org.

Internet Indexers and Directories

Many excellent books and online guides are available if you need help finding what's out there. Indexes, catalogs, and resource directories abound on the Internet; some that you may find useful appear in Table 2–1.

TABLE 2–1 Internet Indexers and Directories

<table>
<tr><td>ALIWEB <http://web.nexor.co.uk/aliweb/doc/aliweb.html></td><td>ALIWEB is a cooperative catalog developed by Martijn Koster of NEXOR Ltd. and stands for Archie-like Web. The idea is that it's more useful to index servers by their themes than by every individual file. ALIWEB accomplishes this by asking Webmasters to summarize the various themes or subjects covered in their WWW server and then register so that this index file can be picked up at regular intervals. ALIWEB is a promising idea but it relies on the active participation of Web administrators.</td></tr>
<tr><td>ArchiePlex <http://pubweb.nexor.co.uk/public/archie/archieplex/archieplex.html></td><td>ArchiePlex is an Archie gateway for the World-Wide Web. It can locate files on anonymous FTP sites on the Internet.</td></tr>
<tr><td>CUI W3 Catalog Centre Universitaire d'Informatique World-Wide Web catalog at CERN <http://cuiwww.unige.ch/w3catalog></td><td>This is a searchable catalog that is updated daily from the following sources:
• NCSA What's New
• NCSA's NCSA Starting Points
• CERN's W3 Virtual Library Subject Catalog and selected sublists
• Martijn Koster's ALIWEB Archie-like Indexing for the Web
• Scott Yanoff's Internet Services List
• Simon Gibbs's list of Multimedia Information Sources
• John December's list of Computer-Mediated Communication Information Sources
• Internet Tools Summary
• Marcus Speh's User Documents for DESY and HEP</td></tr>
<tr><td>CUSI <http://pubweb.nexor.co.uk/public/cusi/doc/list.html></td><td>CUSI (Configurable Unified Search Engine) is a configurable search interface for many searchable WWW resources. It allows you to quickly check related resources without having to navigate and retype the keywords. This service was written and introduced by Martijn Koster of NEXOR in 1993.</td></tr>
</table>

EINet Galaxy *<http://www.einet.net/galaxy.html>*	EINet is a commercial Internet provider, and Galaxy is its index and catalog to the Internet. Claiming 140,000 hypertext link titles, this site allows you to add your own annotations and links to its catalog.
GENBBB *<http://www.cs.colorado.edu/homes/mcbryan/public_html/bb/summary.html>*	GENBBB is a system for cataloging WWW resources created by Oliver McBryan of the University of Colorado. It allows you to add WWW titles, reports, and links via an online WWW form. The result is an expanding collection of WWW resources stored in a hierarchical structure that grows like a tree.
Harvest *<http://harvest.cs.colorado.edu/>*	Harvest is an integrated set of tools for gathering, extracting, organizing, searching, caching, and replicating relevant information across the Internet. With modest effort users can tailor Harvest to digest information in many different formats and offer custom search services on the Internet. Moreover, Harvest makes efficient use of network traffic, remote servers, and disk space.
Lycos Carnegie-Mellon University *<http://lycos.cs.cmu.edu/>*	Lycos™ indexes WWW, Gopher, and FTP servers every day and updates the index once a week. It does not index WAIS, Usenet, or e-mail archives.
RBSE Spider *<http://rbse.jsc.nasa.gov/eichmann/ urlsearch.html>*	The index is constructed by a program that walks the world-wide web like a spider building a database, and WAIS indexing the full text of each document. There are currently 36,195 documents in the index.
Veronica *<gopher://veronica.scs.unr.edu/11/veronica>*	Veronica, by Steven Foster of the University of Nevada at Reno, indexes Gopher sites.
W3 Search Engines Page *<http://golgi.harvard.edu/meta-index.html>*	This site collects some of the most useful search services available on the WWW. It groups searches in the following categories: • Information servers • Software • People • Publications • News/FAQs • Documentation • Other interesting things

TABLE 2–1 *(continued)*

WebCrawler *<http://webcrawler.com/>*	The WebCrawler is a tool for searching the Web. It operates by traversing the Web and either builds an index for later use or acts as an agent and searches in realtime for an answer.
Who's Who on the Internet *<http://web.city.ac.uk/citylive/pages.html>*	This is a directory of personal home pages from all over the Internet. "Who's Who on the Internet" is owned and operated by Kirk Bowe at City University, London.
Whole Internet Catalog *<http://www.digital.com/gnn/wic/index.html>*	Based on Ed Krol's excellent book, *The Whole Internet User's Guide and Catalog*.
World-Wide Web Virtual Library *<http://www.w3.org/hypertext/DataSources/bySubject/Overview.html>*	This is a catalog or directory of the Internet organized by subject and maintained by volunteer subject coordinators. In addition to indexing by major subject areas, it offers category subtrees and Library of Congress classifications and is ordered by service type, such as Gopher, WWW, WAIS, and so on. It also offers a search option.
WWW Worm *<http://www.cs.colorado.edu/home/mcbryan/WWWW.html>*	WWW Worm is a resource location tool by Oliver McBryan that indexes more than 3 million URLs. WWWW provides four types of search databases: citation hypertext, citation addresses (URLs), HTML> titles, and HTML> addresses. Using this technique, you can find all documents that refer to your site.
Yahoo—A Guide to WWW *<http://www.yahoo.com/yahoo/>*	This started out as the project of two Stanford grad students attempting to catalog everything on the Internet. It now has more than 32,000 entries, and the students have gone commercial and taken time off from their studies. It is an excellent resource with extensive subject directories, a search index, lists of most popular items, and even a random jump into the Internet.

Make notes as you search through this material, because later you will want to be sure that your service is listed in these indexes, directories, newsgroups, and mailing lists. Plus, the problems you have now will be similar to the challenges facing your potential users. Keep notes and learn from this experience. You'll never be less familiar with the Internet than you are today.

Also, learn from your competitors. Pay attention to how servers are set up and how documents are arranged, as well as what special features they provide to their users. For example, many sites allow you to search by key term, but one equipment manufacturer allows you to search by picture. You start with general categories and narrow down to the specific part. The company also has built and patented its own searching system.

Pay attention to feedback, searching, and charging mechanisms to see how easy and intuitive they are to use and which charging systems they are using.

Netiquette

Netiquette, short for network etiquette, is important. It is far easier to offend someone or tread on someone's toes when you can't see their face. Likewise, it is far easier to take offense because online interaction excludes nuances of rhythm, mood, and context and all body language. Here are some rules to live by:

1. Never respond rashly to provocation on the Internet. Although "flame wars" (angry messages are called *flames*) have often broken out on unmoderated mailing lists and Usenet newsgroups, no one encourages the practice. If you must respond, do it offline (that is, in private e-mail, not to the group).
2. Criticize ideas, not people. Try to be as constructive in your criticism as possible.
3. Watch or lurk for a while in any mailing list or newsgroup to get a feel for the tone and to avoid asking "newbie" (newcomer) questions.

4. Do your homework before asking questions in a mailing list or newsgroup. Look for the relevant FAQ files and archives to avoid asking questions that have already been answered millions of times.
5. Think carefully before sending a message. Remember that you are making your reputation internationally through the messages you send out. And messages last far longer than you'd expect.
6. When you ask for responses and say you'll summarize for the list, do it.
7. Answer questions when you can, but check whether others have already supplied the information.
8. Stay on the topic of the newsgroup or mailing list. No matter how strongly you feel about a subject, it is not appropriate to send information or opinions about it to unrelated groups.

Most books about exploring the Internet talk about Internet manners, but you might want to look at *Netiquette* by Virginia Shea, published by Albion Books. Both online and print versions are available. <***http://www.bookport.com/Albion/catNetiquette.html***>

Identifying Your Competition

A word about competition might be appropriate here. Remember that the Internet was built, and continues to expand, on the basis of cooperation. You should think about this if you find other services offer similar information or competing products on the Internet. Perhaps you can offer to link to their service if they'll link to yours. Or you might want to join forces with your competitor to form a more comprehensive subject-oriented server. Remember that this is a new medium and the old rules don't always apply.

Competition may not be quite the right word in your case, depending on the nature of the server and service you want to establish. But it is important to be aware of what similar servers already are doing on the Internet. Ideally, your server can work in combination with others to provide broader, more detailed resources to the Internet community instead of striving to kill someone off. Remember, the Internet has reached today's interesting state only because of the incredible spirit of cooperation that it has somehow inspired.

Finding what's out there in your area of expertise is essential. For example, suppose for some reason you decided that your goal in life was to put up a WWW site dedicated to the comic strip "Calvin and Hobbes" by Bill Watterson. Once you were finished, wouldn't you be surprised to learn that five other sites (one each in the United States, France, Holland, Sweden, and Norway) already are dedicated to "Calvin and Hobbes"? This is where the Internet gets cooperative: they all link to each other. <*http://www.eng.hawaii.edu/Contribs/justin/Archive/Index.html*>

Defining Your Goals

What can you sensibly hope to attain by publishing on the Internet? Why do you want to publish on the Internet? Do you really know what you hope to gain? Here are a few services that you might be able to offer:

- Special information not available elsewhere
- Collation and organization of information and links to information in a specific subject area
- Advertising for your business or organization
- Advertising of your own expertise

Or you might want to publish on the Internet because doing so decreases the amount of time your staff spends searching for or providing information, because you want to experiment with new technology that may benefit you or your company, or because you want to sell things and make money.

One advantage of defining your goals early is that it enables you to look at how others are achieving similar goals. You can become more analytical as you scour the Internet, noting the techniques each site uses and adding them to your repertoire.

And I should say something about experimenting and keeping your goals loosely defined. The Internet is in its infancy as a method of communication, and all the implications are not yet clear. More than one company has found that a side benefit of publishing on the Internet became more important and potentially more profitable than its original goal. AMP, Inc., a builder of electrical connectors, started with the idea of putting its catalog of 80,000 parts on CD-ROMs. Then its customers (mostly high-tech companies) urged AMP to go to the Internet. In the process the company developed a unique scheme for finding exactly the right part by picture, name, or part number. Among other things, AMP found that its sales personnel started selling a wider range of parts than before. AMP has patented the interface it developed and is starting to sell it. You never can tell what you're going to learn and how useful it will be for others.

Identifying Your Audience

What do you know about your audience? If you want to publish information about Macintosh computers, you'll be able to store files in Macintosh formats and ignore other file formats. On the other hand, if you want all those interested in political science to read your work—no matter whether they're coming from a Macintosh, Sun Microsystems workstation, PC, or mainframe—you should plan to put all your documents in a portable format such as plain text or HTML or in a variety of formats.

Who is going to be happy to see your information on the Internet? Or whom do you want to come to your site? The time you spend thinking about your audience will pay off. If the members of your audience tend to flock to certain newsgroups or e-mail lists, you'll want to be sure to announce your server in those places. And you might want to consider offering to archive those newsgroups or mailing lists as a service (and good advertising). If someone is already doing this, you might consider offering to **mirror**, or duplicate, their service as a way to decrease the load on their server or staff. Here are some questions to ask yourself, broken into categories:

LOCATION

- Is your potential audience limited to a certain geographical area?
- Will there be any overseas interest in your site?
- Is your audience limited to certain identifiable subnets? For example, if you want to sell a service to an institution with a clearly defined range of Internet Protocol (IP) addresses, you could rely on the IP screening capabilities in almost all Gopher, WWW, and WAIS servers. However, if your users will be scattered all over the Internet, you might have to use individual password-based authentication instead, which is technologically more difficult and requires much more administrative overhead. (For an explanation of subnets see IP Addresses, Subnets, and Domains, a sidebar later in this chapter.)
- Is this site going to be internal, reserved only for your company or organization?

EQUIPMENT

- Do you have any reason to expect that your audience will use a certain type of computer?
- Does your audience have hardware or software limitations that would affect how you design your server?
- Do you expect that your audience will primarily be dialing in from home, or will your clients have direct (cable) connections to the Internet? For dial-ins you'll want to make sure that downloading information over a slow modem does not take forever (more than a minute or two), and if it does, perhaps you should rethink the information you want to display. Don't make your files any bigger than you have to.

CHARACTERISTICS

- Is there anything that members of your audience have in common?
- Which foreign language(s) will be necessary?
- Do all your potential clients follow a certain newsgroup or e-mail list?
- Do they all use similar computers or software?

SECURITY AND ACCESS

- Is your site open to anyone, or will you be limiting access?
- Do any IP subnets clearly define your groups? Providing or limiting access to all or part of your server is possible with most server software. You often can designate different access restrictions for different directories of your server.

What If I Don't Know?

If you don't know what kind of audience to expect, you should consider adding a poll to your server. That way you can learn more about the people who connect to your server and decide later whether to focus more narrowly or broadly. Depending on the audience, you might post some questions to a newsgroup or mailing list. Or you might persuade someone already running a server to let you post your questions. The responses could be e-mailed to you. Don't forget the possibility of contacting other, more experienced Web, Gopher, or WAIS providers to find out what they think you might expect.

Identifying Your Data

The point I'm trying to make is that you need to identify and analyze the type of information files you want to make available on the Internet. This decision has implications for your server type and size and for what sort of user interface to design. You will need to be able

IP Addresses, Subnets, and Domains

Internet Protocol (IP) addresses are the one constant on the Internet. Every machine that sends messages over the Internet (and connects to a Web, Gopher, or WAIS server) has an IP address even if only temporarily (some dial-up services assign you an IP address for that session only). IP addresses are like telephone numbers—each machine has one, and it serves as its unique identification on the Internet. An IP address is assigned to a machine by a network administrator; you can't just make one up on your own. Usually, they consist of four numbers separated by dots, such as 192.207.117.2. The number at far right is the most specific, designating a particular machine.

The dots separate the millions of IP addresses into networks and subnetworks (or subnets). Subnets are what make the entire Internet addressing scheme workable. Dividing IP addresses into subnets at deeper and deeper levels enormously simplifies the problem of keeping track of them. Each subnet has a computer (called a router) that keeps track of the IP addresses in its subnet and the IP address of the router one level up. Messages between computers simply go from router to router until they reach the correct subnet and find their intended recipient.

Because numbers are not easy to remember, the Domain Name System (DNS) was invented to allow the use of words instead of numbers. A typical host name would look like *mike.sscnet.ucla.edu.* Note that these names are also divided by dots, except in this case they are called domains and subdomains. In this example the computer called mike is part of a network of computers called sscnet (short for Social Sciences Computing, where I work). That network in turn is part of a much larger network of computers at UCLA, which in turn is an educational institution, so it belongs in the edu domain. Unlike IP addresses, the most specific part of a name, which refers to a particular computer, is on the left. The names are called **host names** when they apply to a computer and **domain names** when they apply to a subnet or group of subnets. Domain name servers provide the lookup service (called DNS Lookup) that takes a host or domain name and looks up its IP address. If it doesn't have that address in its domain, it passes the request along to the appropriate domain name server.

Top-level domains (those that appear at far right in the name) are usually country codes (Australia = .au, France = .fr, Canada = .ca) except in the United States, where the Internet started. In the United States the domains are edu (educational), com (commercial), gov (government), mil (military), net (network), and org (organizational). There is a move to bring the United States into line with the rest of the world in using a top-level domain of .us, but this would require so much renaming that it's unlikely to happen.

to answer the following questions for each type of information you plan to publish:

- What kind of information will you offer? Will you be making announcements, offering catalogs, posting press releases, product information, technical documents, collections of quotations, collections of photos, previews of movies, or the latest stock market quote?
- What format will you use to provide that information? Will it be plain text, formatted text, hypertext, sound, picture, video, program to be run, program to be downloaded, or something else?
- What size files will you offer?
- How generally available is the format you have selected?
- Is there a natural grouping of files—will certain files always be downloaded together?
- How often does the information in the files change?
- Who owns the information? Is **copyright** an issue?
- Who will update it?
- How much will you charge for it, if anything?
- What is your goal in publishing this information on the Internet?
- How will you evaluate whether you've reached that goal?

In addition, think through what happens after your server is set up. If your data are timely, you should plan to update regularly, and be sure that the date you last updated the file is a prominent feature. You will also have to think about what this means in terms of staff support.

Another part of identifying your data consists of finding and recruiting information providers, or those people or organizations that will provide you with what you plan to publish. For example, you might provide company press releases and arrange for the public relations departments to supply them to you with dates for posting and

> **Giving Something Back to the Internet**
>
> Here's where I make the pitch for contributing to the Internet. You may be publishing on the Internet for highly commercial reasons, which is fine. But you will fit in with the Internet community only to the extent that your organization is seen as contributing to the general resources freely available on the Internet.
>
> In other words, if you plan to sell something on the Internet, you should also plan to give something of value for free. The form this takes is up to you and your imagination. But remember that this is not the traditional marketplace in which traditional advertising techniques hold sway. This is a new medium and all the rules are different. If you come in thinking that you'll flood the Internet with advertising, you'll get more bad publicity than you could ever dream of. You'll end up making your company's name well known on the Internet but for all the wrong reasons. The Internet is a cooperative place, where the emphasis is on providing tools and information to those who take the trouble to look for them. You might think of the Internet as a free focus group. You don't have to pay customers to come and talk about your product. If you publish on the Internet, you can get international and technically literate feedback for free.

removal. You might start a literary magazine and collect short stories from high school students in your area. Or you might have a companywide telephone and e-mail directory that might be kept current by the department administrators. Be careful to verify the ownership of the files and data you publish and check for any copyright issues. Don't assume that because it's already on the Internet that it's freely available for your use. See Chapter 9 for a discussion of copyright and the Internet.

Identifying Your Needs

Internet publishing can be done with little cost and time, or it can be a massive million-dollar effort.

Hardware

Given the kind of information you want to publish and the size of the audience you think you might expect, what kind of computer system is available to you to meet those needs? You can set up a server with low-powered computers, and initially that may be the quickest approach. However, if your service becomes popular, it will demand much more computing power. In either case, consider the cost as well as your familiarity with each type of hardware.

For example, you might start out with an inexpensive PC running Windows or with a Macintosh. These systems are familiar to many and are easy to set up to run Gopher or Web server software (or both in combination). This will let you get your feet wet and explore the possibilities without investing a lot of money. Or you might make space on a PC running Microsoft Windows NT. Apple sells a version of its Macintosh that is optimized to run as a WWW server. If usage exceeds the capabilities of your machine, you can move into more powerful hardware.

Note that larger, more powerful UNIX-based machines are getting easier to use. Sun Microsystems and Silicon Graphics are starting to bundle some models with Web server software and management tools to simplify server administration. See Chapter 11 for a discussion of future trends, but expect that you may end up using a combination of servers of all shapes and sizes.

Network Connection

Do you have a dedicated Internet connection, or do you dial in for Internet access? In the latter case, you wouldn't want your home machine to be your server, because it wouldn't be available most of the time. So you'll need to determine whether Internet publishing is a service your Internet provider offers. Or you can negotiate with a service that, for a fee, will run your server on its equipment. Be sure to clarify what access you'll have for updating your information. See Chapter 8 for a discussion of finding and selecting an Internet service provider.

Software

It may be obvious to you which server (Gopher, WWW, or WAIS) or combination you want to use, but review your decision before you take the plunge. Look through Chapters 3 (Gopher), 4 (WWW), 5 (WAIS), and 6 (Other Tools)—including the servers you don't intend to use—and take a particularly close look at the examples in Chapter 10 for what others did in similar situations. And after you decide which type of server software you'll use, you'll have to decide which version is for you.

Human Resources

Do you have the expertise and time in-house to comfortably run your server? Depending on the size and complexity of the computer system you'll use for your server, you may need to recruit the assistance of a system administrator. The **system administrator** is the person in charge of all technical aspects of running the computer system. Some of the Gopher, Web, and WAIS software discussed in this book require a system administrator to get it set up. But once it's running, the **data librarian** steps in. This is the person or persons who do most of the work involved in collecting, organizing, and preparing the data and documents that go on your server. They don't need much system experience at all, because the process of loading the data into the correct directories can be made quite simple. You may indeed want everyone in your organization to add and keep track of their own files on your Gopher, WWW, or WAIS server. However, you should plan to entrust someone with the overall structure and organization of your server, and that person would be the data librarian.

Make sure you have the technical support you'll need. If you plan to run a server on a system with which you are not familiar, and your system administrator is too busy to help, you should think carefully about what support you'll need and where you'll get it. Check the documentation and the newsgroup or mailing list for the type of server you plan to use to get an estimate of the technical expertise it requires. Internet server software doesn't always require a system administrator, although it's often helpful. It is possible, even preferable, to have your system administrator set up and run the server, then give control of various sections to the data owners or maintainers. In many cases, new files can be published by simply moving the files to a particular directory on the server. Remember, one goal of each of the three main server protocols, Gopher, WWW, and WAIS, was to increase the ease and access to Internet publishing.

What level of staff effort will be required to keep your information current? Often this isn't an issue, because you'll simply put information on your server and replace it every few months or so when it gets updated. But if your company's reputation depends on the timeliness and accuracy of the information your server provides, it would be a good idea to make sure that the burden won't be overwhelming.

Will you need the services of a graphic designer? If you're planning a WWW site, hire or consult with a graphic designer. Many Web sites show the lack of design expertise. Others use graphic design to grab your attention.

Will you need management to change policies or procedures in order to get the information and updates your server will need? Will other departments need to be involved, either in providing or using the information on your server? Will your server change some systems that are in place? Start early in recruiting management support.

Identifying Available Resources

When identifying hardware for use as a server, think about a backup. What happens if the machine breaks down? Once your server becomes established, you won't want to have any down time, planned or otherwise. The Internet is international so people will be using your server at all hours of the day and night.

Don't underestimate the time and learning involved. The kind of people you recruit should be excited and eager. This will be a learning experience for your whole crew, so be sure that they (and you) are up for it.

Determining How to Make Up the Difference

If you don't have the right computer equipment available, it's often possible to piggyback on another server. The operations can easily be separated from the user's point of view. Users often don't pay attention to which computer they are connected. Another alternative is renting time and space on a commercial service (see Chapter 8).

One advantage of Internet publishing is that, for the most part, it requires no specialized skill to format and prepare the information. For that reason you might include a broader range of your staff and personnel as data suppliers than you might first have expected. Ideally, the author of each document can be responsible for putting it on your server and keeping it current.

Identifying Charging Mechanisms

How to charge for information—if at all—is an area that is changing rapidly. First, I'd like to make a case for providing some real content or information on your server for free. You don't have to give away your product to be part of the Internet community, but try to offer more than just advertising and order forms. You may well find that by putting up detailed and useful information, you increase your business in other ways. This is the strategy that GE Plastics takes in providing hard technical information about its products and its design guides on its site, which has no ordering or charge-account mechanisms. <*http://www.ge.com/gep/homepage.html*>

Microsoft provides access to much of its technical support Knowledge Base via the Web although it also sells the information on CD-ROM. The CD-ROM version does have some extras, but an enormous amount of information is available for free online. <*http://www.microsoft.com/pages/kb/kb.htm*> Putting the information on the Internet also provides customers with an alternative to Microsoft's phone and fax support.

Or you might use your company's server to sponsor a community organization or just provide information about your area as a gesture of community support. Some companies have offered specialized services, such as mortgage calculation or an index to 800 numbers.

But if you absolutely have to charge, some techniques are in use and others are in the advanced planning or testing stages. This is an area that is changing rapidly, so pay close attention to the sites and discussion groups you find that deal with this. Chapter 7 describes and summarizes the different approaches available.

Identifying Security Risks

Methods exist for limiting access to all or part of your server from certain Internet subnets. Be aware of this possibility when laying out your server, because you might want some sections to be available only to those on your system and others to be available to everyone. However, whenever you screen out IP addresses or subnets, you should be aware of the gateway chaining problem. Basically, this means that any gateways (for example, proxy, caching, and e-mail) to your Gopher, Web, or WAIS server should block out the same IP addresses that your server restricts. Otherwise you're leaving a back door open.

The extent to which security is an issue for you depends on the nature of your organization and computer system. For high security you could put up a firewall to protect the rest of your network from unwanted intrusion. A **firewall** is a method of isolating your company's or organization's computers behind a computer that acts as a gatekeeper, or firewall. All outgoing requests for information or services go to that one machine, which hides the sender's machine address but passes on the request. Any incoming information is sent to the firewall computer, which passes it on to the appropriate internal machine. See *Firewalls and Internet Security* by William R. Cheswick and Steven M. Bellovin, published by Addison-Wesley in 1994, for an in-depth discussion of this technique.

For lower security you still must ensure against unauthorized alteration of your server files and operating system. Several software developers for Gopher, WWW, and WAIS have already started posting detailed analyses of their server software's security holes and risks, as well as their recommendations. Those links, where available, are described Chapters 3, 4, and 5 on Gopher, WWW, and WAIS.

Estimating Your Costs

Like anything else, what you will spend depends on what you want to do and, in this case, how many people will come to see what you've done (i.e., browse your Gopher, Web, or WAIS server). Many people mistakenly assume that because dial-up Internet-browsing accounts can cost as little as $15 per month, Internet-publishing accounts are just as inexpensive. The type of Internet access account needed to do what's described in this book is much more expensive, sometimes running hundreds or even thousands of dollars per month, with additional hardware and line installations adding to the cost. That higher price has to do with the types of service available in your area and the Internet throughput (size of the pipeline) you'll need. See Chapter 8 for more information about finding, selecting, and working with an Internet service provider.

The Gopher, WWW, WAIS, or other server software you may use varies widely in price as well. Some of it is available for free, and other programs cost $5,000 to $15,000 plus annual maintenance charges of $1,000 or more. The free software may not be such a bargain when you factor in programming and debugging time.

The type of computer you use will also be an expense, but thankfully there is a movement toward using less expensive PCs and Macintoshes in the place of the larger, more support-intensive UNIX machines. Staff support costs are often underestimated. In the case of WWW servers, you'll want to consider hiring a graphic designer.

And editorial staff is usually much more important in Internet publishing than programmers are.

Don't let these costs scare you off. In its June 19, 1995, issue *InfoWorld* published a poll that showed cost expectations vary widely. Nineteen percent of respondents expected to spend less than $5,000, 13 percent said more than $45,000, and 35 percent didn't know.

Planning the Presentation of Your Data

A dedicated individual, or a team of editorial consultants, graphic artists, and programmers, can develop a sophisticated well-organized information server. Christine Quinn, Stanford University's director of electrical engineering for computer and network services, describes Stanford's attempts to put a consistent "Stanford" face on its collection of Web servers in an article titled "From Grass Roots to Corporate Image—The Maturation of the Web," which she presented at the 1994 WWW conference in Chicago. Because Stanford was looking for a unifying theme, the university hired a graphic artist to insert pictures of Stanford's famous architecture in its home pages. Quinn says that if you're ready to spend thousands of dollars on a brochure that will be seen by hundreds, why not spend an equal amount to do it right on the Internet, where it will be seen by thousands? ***<http://www.ncsa.uiuc.edu/SDG/IT94/Proceedings/Campus.Infosys/quinn/quinn.html>***

Dale Dougherty of O'Reilly and Associates, publishers of UNIX administration books, describes Internet publishing as a collaborative art. At the 1994 WWW conference in Chicago he recalled how his company's extremely popular *Global Network Navigator (GNN)* site needed more editorial and production people than technical staffers. Having a graphic artist on board was essential. According to Dougherty, a publisher "organizes an audience," and publishing on the Internet has the same requirements of any publishing enterprise:

- Editorial requirements include a point of view, goals, the writing and editing of new material and updating of old material.

- Strong graphics allow the publisher to create an identity—"define our space," Dougherty says.
- Technical requirements are constantly changing and not to be ignored—publishers do so at their peril.
- Business requirements include paying attention to costs. If they are high, subscriptions and advertising can defray the expense, just as they do for print.
- Sales and marketing techniques may be different but remain essential.

Even the presentation of your menus and the design of your hypertext require consideration. Are your users quickly finding the information they want from your server, or are they getting sidetracked by confusing menus?

How the information is presented—known on the Net as the metaphor that is used—can make a big difference in how easily and quickly newcomers learn their way around your information server. A **metaphor** is a way to describe the information server or how it is arranged by comparing it with something commonly understood. For example, a directory structure is often described as treelike, with a root and many branches. A book is another metaphor; although a book can be emulated in hypertext and has certain advantages, the flexibility of Internet servers may lead to even easier ways to organize information. The Open Software Foundation Research Institute, a nonprofit research and development organization based in Cambridge, Massachusetts, has collected ideas, analogies, and metaphors that might be useful in describing data and its relationships. *<http://riwww.osf.org:8001/www/InfoPresForm/>* Some of the ways of organizing information that researchers at the institute have come across on the World-Wide Web are shown at *<http://riwww.osf.org:8001/www/InfoPresForm/results.html>*.

The structure of your organization might provide an obvious structure for your server, but you may prefer a more subject-oriented model based on the main areas your server covers. Here are some examples:

- If a company is composed of different divisions, its server might be split up that way as well, with branches leading off to areas that represent each division.
- If a company is global, the server might have links leading to the different geographic regions and then to the countries (and company offices) within those regions.
- If a company or organization offers a variety of services or functions, it could split its Gopher or Web server along those lines.

Extensive testing is one of the best ways to make your server and data presentation user friendly. By testing I mean trying out all the links and menus yourself from a variety of browser programs. And keep testing once your server is in use. Links can die or change on you—that link you thought was fascinating and pertinent two months ago may have changed focus or moved to another site. Also test your server's presentation by asking novice users to explore it, and then ask them to summarize what your server contains. You might be surprised by what they miss.

Always keep in mind that users are a resource. They can provide helpful information. On the Internet the bias is toward criticism and feedback (with the assumption that you'll fix what's wrong), so take advantage of that, as well as the ideas your users may provide. In their travels through the Internet they may have come across a design or presentation solution that could be useful to you. Don't forget that they may have seen and used many more servers than you have. Actually, it's common to borrow techniques from others on the Internet.

Another method is to try different approaches to presenting the same data and then use your system's logs to determine which route browsers use most.

Different people tend to learn in different ways. Psychology tells us that people have four basic learning styles:

- Reflective people relate everything to their own experience: why would I publish on the Internet?

- Conceptual people want to know the big picture: what is the significance of Internet publishing?
- Practical people seek usable information: how do I do it?
- Creative people are easily bored and tend to learn by trial and error: what if . . . ?

Keep these styles in mind when designing your server. It might behoove you to present your crucial information in several different ways. For example, you could present a single concept with a written explanation, a diagram, a step-by-step example, and a discussion of the benefits and implications. Cater to the different types of learners in your audience.

Preparing Your Data

Gopher servers generally need less data preparation than WWW and WAIS servers. Usually, you just pop the file in place and it's instantly available on your server. But even with Gopher servers many questions come up about the preparation of material.

Acquiring the Material

You should analyze the need for

- Scanning in text and images from paper copies
- Optical character recognition
- Uploading existing files to your server

Formatting the Material

Formatting concerns include

- Whether to crop or edit images (retouch the boss's picture?)
- Whether to translate materials to a different format
- Which text formats to make available (for example, WordPerfect 5.1, Word for Windows 2.0, PostScript, and so on)

- Whether those formats exclude use of those files on other types of computers, such as Macintosh, UNIX, VAX, and IBM mainframe
- Whether to append a company logo, copyright statement, or author and date (can this be done automatically?)

Access to the Material

In determining which image file formats to use, you should ask whether

- Accepted standards exist for the machines you plan to use
- Your data need to be indexed, filtered, or generally cleaned up

Future

You also need to consider your needs in the future:

- Can indexing and cleanup be handled automatically by scripts or programs?
- Do you need to convey information that isn't yet standard on the Internet, such as tables and formulas that aren't easy to format on Web servers using HTML 2.0?
- Is there any provision for removing information that becomes dated?
- In what ways might the size of your server grow?

Indexing Your Data

You might consider indexing the contents of your Gopher and WWW servers (WAIS servers have built-in indexing), although it's not required or even always necessary. If you have just a few documents and your menus aren't very deep, users are unlikely to get lost or miss items on your server. However, if you have an extensive menu structure, a large collection of documents, or large documents, you should consider an index. The usual practice is to place a search link at the beginning of your opening screen that offers users the chance to search the contents of your Gopher or WWW server. Users then can search quickly through the index for what they want, instead of working their way through various submenus or hypertext links.

If you've ever been unable to find something on a server that you knew was there, you'll appreciate what a convenience the ability to search the contents of a server can be. Jughead, developed by Rhett "Jonzy" Jones, a programmer at the University of Utah, is one tool available for indexing UNIX Gopher server menus. As discussed in Chapter 1, Veronica also does this kind of indexing, although for thousands of Gopher servers. We'll talk about Jughead and Veronica and other such tools and techniques in Chapters 3 and 4.

You also can index the full text of documents on your Gopher and WWW servers. Full-text indexing is different than indexing by menu item or file name. **Full-text indexing** means that every word in each document is indexed, not just the menu description line (for Gopher servers). For example, if you have a document summarizing the history of the conflict in the Middle East and it mentions Syria, the menu line might say only "Middle Eastern Conflict—History." Someone searching for everything she can find about Syria won't turn up that document. But with full-text indexing a search on *Syria* would retrieve it. Some Gopher and WWW servers, such as GN, WN, TurboGopher, and MacHTTPD, offer the ability to do full-text indexing. Others allow links to WAIS to accomplish this.

You'll want to think about what kinds of searches your users might make and whether you'll need sophisticated indexing features such as **structured field searching**, which means that users can search fields or certain parts of the text, including title, author, and date. **FreeWAIS-sf** adds structured field searching to the **freeWAIS** indexing software, which is available for UNIX systems. Libraries and large databases will want this level of sophistication. Whenever the text information you are publishing is so big that searching on a simple word or words fails to narrow the field, you need to consider whether fields are available and field searching is necessary.

Menu and full-text indexing are not the only kinds of indexing. If you plan to provide a large number of nontext files, such as programs, pictures, sound, and video, you will want to index them. You might index only their file names (or menu items), but if you have explanatory blurbs about each one, you will want to index the explanations so that indexes retrieve the nontext file as well.

External indexers are usually programs that attempt to go out and collect information from all over the world and then make that index available from one server. Veronica (for Gopher sites) and Archie (for FTP and Gopher sites) are the most famous examples of external indexers. External indexers are a crucial element in indexing Gopher and Webspace (Webspace means the content of all the servers browsable with WWW browsers). They are analogous to listing a book in an international card catalog system. WWW Worm (WWWW), ALIWEB (Archie-like Web), and assorted other search programs traverse the Web to develop similar indexes. Learning the techniques and philosophies behind each of these external indexers is quite useful. The best way to do this is to look at the descriptions in Table 2–1, follow the links to each one, and then read more about them. Sometimes you'll find theoretical papers discussing search strategies, but usually you can learn their approach within a few minutes. Then you should register your server with all those indexes that you deem appropriate if you want your server to be truly internationally available.

Indexing has many advantages for both you and your users. It can lessen the load on your server and ease the frustration and complaints users have about getting lost in large servers. But indexing can be difficult to install and complicates server administration, one responsibility of which is ensuring that the indexes are always up to date.

Registering or Announcing Your Server

Gopher, WWW, and WAIS all have free central registries that attempt to keep track of all the servers in the world. You should register with them and apprise them of any server name changes you make. You also should be aware of the subject indexes and automatic and voluntary indexing servers. Register with them as appropriate.

See the indexing sections of the Gopher, WWW, and WAIS chapters (3, 4, and 5) for a list of these services and an explanation of their philosophies and indexing techniques.

If your server performs a service or acts as a resource for a certain population on the Internet, post information about it to the relevant Usenet newsgroup and e-mail the appropriate mailing list. Keep your announcement short and to the point, and try to avoid boasting. Asking for feedback and additional links is both good netiquette and good business—it will help you improve your server. Finally, contact other similar Web, Gopher, and WAIS sites and invite them to link into your server. The easiest way to find related sites is to search the Internet directories and indexes using terms that describe your own server.

Maintaining Reliability

A reachable site is a well-maintained site. You should plan to budget for maintenance and hardware sufficient to handle the load. If your Gopher, WWW, or WAIS server is often down, unavailable, or filled with links that don't work or data that are out of date, your company's reputation could be hurt. Servers go down because of power failures, machine malfunctions, software bugs, human error (someone turns it off), and overload. Although nothing is fail-safe, you need to plan for monitoring and maintenance of the server hardware and software. Some sites set up automatic programs that let them know if their server is down. I've even heard of someone who set up a machine to do this monitoring and page him if something is down.

Links can be incorrect if they were entered incorrectly and never checked or they changed without notification. A server has no way of knowing all the sites that link to it, so posting notices of changes to everyone who needs them is impossible, although some server administrators attempt to notify all sites they are aware of. Obviously, this requires a certain amount of personal attention. Plan to regularly verify and update your server's data and links. Some free UNIX programs for Gopher and WWW servers that automatically attempt to verify that all your links are working include:

Go4check—<***gopher://tjgopher.tju.edu/00/networks/internet/tools/gopher/go4check***>

Anchor Checker—<***http://www.ugrad.cs.ubc.ca/spider/q7f192/branch/checker.html***>

Link Verifier—<***http://wsk.eit.com/wsk/dist/doc/admin/webtest/verify_links.html***>

You should consider mirroring to another site or backup server if you expect to have a popular server. There are actually several kinds of **mirroring**. One type negotiates with another site to maintain a duplicate of its site or service. These sites are often on different continents to ease the load on international links. LeWeb Louvre does this with the original site in France and the mirror in North Carolina. The Internet Movie Database started out in Cardiff, Wales, and now has mirrors in Australia, the United States, Germany, and Japan. All sites offer the same data.

In another mirroring arrangement one site maintains several machines in parallel, each acting as the Gopher or WWW server. This is what the University of Minnesota Gopher crew had to do to handle the extreme load on its Mother Gopher server (because Gopher was invented there, the University of Minnesota's site is called the Mother Gopher). The university runs 10 Mac IIc's (running the A/UX operating system) in parallel, each with an 80MB hard disk just to support the top level of its Gopher server. Below that the university has a variety of machines, including Sun Microsystems and NeXT workstations and more A/UX machines.

Evaluating Server Performance and Audience Response

Evaluation is an important but often ignored component of any process. In this case most of the servers come with some sort of log file, which is easily activated if not so easily analyzed. Chapters 3, 4, and 5 on Gopher, WWW, and WAIS servers detail what is possible with those servers, but check to see whether this information can be gleaned from the log file:

- The number of connections your server supports per hour, day, week, or month.
- Origins of connections. This shows up in the logs as host names or subnet addresses of those making connections.
- Items accessed most often.

Turning log files into useful reports is sometimes more difficult than you'd expect, and some utilities have been written to simplify this process. Those currently available are described in Chapters 3, 4, and 5 on Gopher, WWW, and WAIS. Again, it's important to check with the Usenet newsgroup or e-mail mailing list for your particular brand of server to stay current with what these utilities can do. They are often written by administrators facing problems similar to yours.

Because Gopher, Web, and WAIS servers routinely log the host name (and IP address) of each user's computer, along with the items retrieved, you do need to be aware of the potential for invading users' privacy. To protect users' privacy many log analysis programs automatically strip off the lowest level of IP address in their reports, which removes this link to individuals. You need to know who your audience is, but you don't need to know who each user is. You might also consider modifying the server software to remove the link between users and items retrieved.

Nothing prevents you from building your own evaluation tools into your server. For example, some servers allow users to fill out a questionnaire. See Figure 2–3 for an example of an online comment form from a Web server. The answers can be stored in a private file, e-mailed directly to you, or posted right back on your server. One WWW site has a "sign-in sheet" that allows users to leave a comment as well as their name and e-mail address, data then added automatically to what is displayed on the server. Be aware that not all browsers support online forms, so always give your users an alternative, such as a way to e-mail their comments.

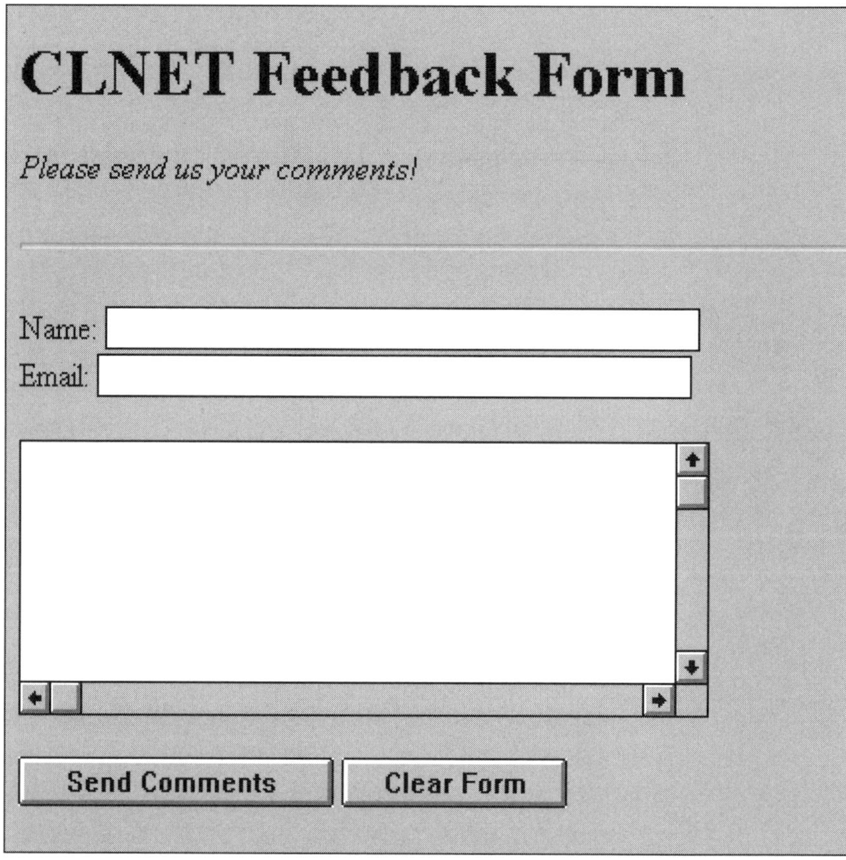

FIGURE 2–3 CLNET Feedback Form

Another option is to provide users with a voice telephone number, fax number, e-mail address, and/or postal address from which they may obtain further information. Although this somewhat defeats the purpose of publishing on the Internet, responses can be an objective measure of the interest generated by your server.

Or perhaps you've posted a catalog, and users place their orders through an existing telephone or fax order system. In that case make sure that the order form or telephone operator asks for the source of users' information, so that you can accurately evaluate your server's contribution.

Using What You've Learned

You may or may not have planned to implement your Gopher, WWW, or WAIS server in stages, but almost certainly you will learn from the process and find better ways to accomplish your goals. Given that this is a most malleable medium, you should plan to continually check, revise, update, and perhaps redesign your server. It is an artificial restriction to say that once it's up it can't be changed. That logic may apply to print versions, but with the Internet there's no such thing as final.

However, if you change information or remove menus that may have been linked by other servers, you should post explanatory notes. In such cases it is helpful to leave a link in place that describes the change and gives the new link information. You may also find it helpful to keep an administrator's log, describing the changes you make to software and hardware and particularly any changes in philosophy on menu arrangement or hypertext design. Also record any addition of other resources, such as a searchable index or major bodies of information, such as new departments. You may find the log useful in the future, or it may give another administrator an insight into your server's design. Much of this is of interest to your users as well, so you should consider adding a "What's New" section to your server for providing this information online. If you do, you should still keep a separate and private administrator's log in which you record changes or upgrades in your system or server software as well as problems you encounter and their solutions.

Summary

This chapter is about the groundwork you should do before you start publishing on the Internet. This includes exploring Gopher, Web, and WAIS sites both in your subject area and in others to get ideas and techniques you can use in your server. And keep notes of the problems you have and what helped and didn't help in your searches. Become familiar with FAQs, mailing lists (and their archives), and Usenet News, as well as the various Internet indexers and directories listed in Table 2–1. These are your tools on the Internet and you should know them well.

You will need to answer many questions—about your audience, your competition, charging policies, and how the information you publish will be gathered as well as maintained. You may need to think about a graphic designer. Are there any special security issues?

The presentation and organization of your data can be an important factor in your site's success. Do you have a design team or will you need one? Think about indexing the contents of your server wherever you have a large amount of material. Both internal and external indexes are important, so be sure to register your server. Also plan for continual maintenance and testing of your server's links. They can go out of date quickly, but tools are available to help you do the testing automatically.

Evaluate your server log files, particularly the error logs. Ask for feedback from your users (by e-mail, online forms, or even phone or fax). Users are a resource; don't waste them. This is a growing medium, so assume that your server will need to be redesigned regularly, that it is a perpetual work in progress.

Finally, remember that the Internet is not just millions of potential customers; it's also a network of people with varied interests, enthusiasms, and talents. Contribute something to the Internet to help it grow.

CHAPTER 3

Gopher and Gopher+

Depending on whom you ask, Gopher and its newer version, Gopher+, are in the midst of either their growing pains or their death throes. Gopher has already been surpassed by WWW in total number of servers and amount of traffic on the Internet, but with more than 7,000 servers worldwide and an extremely active development community, Gopher is an Internet publishing method that is hard to ignore. Here is a summary of Gopher's pros and cons:

ADVANTAGES

- Easy set-up and low maintenance.
- Little or no document preparation necessary.
- Light load on network because of small file sizes.
- Facilitates automatic indexing of server menus.
- Servers available for many types of computers, including mainframes.
- Client can run on old, slow computers.
- Gopher+ can serve up multiple versions of the same file.
- Client software available in English, Chinese, Japanese, Spanish, French, and Finnish.
- Strong development community.

DISADVANTAGES

- Can't mix graphics and text on same screen.
- Gopher client can't view HTML.

- Commercial users of University of Minnesota server software must license it.
- Gopher is divided between Gopher0 and Gopher+, and not all clients (browsers) handle Gopher+.

But even if you're enticed by WWW, don't pass Gopher by too quickly. Graphics are nice, but for a large percentage of Internet users, graphics are a luxury that their modem speed can't support. For these users Gopher is an excellent tool. Considering that preparation of material for Gopher is extremely simple and the Gopher software is easy to install and maintain, like FTP, Gopher will probably always have a place on the Internet. Gopher is an excellent choice when graphics are not an issue and a wide variety of people with little or no training need to add their files to the server. If you just want to get the information out there, Gopher is likely your best choice.

Gopher: Pros and Cons

Gopher has the advantage of being a simple protocol that is easy to set up and maintain. Adding documents and files to a Gopher server is usually a matter of just copying them into the Gopher directory structure. Unlike WWW servers, Gopher servers don't need special formatting or linking. Just drop the file in a Gopher directory and it will show up in the Gopher menu.

The average size of Gopher menus is small, usually 2K to 6K, whereas WWW home pages are usually 5K to 10K or more, and **inline images** (graphics that appear within a Web document), can increase that size to 100K or more. The smaller size of Gopher menus translates to quicker response to the user and less load on the Internet.

Gopher also does not require the user to have an extremely fast computer. Because the principal element of Gopher is a menu, it can be conveyed in text as easily as in graphics. So graphics monitors aren't even necessary.

A Gopher server is also flexible—it can serve up almost any type of file; **Gopher+** allows you to offer different versions of the same file (for example, WordPerfect, PostScript, and plain text versions of the same document, or Spanish, French, and Swedish versions).

The biggest drawback to Gopher is that it just isn't as sexy (or impressive in appearance) as WWW can be. Although it can make picture files available for downloading, it can't mix the pictures and text together in a glossy brochure-like presentation as WWW can.

One drawback to Gopher as a client program is that Gopher client programs can't browse WWW servers, although WWW client programs can view Gopher servers and retrieve data. Nevertheless, Gopher remains an extremely powerful and useful Internet publishing tool, with thousands of Gopher servers worldwide.

How Gopher Works

For technical details on the operation of Gopher, see "The Internet Gopher Protocol" and "Gopher+—Upward Compatible Enhancements to the Internet Gopher Protocol," both available at <*gopher://boombox.micro.umn.edu:70/11/gopher/gopher_protocol*>.

Here's a simple description of what goes on between a Gopher server and client:

1. Person selects an item on a Gopher menu.
2. Person's Gopher client reads the Gopher server address and port number in the link the person selected.
3. Gopher client contacts Gopher server on that port.
4. Gopher server accepts connection.
5. Gopher client asks for directory or file.
6. Server either fulfills the request or reports (via an error message) that it's not there.

If you want something else, you repeat the process. The Gopher server finds it an efficient process because it doesn't have to keep track of ongoing requests. Answer a question and wait for the next question—that's all it does. This can happen hundreds to thousands of times per day, depending on the popularity of the Gopher server. There is an agreed-upon list of the "types" of items that the system can convey, and the list is open-ended. It is administered by the University of Minnesota and is listed in the Gopher FAQ. You need to study the exact language or syntax used in the Gopher protocol only if you're writing Gopher server or client software.

Gopher and Gopher+ Features

Unfortunately, it's not enough to decide you want to run a Gopher server. You then have to choose Gopher0 or Gopher+. (The original Gopher protocol is referred to now as *Gopher0.*) Whether Gopher+ is an option depends on the type of computer you're going to run your server on. Gopher+ is the newer definition, or standard, toward which the Gopher community is moving. Gopher+ adds some nice features to Gopher, such as interactive online forms, multiple versions of the same file (called *views* in Gopher+ documents), and additional meta-information (or information about the files, such as administrator, date updated, and so on).

Gopher simplifies downloading from FTP servers because you immediately view what you download and then download more. This is particularly helpful because most FTP sites have readme and index files that you need to read.

Shell scripts are specially written programs that allow you to add other functions to your Gopher server. Scripts have been written to connect Gopher servers to database programs, for example.

The list that follows details features of both Gopher0 and Gopher+, but be aware that some Gopher servers may have additional features. Others may not have all the features listed here.

Gopher0 FEATURES

- Provides users with a menu of items available on Gopher server.
- Delivers directory indexes.
- Delivers files of specified types.
- Delivers telnet or tn3270 sessions (remote login) to another computer.
- Delivers links to items on other Gopher servers.
- Delivers links to files on anonymous FTP servers.
- Delivers results of index searches.
- Runs scripts on server.
- Answers requests in one step and then disconnects, which allows the Gopher server to run faster and handle more requests.
- Uses easily understood directory structure to store files on server.
- Permits system to define other item types at a later date.
- Configurable for querying remote WAIS servers and funneling the results to Gopher clients.
- Configurable for searching local WAIS indexes and indexing your own information.
- Queries remote FTP sites and funnels the results to Gopher clients.

Gopher+ FEATURES

- Provides administrator contact information for each item as a way to track the sources of information.
- Provides the date on which the document was last modified.
- Provides abstracts of items, especially useful for long documents.
- Provides online forms (called **ASK blocks**). This lets you ask your users to fill out an online form.

- Provides alternate views or file formats for Gopher items. This simplifies the process of providing documents in different word-processing formats.
- Permits system to define other item attributes and easily add them at a later time.

Gopher Resources

One way to learn about Gopher is to download the server software and set one up. It's easier than you think. But for those of us who like to test the waters first, see Table 3–1 for some sites and resources that will tell you a great deal about Gopher matters.

Note that some of the mailing lists are duplicates of Usenet newsgroups. And both are often archived at sites that provide indexed searching. Learning how to search these is one of the first skills you'll want to acquire. As you will see, Gopher servers can be run on many different types of computers. Some mailing lists and Usenet newsgroups have sprung up around different versions of Gopher servers. They may have a narrow focus, but they can be extremely rich in expertise and experience.

Generally, your plan to learn more about Gopher and Gopher+ should be to

1. Read the FAQs.
2. Look at existing servers and note features that you like.
3. Follow related Usenet newsgroups and list servers.
4. Install and run the Gopher software.

Learn how to use the bookmark feature in your Gopher or WWW browser. Then use it to "capture" (keep a record of) links to any site that might be useful to you later. It's possible to learn a lot from existing Gopher servers, both in style and in technique. Look at how they are laid out, and watch for techniques that make it easier or harder for you as a user to find information. If you have questions about how something was done, send e-mail to the

Gopher administrator and ask. And if you like what you see, say that too. Don't be upset if you don't get a response (they are probably as busy as you are), but it's very much within the culture of the Internet to ask how something is being done. No one waits for an introduction.

TABLE 3–1 Gopher Resources

Online Documents and Useful Sites	
Mother Gopher at University of Minnesota: <*gopher://gopher.tc.umn.edu*> and for software: <*gopher://boombox.micro.umn.edu*>	Start here! It has current versions of Gopher servers and clients, Gopher tools and documentation files and links to all the registered Gopher servers in the world, as well as the Gopher News Archives.
Gopher FAQ <*gopher://mudhoney.micro. umn. edu/00/ Gopher.FAQ*> or <*ftp://rtfm.mit.edu:/ pub/usenet/news.answers/gopher-faq*>	This FAQ file won't have everything you need, but at least you'll be able to say you read it.
VMSGopher–L FAQ <*gopher trln.lib.unc. edu*>	A FAQ file for the operators of VMSGopher Server software.
VMSGopher Server Archives <*gopher:// psulias.psu.edu*> or <*gopher://niord.shsu. edu*>	Archives for the operators of the VMSGopher Server software.
Gopher Conference '93 Trip Reports <*gopher://gopher.ucla.edu:70/11/gopher/ gopher93*>	These reports give a bit of the flavor of how Gopher developed.
Gopher Conference '94 Papers & Presentations <*gopher://boombox.micro.umn.edu: 70/11/gopher/Gopher_Conference_94/*>	The Gopher conferences are a hoot to attend but if you can't, at least some papers have been stored online.
Veronica FAQ <*gopher://veronica.scs.unr. edu:70/00/veronica/veronica-faq*>	Veronica is important because it goes out and indexes most Gopher servers in the world. This FAQ tells you how to register your Gopher server, among other things.
"Well-Constructed Gophers: Is Your Gopher Golden?" by J. E. Kosokoff in *Computer-Mediated Communication Magazine* <*http://sunsite.unc.edu/cmc/mag/1995/ mar/kosokoff.html*>	This short online article describes some factors that make a well-designed Gopher site. The issues raised are useful for Web administrators as well.

TABLE 3–1 *(continued)*

Usenet Newsgroups	
Comp.infosystems.gopher	The official Usenet group for discussions of Gopher matters.
Alt.gopher	The alternative Usenet group for Gopher matters
Vmsnet.infosystems.gopher	Discussion group for VMSGopher developers and administrators. It mirrors VMSGopher-L.
Electronic Mailing Lists	
Gopher-announce To subscribe send e-mail to *gopher-announce-request@boombox.micro.umn.edu*	The University of Minnesota uses this e-mail lis to announce new versions of its Gopher software.
Gn-maint To subscribe send e-mail to *listserv@netcom.com* containing the line *subscribe gn-maint*	This mailing list is for those running GN, a combination Gopher and WWW server.
GO4LIB-L To subscribe send e-mail to *owner-go4lib-l@ucsbvm.ucsb.edu*	Serves as a forum for library Gopher developers.
Gopher-news To subscribe send e-mail to *gopher-news-request@boombox.micro.umn.edu*	Gopher discussion also takes place on the mail ing list gopher-news.
VMGopher To subscribe send e-mail to *listserv@pucc.princeton.edu* with the following: *subscribe vmgopher [your name]*	This is a discussion list for the Rice CMS Gophe
VMSgopher-L To subscribe send e-mail to *listserv@trln.lib.unc.edu* with a message that contains *sub VMSgopher-L [your name]*	This is a discussion list for VMSGopher developers.
MVSGopher To subscribe send e-mail to *listserver@lists.acs.ohio-state.edu* containing: *subscribe mvsgopher [your name]*	A mailing list for MVSGopher developers and users.
Jughead-news To subscribe send e-mail with the subject subscribe to *jughead-news-requests@lists.utah.edu*	A mailing list for users of the Jughead indexing tool for Gopher servers.
Books	
The Internet for Everyone—A Guide for Users and Providers by Richard W. Wiggins	Among other things, this book gives example of UNIX and non-UNIX Gopher server set-up. It also details the GN server.
Managing INTERNET Information Services by Cricket Liu et al.	For UNIX administrators, this book gives detailed set-up and configuration instructions for Gopher servers, as well as WWW and WAIS.

The University of Minnesota's Mother Gopher site is the first listed in Table 3–1 because it is the official Gopher archive. Among other things, the Gopher team has set up examples of how all Gopher data types show up. These demonstrate each capability of Gopher.

Types of Items Gopher Handles

Gopher item types are important because they describe the kinds of information and services Gopher servers can deliver. You may think you just want to put text files and images on your server. But the Gopher server has to tell the Gopher client exactly what type of information will be sent out if the user's Gopher client program is to transmit and display the text file or image correctly. Most Gopher browsers (the terms **browser** and **client program** are used interchangeably) use a different symbol for each type of information they show. The users don't actually see the type codes listed in Table 3–2, but as a Gopher administrator, you will be dealing with them often. In many cases part of putting something on your Gopher server means specifying its type. It is important to understand the different types so that you can use them appropriately. Right now the key thing to know is that Gopher has a wide variety of types; you can come back and learn the details later.

See Table 3–2 for the current list of the many types of data and services Gopher servers can provide. The University of Minnesota's Gopher team keeps track of additions to the list. Some types aren't files at all. They represent some other kind of action that the Gopher server can provide, such as a telnet session and a tn3270 session type. They are both methods of logging in remotely to another computer. When a Gopher browser program sees type 8, which signifies a telnet session, it takes the host's name and port number provided and starts its own telnet session to that host computer. Type 7 signifies that a search will be initiated. For an explanation of **MIME** types, see Table 3–3. You can create your own data type too, although if you want anyone else to recognize it, you should register it and make sure their browser programs know how to handle it.

TABLE 3–2 Gopher Item Types

Type	Description	Explanation
0	File.	Almost always plain ASCII text files. Aliases allowed.
1	Directory.	Directory contents show up as a Gopher menu in alphabetical order, unless specified otherwise.
2	CSO (qi) phone-book server.	This is a special campus-directory type of application used at University of Minnesota when Gopher was first developed.
3	Error.	
4	BinHexed Macintosh file.	BinHex is a specific method of converting a Macintosh file or document to make it safe for transport across the Internet.
5	DOS binary archive of some sort.	This is for an uncoded, "as is," nontext file from a PC.
6	UNIX UUENCODED file.	UUENCODE is a specific method of converting files to make them safe for transport across the Internet.
7	Index-Search server.	Leads to a search program in which the user enters a query and the Gopher server responds with links to the files that matched.
8	Text-based Telnet session.	A user choosing this item will head off into another computer system via a remote login program called Telnet.
9	Binary file client must read until the connection closes. Beware!	Leads to a binary file with no operating system specified. Gopher browser program writers are warned that this Gopher type won't have the usual end-of-message confirmation.
T	tn3270 connection.	As in the Telnet type (type 8), this item leads off to another computer system via a remote login program called tn3270. That is a particular type of telnet that emulates an IBM 3270 terminal common to IBM mainframes.
s	Sound type. Data stream is a mulaw sound.	This returns a sound file that is a recording (or digital synthesis) of a particular set of sounds. Mulaw is a standard used on many DSP (digital signal processor) chips.

TABLE 3–2 (continued)

Type	Description	Explanation
g	GIF type.	GIF (pronounced *jiff*) stands for Graphic Interchange Format and was developed by CompuServe (a commercial bulletin board service).
M	MIME type. Item contains MIME data.	Multipurpose Internet Mail Enhancements include a large variety of file types to allow transmitting multimedia more easily.
h	HTML type.	HTML, or HyperText Markup Language, is the principal document type for WWW servers with links contained within the text. HTML viewers may soon be available for Gopher clients now that URLs have been standardized.
I	Image type.	The image viewer program has to detect from the file's internal structure exactly which type of image.
i	"Inline" text type.	These are nonselectable items in a menu. Think of them as information items that show up in the menu but don't link anything.
P	PDF—Portable Document Format.	PDF is Adobe Systems, Inc.'s proposed method for making graphical documents display equally well on Windows, Macintosh, and UNIX machines. The viewing program, Adobe Acrobat, is free. This is seen as a potential alternative to HTML.

The list of Gopher item types has grown since Gopher was originally created. New types such as MIME, HTML, and GIF have been added because users expressed the need for them. This flexibility is extremely important, because it means that Gopher has the capacity to grow and adapt and allow you to connect your users to many, if not all, existing Internet services.

Given the wide variety of formats in which you can publish using Gopher, don't forget the lowest common denominator, plain text. Gopher was designed for the low-end machine with a slow

TABLE 3–3 MIME Types

MIME stands for Multipurpose Internet Mail Extensions, a protocol designed for sending mixed media files across the Internet. MIME represents a large (and still growing) list of file types. Here are a few examples of MIME types.

MIME Type List (Excerpts)

TYPES/SUBTYPES	EXPLANATION
Text—plain	Text, plain and simple, like what you are reading now
Text—tab-separated values	Text items separated by tabs: California Oregon Michigan
Application—PostScript	Adobe PostScript file
Application—WordPerfect 5.1	A file ready for use in the application WordPerfect 5.1
Application—PDF	Adobe Portable Document Format (PDF) file
Application—ZIP	A compressed file that can be uncompressed with PKUNZIP
Application—MS Word	A Microsoft Word file, although which version is not clear
Application—Mathematica	A file that can be used in the application program Mathematica
Image—JPEG	An image file in JPEG format
Image—GIF	An image file in GIF format
Image—TIFF	An image file in TIFF format
Video—MPEG	A video file in MPEG format
Video—QuickTime	A video file in QuickTime format

To see the full registered list of MIME types (also used as Gopher+ view types), download it from <*ftp://ftp.isi.edu/in-notes/iana/assignments/media-types*>.

connection to the Internet. Also, Gopher is so widespread that you can never tell what kind of computer your viewers will be using. Although PostScript, Portable Document Format (PDF) from Adobe, and various word-processing formats make documents look much nicer than plain text, only plain text will be viewable if the user is on a mainframe Gopher client.

Gopher Servers

Gopher servers have been written or ported (short for *transported*) to many different types of machines. The University of Minnesota's Gopher Development Team started with a version for machines running the UNIX operating system, which includes Sun Microsystems, Silicon Graphics, IBM RS6000, and NeXT computers. Then the team wrote a version to run on Macintoshes, Gopher Surfer, which now has full-text searching. Other groups then wrote versions for their favorite machines, including DEC Vaxen, IBM mainframes, PCs running Windows NT and OS/2, and even lowly DOS machines.

Some servers run only the basic Gopher protocol, but many have moved on to Gopher+. Other servers offer more advanced functions. GN, from John Franks (no relation to the author), a professor at Northwestern University, is a combination Gopher and HTTP (WWW) server.

As with any software you need to address at least these five concerns when choosing a Gopher server:

Function—Look at the functions supported, the extra capabilities the server provides, as well as its record of compatibility with add-on indexing programs.

Platform—Check the platform (operating system and hardware) required, such as UNIX, Windows, and Macintosh, and its relative stability. Be aware of the difficulties in supporting platforms you're not familiar with.

Load—Investigate the load this server/platform can be reasonably expected to handle. Be sure it is high enough for two to three times the load you expect.

Support—Verify the level of support and activity this software enjoys, including newsgroups and mailing lists, as well as more formal commercial support mechanisms. An active newsgroup of technical administrators can be better than many companies' tech support desks.

Price—Determine the licensing policy. If it's freeware, check that it's not limited to educational organizations. Many free programs have a different policy for commercial uses.

The section that follows discusses the capabilities of many existing Gopher server programs.

UNIX

UNIX is the most powerful and flexible operating system available for Gopher servers. It is also extremely widespread. For this reason most new development is for UNIX first. Maintaining a UNIX system does require quite a bit of technical knowledge and experience.

Gopherd. Gopherd is a UNIX-based Gopher+ server from the University of Minnesota and is the leader in the development arena. This server always gets the new features first. Contact the university for licensing information. <***gopher://boombox.micro.umn.edu:70/11/gopher/Unix***>

GN. GN is a free UNIX-based multiprotocol server from John Franks at Northwestern. This server is unique in that it serves both the Gopher and WWW worlds, sending the same documents out via either protocol, depending on the type of request.

The GN server can act as both a Gopher (but not Gopher+) and WWW (HTTP) multiprotocol server and has been recommended as an intermediate step between Gopher and WWW. The support newsgroup gn-maint-l is very active and enthusiastically supports GN. An FAQ file on GN is available at <***http://www.unicom.com/1/FAQ***>, whereas the software can be found at <***http://hopf.math.nwu.edu:70/***>. John Franks has stopped development of GN and moved onto a Web (HTTP only) server called WN. See Chapter 4 for a list of Web servers grouped by computer platform.

VMS

VMS, short for Virtual Memory System, is Digital Equipment Corporation's multi-user, multitasking operating system. It runs on

DEC's VAX series of computers, from the smallest minicomputer to the biggest mainframe.

VMSGopher Server. VMSGopher Server 0.6b is a free Gopher server for the VMS operating system. The "tweaked" code is not always available at Boombox, so check other sites as well. Check out the Gopher FAQ and VMSGopher Server Archives (see Table 3–1). Several sites have beta-test source code for VMS, which is often ahead of the version stored at the University of Minnesota. <*gopher://psulias.psu.edu*> or <*gopher://niord.shsu.edu*> or <*gopher://gopher.wfeb.edu*>. Precompiled (ready to run) executables are available at <*gopher://trln.lib.unc.edu*>. The Minnesota archive is available at <*gopher://boombox.micro.umn.edu:70/11/gopher/VMS*>.

Macintosh

Macintoshes are a user friendly place to set up a Gopher server. You can manage quite a bit of customization by using AppleScript (a command language that comes with System 7) and MacPerl (a free Macintosh port of the Perl language). An alternative to mounting a Gopher server on a Macintosh or PowerMac is to run A/UX (Apple's UNIX) instead of the normal Macintosh operating system. Then you would choose a Gopher server from the UNIX section.

Gopher Surfer. Gopher Surfer is a Macintosh-based Gopher+ server from the University of Minnesota that requires System 7.0. It uses AppleSearch to provide full-text searching. Contact the university for licensing information. <*gopher://boombox.micro.umn.edu:70/11/gopher/Mac_server*>

Windows NT

Microsoft Windows NT 3.5 is now a serious choice for Gopher administrators, primarily because of the ease of installation and administration. Windows NT also offers the ability (on some servers) to interact with Visual Basic and data in regular Windows applications such as Microsoft Excel and Access.

EMWAC GopherS for Windows NT. GopherS, pronounced *Gopher-ess,* is a Windows NT–based Gopher0 server (not Gopher+) that runs as a Windows NT service so you don't have to remain logged in. It handles multiple simultaneous connections using multiple threads and can handle WAIS database searching if you use its WAISTOOL tool kit. It has a UNIX compatibility mode, which will be helpful for those familiar with UNIX Gopher servers. FTP from <*emwac.ed.ac.uk*> in the directory pub/gophers. <***http://emwac.ed.ac.uk/HTML/internet_toolchest/top.HTML***>

DOS and Windows

DOS runs on a minimal PC so it is ideal for setting up extremely inexpensive Gopher servers. Windows has the advantage of being widely used (even if it's not always stable), so it is an easy platform to begin with.

KA9Q NOS. KA9Q NOS is a DOS-based Gopher and e-mail (POP2/POP3/SMTP) server written by Phil Karn. It requires at least a 286, but a 386SX with 2MB of RAM is recommended. <***gopher://boombox.micro.umn.edu:70/11/gopher/PC_server/ka9q***>

GO4HAM. GO4HAM is a Windows Gopher server (using WINSOCK.DLL) written by Gunter Hille of the University of Hamburg. It includes full-text search capability and gateway to the Borland Paradox database program. Available from <***ftp://ftp.informatik.uni-hamburg.de/pub/net/Gopher/pc/go4ham***> or from <***gopher://boombox.micro.umn.edu:70/11/gopher/PC_server/hamburg***>.

OS/2

IBM's OS/2 version Warp 3.0 has the advantage of being relatively stable while running on PCs with less memory than Windows NT requires.

GoServe. GoServe is a Gopher server designed to run on IBM's OS/2 2.x operating system. It provides for an audit trail of requests and actions. GoServe is free. <*gopher://boombox.micro.umn.edu:70/11/gopher/os2*>

Other Platforms

MVSGopher Server. MVSGopher Server runs on the MVS operating system, which usually means large IBM mainframes. <*gopher://boombox.micro.umn.edu:70/11/gopher/mvs*>

Rice CMS Gopher Server. Rice CMS Gopher Server runs on the CMS operating system. Check the resource table (Table 3–1) for the list server information. <*gopher://boombox.micro.umn.edu:70/11/gopher/Rice_CMS*>

VieGOPHER. VieGOPHER runs on the CMS operating system and was written by Gerhard Gonter of Vienna. <*gopher://boombox.micro.umn.edu:70/11/VieGOPHER*>

Other Servers

The best way to find out about new Gopher servers is to go looking on <*gopher://boombox.micro.umn.edu*>, check the Gopher FAQ periodically, and watch the Gopher newsgroups (see Table 3–1).

Installing Gopher Server Software

Gopher and Gopher+ are protocols. The Gopher protocol is a defined way that the server and the client communicate. The protocol does not specify how information is to be stored on the server, nor does it in any way define how the Gopher server should go about doing its job.

The programmers who wrote each of the Gopher servers had a lot of leeway to do things in a way that made the most sense for the machine and operating system they were using. A Macintosh-based Gopher server will look very different (to the administrator) from one designed for a mainframe. Basically, each version of the Gopher server software is different, and the installation instructions are different as well.

For these reasons I won't give you step-by-step instructions. We'll go through the basic steps of installing and setting up Gopher server software, using the UNIX Gopher server as a model. The point here is to understand what options are generally available and the kinds of decisions you'll have to make, no matter which type of Gopher server you choose.

If you have problems, check the mailing list or Usenet newsgroup (and their archives) related to your server software to see whether someone offers a solution. Providing step-by-step installation instructions for each version of Gopher server software is beyond the scope of this book. Instead, I assume that you or the person who will be responsible for your server will be able to use the software documentation to install it, and I will concentrate on providing you with an explanation of the concepts and techniques that you'll begin to use once the software is installed.

Downloading, Uncompressing, and Compiling the Software

You have to get your software from somewhere, and usually that means you're getting it by Gopher or anonymous FTP from one of the sites listed earlier in this chapter. The most common error is to forget to switch to binary mode before FTP-ing the software down to your machine.

On UNIX the files come in the form filename.tar.Z, which means they've been both tarred and compressed. (**Tar** is a UNIX command for combining zillions of tiny files and directories in one big file.) Make sure you have plenty of disk space, then type Uncompress filename.tar.Z, which will replace your compressed version with a much larger file without the .Z at the end. Then make sure you are sitting in a directory one level above the directory into which you want to put your files, and type tar -xfv filename.tar, which will create the subdirectories and unpack all the files that go into them.

Macintosh files usually come in BinHex format (.hqx) to travel safely across the Internet, and sometimes they are also in a self-extracting archive (.sea). Often these two are combined so that the file would look like filename.sea.hqx, but unloading it is easy with the shareware BinHex program (use Archie to find it on the Internet).

UNIX and VMS versions usually have to be compiled before they can be run. Before you compile, determine which additional gateway features you want your server to have. WAIS is the program most commonly added to Gopher, and it's essential for some of the indexed searching functions you may want. Compilation problems are one of the most talked-about issues in the Gopher newsgroups. The best thing you can do is read the documentation carefully and take careful notes of each step in the compile process. If you do have to go asking for help in the Gopher newsgroups, you'll be able to accurately summarize your situation (don't leave out the details of your operating system). And when the next release of your Gopher server software comes out, you'll be able to avoid the mistakes you made the first time around.

What's Involved in Gopher Server Configuration

Gopher server configuration refers to editing certain configuration files to add information about your site and decide how the server should behave in various situations. The information specific to your site is easy. It consists of such things as the server's name, administrator's name and e-mail address, time zone, default language, location, latitude/longitude, and other identifying factors.

The hard part of configuration is understanding what each configuration option means and deciding how important it is in the operation of the server. Some options affect performance, and others can affect your system's security and may require consultation with your system administrator.

The configuration information will be in different locations and may have different names, depending on the version of Gopher server software you use. (In the UNIX version the files to be edited are gopherd.conf, makefile.config, and conf.h.) There also are some command line options when starting the Gopherd program.

Configuring Site-Specific Information

The site-specific information for the Minnesota UNIX Gopher includes such items as organization, site, administrator, latitude/longitude, time zone, host alias, and language.

Organization is the group that owns the **site**, such as UCLA or Addison-Wesley. The site is the name you want to appear when your server is contacted, such as Social Sciences Computing for my Gopher server. **Administrator** and **admin-email** refer to the name and e-mail address of the person who administers your Gopher server. This information is required under the Gopher+ protocol because it will be listed for every menu item on that Gopher server that does not specifically have its own administrator information. It's common to use an alias such as Gophermaster and have the mail forwarded from there to a real person. *Note:* With this server you can have different administrators for different subdirectories. To do this, see auxconf in the gopherd.conf file.

The 3-D version of Gopher, which is in development, will use **latitude** and **longitude** to provide a graphic display of the server's geographic location. Check an atlas or these two geographic information servers to find this information for your location: <***http://sipb.mit.edu:8001/geo***> or <***telnet://martini.eecs.umich.edu:3000***>. You can also display the **time zone**, or the number of time zones your server is from Greenwich Mean Time. Minnesota is GMT-6, Los Angeles is GMT-8, Rio de Janeiro is GMT-3, Taipei is GMT+8, Sydney is GMT+10.

Remember that the machine you put your server on today may not be the machine it's on next year. For that reason it's best to set up a host alias, instead of the specific name of the machine on which it resides. For example, we (Social Sciences Computing at UCLA) originally set up our Gopher server on one machine, but instead of registering that name, we used an alias. Within six months we had to move our Gopher server to a machine with a different name, but the alias stayed the same.

Language identifies the default (or most commonly used) language in the text files on your Gopher server. Like the administrator attribute, this meta-information is passed along by Gopher+ servers whenever item information is requested. A different language can be specified for individual files.

Configuring Gopher Performance

Gopher can be configured to behave in different ways in particular situations. Some options affect the speed with which a Gopher server will respond. The following options are available on the Minnesota UNIX Gopher server but may not have an equivalent in other servers. The **cache time** variable sets the amount of time (in seconds) before the server checks whether the Gopher files have changed. Because it's faster for the Gopher server to grab a cache file of a directory list than to actually run a directory listing, this setting affects the server's response time, particularly for large directories. The number of seconds should be low when you expect rapid change in a directory and high when change is likely to be rare.

You can configure your Gopher server to ignore or not include any files that end with a particular extension or that match a particular pattern. This can be a convenience for the Gopher administrator. ViewExt lets you specify certain file name extensions for different views of a similar base file. For example, message.txt.SP could designate a text file in Spanish, whereas message.txt.DE means text in German (Deutsch). When Gopher+ browsers select this item, they see a list of the different Spanish and German views available for that document. Instead of languages, the different views might be different word-processing formats, such as WordPerfect 5.1, Word for Windows, PostScript, and plain text.

The decoder option allows you to run files with certain extensions through certain programs before delivery. One use is storing files in a compressed form with a specific extension, such as .zip. Then the Gopher server will run the decompression file specified with the decoder option when delivering any .zip files. VeronicaIndex determines whether your Gopher server allows Veronica indexing. Veronica is an extremely useful Internet-wide Gopher index collection system. See the Veronica section later in this chapter for limiting indexing to certain directories.

Configuring Access and Security

One of the first things you need to think about after you have the Gopher server running is whether you need to restrict access. If anyone, for any reason, should not see what's on your server, you should consider whether you want to put that information in a public place like the Internet. Don't trust that the server software in its default configuration will be secure on your system. Pay close attention to exactly what options for limiting access your server software provides, and be sure you understand the method in use. Here are three basic techniques for restricting access to your server:

Restrict or allow access by domain name.

Hide your server.

Require a password for connection.

With these techniques you can restrict part or all of your Gopher server. You can have certain information available only to those coming from certain **domains** and have other information sent to different domains. You can require a password for certain items. Remember that each technique has its limitations.

Restricting or Allowing Access by Domain Name. The first method of restricting access is to allow or restrict access based on the Internet domain or subdomain of the Gopher user's machine. You can also restrict by subdirectory as well as the entire Gopher server. For example, in our Gopher server, <*gopher://gopher.sscnet.ucla.edu*>, sscnet stands for Social Sciences Computer Network, which is in the UCLA network, which is in the edu (education) domain, as opposed to the com (commercial), gov (government), mil (military), or .uk (United Kingdom), .fr (France), .au (Australia), .br (Brazil), and .sg (Singapore) domains. Say I have something on our Gopher server that I want to make available only to people from UCLA. I can restrict access to only those users whose computers are in the ucla.edu domain. Further, if I had something else of interest only to those in the social sciences, I could restrict access to only those people whose machines are in the sscnet.ucla.edu subnet.

This method works when you have a small number of local subdomains that can be easily listed and anything else shouldn't be allowed to see your server. This is appropriate when your company or campus is licensed for certain types of things, but you don't want to publish them for the world.

The restricted access option specifies IP addresses or subnet domains that are or are not allowed access to specific directories or the whole server, whereas you can also limit access by type (browse, read, or search only) for certain machines or subnets. "Bummermsg" is the message that goes out to anyone refused access to your Gopher server because of the restrictions you set up. You can make it friendly, authoritative, or mean like a snake. It's your server, your choice.

Hiding Your Server. Hiding your server may seem silly but actually can be quite effective. Because Gopher servers are expected to run (or be listening) on port 70, hiding your Gopher server means running it on a nonstandard port. Each UNIX machine has thousands of ports. They aren't physical ports, just numbers assigned for different purposes. Port numbers 1023 and below are reserved for the system administrator, but others can use ports with higher numbers, so you'll often see personal Gopher servers listed at port 7000 instead of Gopher's usual port 70. Sites that need different features provided by different Gopher servers often run both but on different ports of the same UNIX machine.

Although the degree of safety obtained by running on a nonstandard port number is not great, it does keep casual browsers out, simply because they would have to try all your ports to find your Gopher server. Of course, once someone sees a link (or URL) to your server, nothing prevents that person from copying it and linking to it. But if you don't publicize this number, it is extremely unlikely that someone will search all possible ports on your machine just to find a hypothetical Gopher server.

Requiring a Password for Connection. Requiring a password (sometimes called a *ticket*) for connection to the Gopher server is basically a low-security method of validating users. Different techniques are discussed more fully in Chapter 7. But for now you should know that this capability is built into at least the University of Minnesota UNIX Gopher server.

Startup: Stand Alone Versus Inetd

(This section applies only to UNIX servers.) Obviously, you want your Gopher server to come up automatically whenever your server is rebooted. This is handled differently on different platforms, but UNIX has two options, stand alone and inetd (Internet Daemon). They determine which part of the operating system has actual control of the Gopher server process.

Inetd is a special process on UNIX that listens for a call on various ports and, when it finds one, starts up the appropriate program, in this case the Gopher server program Gopherd. This would seem sensible, because the Gopher server runs only run when a request comes through, but unfortunately the time delay to start up the Gopher server program, as well as other factors, make this the less desirable alternative.

Standalone mode means that your Gopher server is running all the time, sitting and waiting for someone to talk to it on port 70 or whichever port you've assigned it to watch. The important thing here is to make sure that the Gopher server is not offering too many privileges. You don't want your Gopher server to be subverted by a hacker who gains enough access to damage your system. That's why the UNIX Gopher documentation strongly suggests that you run your Gopher server from a limited privilege account, with only enough privileges to access the directories it needs.

Setting Up the Gopher Data Directory

No matter what version of the Gopher server software you use, you will need an area in which to store files and documents. This is called the **Gopher data directory**, and it's where you'll do the bulk of your work. Each directory acts as sort of a submenu; the files in that directory show up as menu items. You might, for example, have a subdirectory for each department in your organization. These departments might then have subdirectories for different content areas. See Figure 3–1 for a sample directory structure for the UCLA Social Sciences Computing Gopher. (*Note:* The list of departments is shortened.)

You are not obliged to have many subdirectories, but subdirectories often help to keep things organized and keep your Gopher menus from getting too long. And using different subdirectories for different departments makes it easy to set up group permissions (if your operating system allows it) so that one department can update its own material but not another department's.

FIGURE 3–1 Sample Gopher Data Directory

```
Top-level  ──► /gopher-data
menu items
               |──anthro
               |──econ
               |   |──announcements  }
               |   |──data           } ◄── Appears under econ menu
               |   |──faculty        }
               |──geog
               |──|──climatology ◄── Appears under geog menu
               |──sscnet
```

Figure 3–2 shows how the first-level directory from the example in Figure 3–1 would look in Gopher. Note that the directory and the one file name, welcome, appear in alphabetical order.

Short names for directories and files are convenient for Gopher managers, but users like longer names that include some description. Also, the order here isn't right. The welcome message should be the first item on the menu, not the last, as it appears alphabetically. The UNIX Gopher+ server lets you make such cosmetic changes via the .names file. *Note:* Different Gopher servers use different techniques to make these changes. This section isn't meant as a tutorial but rather as an example of the kind of control almost any Gopher server allows you.

When using the University of Minnesota's UNIX Gopher server software, putting a period at the front of a file name makes that file invisible to Gopher. It also means the Gopher server will check on whether it contains valid instruction statements. These instructions can do three things:

Give longer names or titles to items (directory and file names).

Specify the order in which items appear.

Link to other locations for items.

The example in Figure 3–3 uses the first two of these and shows a .names file setup to give longer names and change the order. Figure

FIGURE 3–2 Sample Data Directory as Seen by Gopher User

```
Internet Gopher Information Client v2.0.16

                                      Social Sciences Gopher

-->    1.  anthro/
       2.  econ/
       3.  geog/
       4.  sscnet/
       5.  welcome  [ 5Mar95, 1kb]
```

3–4 demonstrates the results of using the .names file to make these cosmetic changes.

Note how much more descriptive that Gopher menu is now. And the welcome file has a longer title and shows up at the head of the list. The Numb=1 command for the welcome file in Figure 3–3 made that happen. The rest of the items are alphabetized—by their new descriptive titles, not by their file names.

FIGURE 3–3 Cosmetic Touches—.names File Adds Titles and Reorders Items

```
#
Name=UCLA Anthropology Department  <---  Longer, more descriptive name.
Path=./anthro
#
Name=UCLA Geography Department
Path=./geog  <---  Path to file or directory being renamed.
#
Name=UCLA Economics Department
Path=./econ
#
Name=Social Sciences Computing
Path=./sscnet
#
Name=Welcome to the UCLA Social Sciences Computing (SSCnet) Gopher
Path=./welcome
Numb=1  <---  Path to file or directory being renamed. This item
#             becomes first in Gopher menu.
```

FIGURE 3–4 Sample Data Directory After "Cosmetic Touches"

```
Internet Gopher Information Client v2.0.16
                                        Social Sciences Gopher

-->     1.  Welcome to the UCLA Social Sciences Computing (SSCnet) Gopher
        2.  Social Sciences Computing/
        3.  UCLA Anthropology Department/
        4.  UCLA Economics Department/
        5.  UCLA Geography Department/
```

For the final step in this example let's add a link back to UCLA's main Gopher server, so that our users can find their way out to other parts of the campus. Also, the Chicano Studies Research Center has its own Gopher server, and because that's one of the departments we support, let's link to it as well. These links can be added to the .names file or to another file that starts with a period. Let's call our other file .links and keep it separate. Figure 3–5 shows the .links file, and Figure 3–6 shows the results of adding the two links.

Figure 3–5 shows how to add information that describes how and where to locate the other Gopher servers. And the Chicano Studies Gopher server is a Gopher+ server, which allows us to add the administrator's name and contact information. This shows only when the user requests information on this link.

Figure 3–6 shows the two new link items in alphabetical order as items #2 and #5 on the Gopher menu, the result of the Gopher server program's doing its job of coordinating the various files and items to make a useful Gopher menu out of them. One advantage is that you can group your links in different files without having to worry about combining them.

FIGURE 3–5 Adding Links to Sample Gopher Menu

```
#
Name=Info UCLA - UCLA's Gopher Server
Type=1
Port=70
Path=
Host=mic.ucla.edu
#
Type=1+
Name=UCLA Chicano Studies Research Center
Path=1/Directory/Research/UCLA_CSRC
Host=latino.sscnet.ucla.edu
Port=70
Admin=Richard Chabran, Chicano Studies Research Center,
UCLA <chabran@latino.sscnet.ucla.edu>
```

Items with these titles will appear on Gopher menu.

FIGURE 3–6 Menu After Adding Links to InfoUCLA and Chicano Studies

```
Internet Gopher Information Client v2.0.16

                                Social Sciences Gopher

-->     1.  Welcome to the UCLA Social Sciences Computing (SSCnet) Gopher
        2.  Info UCLA - UCLA's Gopher Server/
        3.  Social Sciences Computing/
        4.  UCLA Anthropology Department/
        5.  UCLA Chicano Studies Research Center/
        6.  UCLA Economics Department/
        7.  UCLA Geography Department/
```

The next step in setting up this Gopher server would be to add files and links to each directory (anthro, econ, geog, and sscnet). The procedure is the same, however, and each directory can have its own collection of .names and .links files. If you need to add more directories at the top or in any subdirectory along the way, you're free to do so. Just check it with a Gopher browser to make sure it shows up the way you want it to.

Useful Techniques for Adding Information and Files

The whole point of the original design of Gopher (and WWW as well, for that matter) was to make it easy for people to publish their information. Gopher succeeds at this better than WWW because there is less emphasis on the format of the material. All you have to do is put your files in a Gopher directory and they become available over the server. It is not necessary to format the document in hypertext.

Eventually, you will find that you don't have time to handle all the files and links that need to be added to your server. Because no one knows as much as you do about the operation of your Gopher server, it is important to have easy, convenient, foolproof methods for others in your company or organization to add information to your Gopher server.

What follows are some techniques for adding information to your Gopher server. Some are simple and some are complex.

Group Permissions

If you are using UNIX or any other operating system that allows rights to be assigned to a group of users, take advantage of that feature to allow individuals to update their own areas of expertise in your Gopher server. Set up a group and then give that group access to the files and directories in its area of the Gopher data directory.

The Macintosh Gopher Surfer server administrator can use the User and Group Privileges features of Apple Personal Filesharing to permit participants in a Macintosh Appletalk network to put their files in your Gopher by just dragging them over with a mouse. Be sure that users know what to do if they need to modify the access rights to the files they add. The limitations of this method are that the users need to know their way around your operating system and they have to be familiar with any specific Gopher server set-up instructions your server may have.

Adding Documents with FTP

On UNIX systems you can give users the rights to FTP files into their subdirectories of your Gopher data directory. It is relatively easy to teach users to do this, and they don't need to learn UNIX commands. And users who become familiar with the .names file format can design and upload that file and control the appearance of the file names and order of appearance.

Linking to Users' Directories

You can create links within the Gopher data directory that point out files in other directories, specifically a subdirectory of the home directory of the person you want to administer that section of the Gopher data. This works on UNIX and may work on any other operating system that allows aliases or links to make a file appear to be in two places at once.

Connecting Gopher to a Database

Although most Gopher servers store their data in files, that isn't necessarily the only way to go. Some Gopher servers are built on top of databases and then use a gateway program between the two. This arrangement allows you to use Gopher to access information in a sophisticated and powerful database package, where it might be used for many other purposes as well. For example, you could keep your company's product information, prices, and inventory in a database that you also make available via Gopher. Instead of scattering files throughout the Gopher data directory, these Gopher servers store at least some data in databases.

This has its advantages, especially if you can link Gopher to an existing mainframe SQL (Structured Query Language) relational database that is already being used for other purposes. This linkup provides broader access to the same data with much less user training. Users find Gopher is much easier to learn than SQL query statements.

The University of Minnesota Gopher Development Team wanted to give Gopher users access to information about campus events that was stored on a mainframe computer. The data was in an SQL database (in this case Sybase), so the team developed the GopherSQL gateway to translate Gopher requests into SQL query statements. The responses from the mainframe database return through the GopherSQL gateway to the Gopher user. This process is described in Paul Lindner's paper presented at the 1994 Gopher Conference, "A Gopher Interface to Relational Databases," which you can find at <*gopher://boombox.micro.umn.edu:70/00/gopher/Gopher_Conference_94/Papers/GopherSQL*>. GopherSQL and other gateways are located at <*gopher://boombox.micro.umn.edu:70/11/gopher/Unix/gopher-gateways/*>.

Getting Others to Collect Links

Encourage your staff and users to suggest links to you by saving them in their own bookmark files and e-mailing them to you. That gives you a group of people scouring the Internet for related resources, instead of just one. And your staff will feel it is participating in the publishing process.

Adding Links via Forms

Build a Gopher+ form on which users or staff members can enter link information. Encouraging others to gather links for you will bring in more than you'd find on your own. The limitations are that users need to have a browser that is compatible with Gopher+ (forms are a Gopher+ feature) and that anyone can add documents to your Gopher server if you have not installed some authorization or password control options.

Using Veronica to Collect Links

Use the Veronica Gopher Indexing program to search out links to related or useful information. Some Veronica servers allow you to download the entire .link file for the entire search (instead of one item at a time) and add those links to your Gopher server.

Adding Documents via E-Mail (GMAIL)

GMAIL is a Perl script for UNIX Gopher servers that allows your data maintainers to send you their additions and deletions via e-mail (see Table 3–4). This script allows you to create a list of e-mail addresses and match each to a directory in which users can deposit messages. The subject line of the message becomes the Gopher menu item for that file, and the rest of the mail header is stripped off for security and appearance. If you put *delete* in front of the same subject line and send it, GMAIL will delete the message. The script even sends back confirmation messages. The limitation of GMAIL is that each e-mail ID can deposit in only one directory, although each directory can have multiple contributors.

Adding Documents via E-Mail (Appending to a File)

On UNIX systems you can set up an alias such that any messages received are added to the end of a specified file instead of being sent to a person. The University of Minnesota's Gopher server displays these files (they are also called *mail spool files*) as a menu of items, using the subject line of each message as its menu item. This is a good way to add the messages from a mailing list to your Gopher server, if you make that alias a subscriber to the mailing list. But be aware that this file can get quite large if it is not monitored. One solution would be to run a cron job (a program on UNIX that lets you schedule certain events at specified dates and times) so that the file is renamed once a week with the week name. You could also instruct the system to delete the oldest week file to save space. One limitation of constantly appending to a file is that the latest items always appear at the end of the Gopher menu.

GopherLunch

GopherLunch is a Gopher data submission system from Arizona State University (see Table 3–4). It runs on UNIX Gopher servers and allows relatively easy submission of documents via ASK block forms, FTP, or e-mail messages.

Gopher Tools

Whenever you get a bunch of programmers interested in something, you'll soon see that they've developed additional programs and tools that make their job easier. Tools like Jughead were developed to index Gopher servers and allow Boolean searches (logical operators, such as search for this AND that OR something else). Other tools make it easier to link to certain types of items or test your links automatically. These tools can make your life as a Gopher administrator much easier and can allow you to improve your server. Table 3–4 lists and describes some of the more useful tools for Gopher administrators.

Gopher Menu Layout

The layout of a Gopher server is not as simple a project as you might think. In fact, it can be the cause of quite heated discussions. Different camps have good reasons for their opinions. Basically, what drives the controversy is which layout works best to communicate to the user. Typical users of a poorly designed Gopher server might

- Get lost and give up in disgust.
- Falsely assume you don't have what they want when they can't find it immediately.
- Look for something by one name or in one category, when you've grouped or named it differently.
- Have to go so deeply into your Gopher menu that they can never get back or tell anyone else how to get there (of course knowledgeable users would save a bookmark to that link once they had found it).
- Spend too much time following links and menus to get to a popular item that should have been near the top of the menu.
- Find an index search of your server's contents but then have no way to understand the terminology you used in your documents, and all their guesses fail to hit.

Here are some guidelines/rules/suggestions for Gopher menu design:

1. Be clear and descriptive in your menu titles.
2. Avoid vague words like *other* and *miscellaneous.*
3. Keep your main Gopher menus to one screen, two at most.
4. Test your menus on novices.
5. Make a searchable index of everything on your server and make it highly visible.

TABLE 3–4 Gopher Tools

Tool	Platform	Description
Minnesota Mother Gopher Site *<gopher://boombox.micro.umn.edu :70/11/gopher>*	Multiple	This is the first site to check for Gopher tools.
Jughead by Rhett "Jonzy" Jones, U. of Utah Computer Center. FTP from *<ftp://ftp.cc.utah.edu/pub/gopher/ GopherTools/>*	UNIX	Jughead lets you index a specified Gopherspace and then provide Boolean searching of those menus.
getLinks by Rhett "Jonzy" Jones, U. of Utah Computer Center. FTP from *<ftp://ftp.cc.utah.edu/pub/ gopher/GopherTools/getLinks/>*	UNIX	getLinks allows you to specify certain menus on another Gopher site and automatically download and duplicate them on your Gopher server.
GMAIL by Prentiss Riddle of Rice University. *<gopher://boombox. micro.umn.edu@/pub/gopher/Unix/ GopherTools/>*	UNIX	This Perl script allows server operators at selected e-mail addresses to send in updates of their UNIX Gopher server via e-mail. Excellent for allowing updates by unskilled staff. Limitation of one directory per e-mail address.
G2NNTP by Martin Hamilton. *<gopher://genie.lut.ac.uk:70/0/g2nn tp>*	UNIX	Every newsgroup appears as a searchable object, which you can make links to, bookmarks of, etc.This use of indexing is limited to the information you see in the directory listings—subject line, author, and number of lines.
GopherLunch *<ftp://info.asu.edu/pub/unix/ gopher>*	UNIX	GopherLunch allows submission of documents via ASK block forms, FTP, or e-mail messages.
go4check by George A Theall. *<gopher://tjgopher.tju.edu/00/netw orks/internet/tools/gopher/ go4check>*	UNIX	go4check automatically checks Gopher links, probing each connection and testing the output received.
gee by Bill Middleton. *<gopher://boombox.micro.umn.edu :70/11/ gopher/Unix/GopherTools/>*	UNIX	gee is a tool that enables Gopher administrators to easily see and make changes to their Gopher data directory. It is written in Perl and was not designed for Gopher+ servers, although it should work with them.

Password Protection

Sooner or later Gopher managers find that they need some sort of password verification to allow only certain users access to particular data files or directories. Providing password protection is a problem endemic to the Internet publishing industry, and some say its solution is the key to making the Internet commercially successful (as opposed to just wildly successful at encouraging cooperation and sharing of information). Needless to say, much research is concentrating on Internet authorization and secure charge-account systems. See Chapter 7, Internet Commerce, for more detailed descriptions of some of these efforts.

However, you should be aware that some Gopher servers offer a "lightweight" security system that exchanges some form of password or token to "prove" the identity of the user. It is called lightweight security because the password is usually sent across the Internet in the clear or with only modest encryption.

Lightweight security systems can be enticing, because they appear to give you at least a certain level of security. But don't confuse the appearance of security with security itself. Although you might be acutely aware of the limitations of your security scheme, your data librarians and others who add items to your server may not always be so cautious.

What Logs Can Tell You

Almost all Gopher servers have some provision for keeping logs, and some utility programs provide statistics so you can analyze those logs. Here's a sample of the information usually available from the log files:

IP address of all clients

Dates and times of connection

Item(s) retrieved (this does not include links to items on other servers, because they would attach to the other server, not yours)

Host names of all clients

These logs make it possible to determine the number of times an item is retrieved and when and its relative popularity. You cannot yet get a reading on the type of clients (Gopher, Gopher+, HTTP, and so on) connecting to your Gopher server. That information would tell you how many of the Gopher+ features you use are beyond the abilities of the Gopher client programs that access your site.

Knowing what files are most and least popular can be useful for measuring utility as well as for redesigning your layout. Perhaps the information you know your users would find most helpful is so far away from the top level that they never find it. Or perhaps the name of the file is not clear enough. You can experiment by listing the file under a new name while keeping the old one. See if the new one gets retrieved more often.

However, you need to be aware of the potential for invasion of privacy inherent in these logs. The logs record the host name (and IP address) of each user's computer, along with the items that person retrieved. Gopher (and Web) administrators often automatically strip off the lowest level of IP address in their reports, precisely to remove this link to individuals. I'm told that at least one Gopher site has had to modify its Gopher server software to remove the possibility of linking this information, because it has a grant that requires absolute anonymity for those retrieving information.

Of course no log actually tells you whether the information downloaded was useful or was even what the user expected. To gather that kind of information you could provide an online form for your users to fill out, asking them specific questions about certain features or selected files on your Gopher server.

Setting Up Forms Using ASK Blocks

Among the most useful enhancements in Gopher+ is the ability to interact with your users. Before Gopher+ the only way for Gopher users to send you a message was by e-mail. ASK blocks in Gopher+ allow the user to fill out a form on your Gopher server online. The information is sent back to your Gopher server to be appended to a file or processed by a shell script or program. Uses of ASK blocks are endless, including asking for comments, filling out an order form, and checking off answers in a multiple-choice questionnaire.

ASK block forms can be built from the following component commands:

- Ask asks the user a question and allows a one-line response.
- AskL asks the user a question and allows a multiple-line response.
- AskP asks the user a question and hides the response (as is commonly done with passwords) so that no one can see the response over the user's shoulder.
- ChooseF asks the user for the name of a local file on her machine. The user can then send this up to the server. This would be a simple way to accept online résumés.
- AskF asks the user to create a new file name on his machine so that the Gopher server can send and store something there. This would allow downloading of data files.
- Select shows the user a set of options. The user can then pick one or more (similar to Macintosh check boxes).
- Choose shows the user a set of options from which the user may select only one (similar to Macintosh radio buttons).

Check out these Gopher+ test sites at the University of Minnesota and the University of Indiana for examples of the latest ASK types. (*Note:* WWW browsers don't accept all Gopher+ features, so use a Gopher+ browser for these sites. For consistency we've given URLs here, but if your Gopher browser doesn't handle them, just connect to the sites listed *(mudhoney.micro.umn.edu)* and *(FTP.bio. indiana.edu)* and follow the menus to the Gopher+ examples.)

> *<gopher://mudhoney.micro.umn.edu/11/gplustest>*
>
> *<gopher://FTP.bio.indiana.edu/11/Gopher+/Gopher+test/ask%09+application/Gopher+-menu%20En_US>*

ASK blocks are fairly simple. Basically, you create two files with similar names. One lays out the form with questions, types of variables, and so on. The other is the script that handles the information the form provides. If you just want the information appended to a file, the script does that. For example, in a sign-in log you'd want to collect the names in a steadily growing list. But it can do much more complicated things as well. For more information look for the latest version of the document called ASK FAQ version 0.5 *<gopher://grace.skidmore.edu/0R50706-69321-/help/Gopher/plus/ask-tips>*.

One big drawback to using Gopher+ ASK blocks is that Web browsers don't support them and it's not certain when or if they will. Because Web browsers are a popular method for surfing the Internet, this is a disadvantage.

Security Holes and How to Prevent Them

To think about security you have to understand where your main points of weakness are and what you might be able to do about them. One main concern is that the Gopher program itself not have too many rights. It's important to prevent a user from somehow subverting the Gopher server to get it to perform actions that you didn't intend.

Another area of security is in limiting the directories that are accessible to the Gopher server program. You don't want your Gopher server delivering up your machine's password file, for example. If the Gopher server can see only the files in your Gopher data directories, no one will be able to trick it into handing over something it shouldn't. And make sure that only those you trust have the right to add items to the Gopher data directories. If, for example, you're laying your Gopher server over an FTP server, make sure that no one can make an anonymous upload. Otherwise, someone could upload a virus into the middle of your Gopher server.

Finally, scripts and programs that are run in response to Gopher requests are always a point of concern. If it's possible to "shell out" or execute other commands via one of these programs, you have to make sure that nothing dangerous can be run via your script.

Different versions of the Gopher server software offer different solutions to these problems, and some may raise additional concerns. Check the relevant newsgroup and list server archives for discussions of these issues, and read through the documentation for the server. Usually, as security problems are found, patches or even new releases are quickly announced. For the Minnesota UNIX Gopher server start by reading "Guide to Safe Gophering" written by Paul Lindner for the 1994 Gopher conference <*gopher://boombox.micro.umn.edu:70/00/Gopher/Gopher_Conference_94/Papers/SafeGopher*>.

Remember that you may have security problems simply by being connected to the Internet. Consult a good Internet security text, such as *Firewalls and Internet Security* by William R. Cheswick and Steven M. Bellovin (Addison-Wesley, 1994).

Running Scripts or Programs from a Gopher Menu

You occasionally may want to provide a Gopher menu option that runs a program or shell script on your server and returns the answer to the user. For example, you could have a menu item that asks,

```
Who is logged onto this machine?
```

When someone chooses this item, it executes the who program to show the list of users currently logged on and sends the results to the client. This can be used with other UNIX commands and programs as well. This permits you to truly provide access to changing data or information, because your server will reply to the user with the most recent information. Some examples of how a script or program might be used include

1. Checking for the latest weather information
2. Displaying the last 10 comments made by users
3. Checking for what has changed on the Gopher server in the last few days

All kinds of scripts or programs can be run behind the scenes by the Gopher server—they need not be interactive, but they should make some sort of text response to the Gopher user. This is the mechanism by which gateways to other systems are added to Gopher servers. For example, a WAIS gateway takes a query by a user on a Gopher server, sends it out to a WAIS server, and returns the answer via Gopher.

Different operating systems have different scripting languages; Perl is available for Macintosh, DOS, and UNIX.

Registering Your Gopher Server

Registering your Gopher server is essential if you want others to be able to find it easily and if you want it to be included in index servers like Veronica. The University of Minnesota maintains a master list of Gophers <***gopher://gopher.tc.umn.edu/***>, which is then referenced by other Gopher lists. You get your Gopher server on this list by sending the university an e-mail message with the following information: server's name, host name, port number, administrative contact, an optional selector string, and an abstract describing the content of your server. According to the Gopher FAQ, if your Gopher server is in Europe, send your e-mail to gopher@ebone.net; otherwise send e-mail to gopher@boombox.micro.umn.edu.

Indexing

Although you will design your Gopher menus for ease of access and the convenience of your users, that's often not enough. As the material you offer grows in size, it increases the size and depth of your Gopher menus. This means people have to spend more time searching through your menus to find the material they want or assume (sometimes incorrectly) that you don't have it.

Minimizing the time users spend and improving the accuracy of their searches are in everyone's interest: yours, because users taking wrong paths tie up your server, and theirs, because they obviously don't want to spend more time searching than they have to.

Indexing the contents of your Gopher server (also known as your section of Gopherspace) is helpful to everyone. It can also compensate for any uncertainties in your Gopher's organization. Gopher indexing usually means that all the menu items and directories in your Gopher site are indexed and available for searching. This allows people to quickly see whether your server has any titles related to their area of interest.

You can get your server indexed in several ways.You can do it, and you can arrange for Veronica to do it. I say *and* because you may well want to index your server both ways.

If you do the indexing, somewhere on your main Gopher menu you'll want to offer users the choice of searching the entire contents of your Gopher site or just going through the Gopher menus. A searcher using Veronica might not know about your Gopher server. Users connect to a central Veronica server to do their search. If the Veronica database shows that your server has something in one of the Gopher menus that matches, the searcher is given links to those items on your server. But if your server is not indexed by Veronica, it doesn't show up in Veronica's database.

The remainder of the chapter briefly summarizes some indexing schemes that are available to Gopher administrators.

Veronica

Veronica is a central indexing service that attempts to index all of Gopherspace each month. It is an extremely useful— indispensable—method of searching for items of interest in Gopher servers around the world. That's why you want your Gopher server to show up in the Veronica database. Think of it as free advertising for your Gopher server.

Getting your server indexed by Veronica is easy. (For the Veronica FAQ see <***gopher://Gopher.scs.unr.edu:70/00/veronica/veronica-faq***>.) Assuming your site is not under restricted access, Veronica will know to index your server if you register it with the Mother Gopher at the University of Minnesota or if your server is linked to a Gopher server that is registered with the Mother Gopher.

The biggest problem is deciding which areas of your Gopher server you don't want indexed. Of course, if you don't want any part of your server indexed, that is easy to arrange as well by using a Veronica control file to leave instructions for Veronica. (For detailed instructions and a sample see <***gopher://gopher.scs.unr.edu:70/00/ veronica/About/Index-control/veronica-ctl***>.) This is a plain text file that is left on your Gopher server for the Veronica **harvester** to find when it comes by to index your Gopher server. Specific instructions to the Veronica server include

VeronicaIndex: no—This command stops Veronica from indexing your server.

Disallow: Gopher menu—Use this command (often more than once) to tell Veronica not to index certain submenus.

Veronica-datafile: URL—This command tells Veronica that it can retrieve a prebuilt index. This saves the search-and-retrieval load Veronica would place on your Gopher server in retrieving all your Gopher menus for indexing. These index files can be created by a program such as Jughead, described later.

Note: If you are running the UNIX Gopher+ server from the University of Minnesota, gopherd.conf gives you the option of completely excluding your Gopher server from Veronica harvesting. But the Veronica control file method works no matter which type of Gopher server you are running.

You might think, "Why not let Veronica go ahead and index my entire Gopher site? It couldn't hurt." But you'll be doing yourself and the Internet a favor if you think this through carefully. Are any menus in your Gopher server of local interest only? They might be course lists or assignments for classes or information of interest only to employees of a particular company. Do you have menu items that change so often that indexing them is not useful? Veronica updates only once a month, so if you have items that will be added and replaced several times within a month (like Usenet newsfeeds), Veronica indexing won't be helpful.

The Veronica control file cannot specify individual files, only menus (directories). Therefore it might be worth rearranging your menu structure if you find that some Gopher menus contain items that should be indexed and others that should not.

Jughead

Jughead is an alternative to Veronica that lets you generate your own indexes of your Gopher menus and items, but unfortunately it runs only on UNIX systems. Jughead's designer meant it as a tool for Gopher administrators, but among other things it builds an index of a selected Gopherspace—titles and menu items only, not full text. Like Veronica, it then can act as an index server by listening for search requests at a certain port and responding with the appropriate Gopher item or document. It allows **Boolean searches** (AND and OR) of the indexed material.

One advantage of Jughead is that it was written by a Gopher administrator specifically for Gopher servers, as opposed to some of the other indexing programs, which are more general. One disadvantage is that Jughead runs only on UNIX platforms.

Glimpse

Glimpse is a powerful full-text indexing and query system that allows approximate matching, Boolean searching, and limited **regular expression** (UNIX-style) searching. It allows for three different sizes of indexes, and the larger the index file, the faster it searches. Glimpse does not directly support Gopher servers, but you may be able to make it work as a back-end indexer for Gopher, which is how WAIS works. One advantage of Glimpse <*http://glimpse.cs.arizona.edu:1994/*> is that development work is continuing, whereas freeWAIS appears to be stalled.

WAIS

WAIS indexing is a powerful way to index the full text of your Gopher server and much more. See Chapter 5 on WAIS for more information.

GN (Gopher/WWW Server)

GN is a combination Gopher and WWW server that has its own indexing scheme built in. <*http://hopf.math.nwu.edu:70/*>

Summary

Gopher is an inexpensive and simple method for publishing information on the Internet that does not require users to have a fast or powerful computer. It uses a text-based menu-oriented hierarchy that is easy for users to follow. Gopher was an amazing step forward in making files and information available across the Internet to nontechnical people. Gopher's ability to link to items on other computers as easily as to those on the same computer freed users from worries about login IDs, passwords, and protocols when moving from system to system. This, more than anything, opened up the Internet as a true information resource.

Indexing programs like Veronica and Jughead increase the utility of Gopher tremendously, particularly because the results of each search become its own Gopher menu. Unsuspecting users might think the Gopher menu of search results they are seeing (see Figure 1–10 for an example of a Veronica search) is stored some place on the Internet, but actually it is created at the time of the search. This means that if the user does the same search two weeks later, the menu that appears might be different, because other resources have been added to the Internet and indexed by Veronica in the interim. The dynamic, ever-changing nature of the Internet is one of its most noteworthy characteristics.

Gopher servers and clients (browsers) come in two forms, Gopher+ and plain Gopher, or Gopher0. The enhancements to Gopher+ include such online forms (ASK blocks), the ability to provide different views of the same document, and the addition of meta-information (information about the item, such as date, author, language, and so on). The Gopher protocol was designed with long-term flexibility in mind—Gopher can deal with all types of data.

Gopher server software is available for a wide variety of computer platforms. UNIX once was the most popular, but the use of Macintosh and Windows bases for Gopher servers is growing. Some people run UNIX on PCs and Macintoshes to get faster performance out of their Gopher (and Web) servers. Configuration of Gopher servers varies by the server software used but often includes some sort of access and security options. Usually, they allow you to restrict (or allow) all or part of your Gopher data directories to machines from certain domains of the Internet. This is only useful when those domains can be identified and are precise enough for your needs. Hiding your Gopher server by running it on a nonstandard port is another way to discourage access.

The virtue of publishing via Gopher servers is that information can be made available simply by dropping the appropriate file into the Gopher data directory. The Gopher server automatically adds it to the Gopher menu provided to users. Often, however, particularly with UNIX systems, nontechnical users will want simpler methods than FTP to move their files and information into the appropriate Gopher data directories. There are many alternatives, including GMAIL, which allows e-mail accounts to be used as trusted contributors to specific directories of your Gopher server.

The design of your Gopher server's menu layout is an important factor in making it easy for users to find what they need. Make the menu titles as descriptive as possible, and make the subject categories clear. Indexing your Gopher server with Jughead (or other indexers) is an excellent way to allow users to quickly search the contents of your server to find out if you have what they want. Registering your Gopher server with the Mother Gopher server at University of Minnesota guarantees that it will appear in the master list of all Gophers in the world. Be careful to use the Veronica control file if you do not want all areas of your Gopher server to be indexed.

Security is always an issue when dealing with the Internet, but properly configured, a Gopher server doesn't add to that risk. Be sure to read the security-related discussions on the Internet and in your Gopher server software documentation.

Gopher is said by some to be dying, but it provides an efficient method for making text, graphics, and other files available across the Internet (although not in one document like WWW). Because Gopher browsers can run on even the simplest computers available (a two-floppy PC, for example) and with the slowest of modems, it will continue to serve a purpose long into the future. WWW browsers can also browse Gopher servers, but unfortunately most cannot deal with Gopher+ features. This is unfortunate, and I hope that will change. Gopher is an excellent choice when your main goals are simply to present text and other files for downloading.

CHAPTER 4

World-Wide Web

People like color and pictures. Graphics have always been more immediate and compelling than plain text. As the saying goes, a picture is worth a thousand words. The **World-Wide Web** (WWW, W3, or the Web) certainly brings us pictures—by the thousands—across the Internet. The Web's popularity stems from the ability to mix pictures and text in a way that is similar to print. The promise of the Internet as a new communications medium has been fulfilled more by WWW than by any other Internet application.

Gopher is easy to use and manage. WAIS is more powerful in its searching capabilities. But WWW is the Internet application that makes people sit up and take notice, because of its colorful graphics and text. It also allows limited document formatting and ad hoc organization through hyperlinks. Although it may not be fair to say that WWW has taken over the Internet, WWW traffic has certainly been increasing astronomically. WWW browsers such as NCSA Mosaic and Netscape are so easy to use that they have fascinated and attracted many new Internet users. The ability of WWW to combine colorful graphics with text has led to extremely creative Web sites put up by companies, organizations, universities, and even individuals.

WWW: Pros and Cons

WWW servers allow you to present information with an impressive mix of graphics and text. Hypertext allows easy linking of documents and makes for an extremely flexible publishing environment.

However, WWW requires greater bandwidth than Gopher to transport its image files across the Internet, and transport can be extremely slow over telephone lines, even with 14,400-baud modems.

WWW server software is available for a wide variety of computers, including UNIX machines, Windows, Macintosh, and OS/2 operating systems. HTML, HyperText Markup Language, which is the basis for most WWW documents, is easily decipherable and written in plain text, portable between operating systems. In addition, most Web viewers allow immediate viewing and saving of the source HTML for any document. This gives users easy access to examples of HTML code. When you find something you like, you can easily see how it was done in HTML.

WWW uses one easily understood interface to connect the user with most types of Internet resources, including Gopher, WAIS, Finger, telnet, tn3270, and FTP. This permits people with little or no computer experience to start exploring the Internet easily and quickly. The creation and free distribution of the NCSA Mosaic software epitomized the WWW ideal of easy access to Internet resources. Unfortunately, WWW browsers have not kept pace with the Gopher world's advance to Gopher+. Specifically, WWW browsers cannot yet use the Gopher+ online forms.

One serious problem with WWW is that HTML is being used as a page layout language when it really wasn't designed for that. Still, WWW offers a number of advantages:

ADVANTAGES

- Impressive mix of graphics and text.
- Servers available for UNIX, Windows, and Macintosh.
- WWW browsers work with many types of Internet resources, including Gopher0, WAIS, Usenet News, Finger, telnet, tn3270, and FTP.
- Easy to learn HTML by viewing source HTML of anything you find.

- Hypertext allows easy linking of documents or sections, regardless of hierarchy.

DISADVANTAGES

- Higher bandwidth required.
- More powerful client machine required (unless text-only browser like Lynx is used).
- Not yet compatible with Gopher+, fails on ASK blocks.
- Files require more preparation than for Gopher.
- Most servers can't limit the number of connections to the server (called *load limiting*) to avoid overloading the network or server.

WWW servers let you think in terms of publishing an electronic version of a full-color brochure. You can embed images for a variety of purposes: logos, place markers, buttons, or as page accents. The text can be displayed in different sizes and different formats.

How WWW Works

WWW works similarly to the Gopher protocol: it waits for requests from WWW browsers and then fulfills the request if it can. Like Gopher, HTTP servers can send anything, but the information usually consists of text files in HTML embedded with inline images. Where Gopher sends plain text files, which the client can read immediately, WWW browser software must interpret and receive the HTML that comes through the Web. That's why Web browsers need a higher-powered computer than Gopher browsers do. (The minimum PC for a graphical Web browser is a 386 running Windows with 4MB of RAM.)

The WWW protocol, HTTP, is a stateless client/server protocol, which means that a Web server does not have a long attention span. It receives a request from a client, such as Mosaic, Netscape, or Lynx, and it processes that request and responds with either the information requested or an error message. Aside from the log it keeps of each transaction, it has no "memory" of encountering a particular client before.

HTTP servers handle a broader range of commands than a Gopher server, and the protocol is slightly more complicated (and still evolving). But they're basically both doing the same thing: providing files or actions upon request, not unlike what the anonymous FTP servers do.

Essential to WWW are Uniform Resource Locators, or URLs, which have become the phone numbers of the Internet. They were invented along with WWW by Tim Berners-Lee as a simple method for describing links to files on other systems. They have proved so useful that they are being incorporated in Gopher servers as well. For a discussion of the related developments of Uniform Resource Identifiers (URIs), Uniform Resource Names (URNs), Uniform Resource Characteristics (URCs), and Uniform Resource Agents (URA), see Chapter 11. These devices solve some of the problems with URLs and add some capabilities.

Here's a simple description of what goes on between a WWW server and client. Basically, the process of a user following a Web link goes like this:

1. A Web client program user selects a link (URL) on a Web menu.
2. The Web client program reads the URL to get the protocol to be used (Gopher, HTTP, FTP, and so on) and the address and port number of the server to be contacted (if it's the same server, it's considered local).
3. The Web client contacts the specific server (assume HTTP for this example) using the protocol and port specified.
4. The Web server accepts the connection.
5. The Web client sends the remainder of the URL text. The URL text usually consists of a file name and/or a directory, but it could also be the name of a program or text for a database query.

6. The Web server passes the file or item on to the Web client if it can or an error message if it can't.
7. The connection is closed.

If the file is in HTML format, the Web client immediately scans it for inline images. If it finds any, it starts the process over again with separate requests for each of those image files (assuming the user has not turned off Display Images). If the item specified by the link was a program, the Web server would run the program and send the output back to the Web client. (For example, the link might start up a special program to calculate and display the latest server usage statistics.) If the item specified was a database query, the Web client would receive the results of the search. If the item specified was a file that the Web client doesn't know how to display, it can pass it off to a "helper application" or viewer program. Web clients often handle different graphics and sound files this way.

If the user wants something else, she repeats the process, starting a new connection each time. From the Web server's point of view, the process is efficient because it doesn't have to keep track of ongoing requests. Answer a question and wait for the next question—that's all it does. This can happen hundreds of thousands of times per day, depending on the popularity of the server.

WWW Features

Although not all WWW servers offer all the features listed here, most will.

- Users see hypertext, that is, formatted text with links elsewhere.
- Images (also called **inline images**) can be embedded within text.
- URLs standardize links to other protocols, hosts, directories, and files.
- Text can be formatted to some degree.
- Directory indexes.

- Files in a variety of types.
- Telnet sessions (remote login to another computer) and tn3270 sessions (another type of remote login).
- Links to items on other servers, including anonymous FTP servers and Gopher servers.
- Runs scripts on or programs WWW server.
- Online forms for users to submit information.
- "Clickable images" that send the x-y coordinates that the user picks back to server for further action. This provides the user with a sort of touch-screen interface; the user can click on different areas of a map (or other image) and get further information on that area.

WWW Resources

Resources for learning how to use and build Web servers are all over the Internet. Pay close attention to the Usenet newsgroups and e-mail list servers listed in Table 4–1, because they'll be a source of ongoing support, ideas, and information as WWW continues to develop.

Web Data Types

Like Gopher servers, Web servers can deliver many different types of data files in addition to HTML, which is the most common.

HTML

HyperText Markup Language, or **HTML,** is a method of marking plain text for both structural and layout elements, as well as links to other documents and images, sounds, movie clips, and so on. At first it is confusing to look at but it is not difficult to learn. And it is completely portable. You can write it on a Macintosh, serve it from a Sun Microsystems workstation, and view it on a Windows PC.

TABLE 4–1 WWW Resources

Documents and Sites	
W3O—World-Wide Web Organization Committee *<http://www.w3.org>*	This organization, under the leadership of Tim Berners-Lee, the author of WWW, was formed to document and encourage the development of a common set of tools and base programs for continued WWW development. W30 is the closest thing to the "owner" of the Web.
WWW FAQ *<http://sunsite.unc.edu/boutell/faq/www_faq.html>*	The World-Wide Web Frequently Asked Questions list, maintained by Thomas Boutell, is thorough, making it an excellent place to start. Written in HTML format, it provides links to the resources it lists. Among other things it lists current clients and servers available, guidelines for publishing, and lists of WWW sites available for leasing.
The International WWW Conference Series *<http://jeeves.ncsa.uiuc.edu/Public/IW3C2/>* or *<http://www.igd.fhg.de/www/www95/www95.html>*	The First International WWW Conference was held in Geneva in May 1994 with 380 participants. The second was held five months later in Chicago and had 1,300 participants with perhaps 1,000 more who could not get in. These conferences are documented online. They are an excellent resource with links to tutorials, trip reports, and announcements, as well as the proceedings.
GVU's WWW User Surveys *<http://www.cc.gatech.edu/gvu/user_surveys/>*	The Georgia Institute of Technology has started doing six-month surveys of Web users and providers. The report includes demographics.
Best of the Web Contest *<http://wings.buffalo.edu/contest/>*	Starting in 1994, the Best of the Web contest has such categories as best document design, best navigational aid, best commercial service, best educational service, and most technical merit. Check out the winners and emulate them.
1995 National (U.S.) Information Infrastructure Awards *<http://www.gii-awards.com/>*	Awards given annually in six categories: arts and entertainment, business, community, education, government, and health.
NCSA *<http://www.ncsa.uiuc.edu/SDG/Software/Mosaic/NCSAMosaicHome.html.>*	NCSA Mosaic brought WWW to the world. Check here for its server and client software, exemplary sites, and list of what's new on the Web.

Table 4–1 *(continued)*

Documents and Sites	
CERN *<http://www.cern.ch>*	This is where WWW was invented by Berners-Lee. It continues to be a repository of programs, archives, and directories of Web sites.
SGML Web Site *<http://www.sil.org/sgml/sgml.html>*	This site links to other FAQs and a wealth of information about SGML.
Web Developer's Virtual Library *<http://www.Stars.com/>*	This is a useful collection of links for Web developers and providers.
HaLSoft HTML Validation Service *<http:// www.halsoft.com/html-val-svc/>*	This essential and free online service is provided by HaL Software Systems, of Austin, Texas. It allows you to check your HTML code against different levels of the HTML standard, including the Netscape extensions. It also allows you to do a quick online check of pieces of HTML code.
Handbook: Running a WWW Server by Brian Kelly of the Computing Service, University of Leeds *<http://www.leeds.ac.uk/ucs/WWW/handbook/handbook.html>* or *<http://scholar2.lib.vt.edu/handbook/readme.html>*	This handbook was written to provide support for British academic institutions that want to run a World-Wide Web service. It is an alternative to the many U.S.-centered advisory documents available online.
Web Tools Review by Philip Greenspun *<http://webtools.com/wtr/>*	This is an online journal for developers of WWW sites by the author of the award-winning "Travels with Samantha" WWW site.
Web Developer's Journal *<http://www.awa.com/nct/software/eleclead.html>*	The Web Developer's Journal is a part of NCT Web Magazine—a computer magazine aimed at small business and home office users.
WebWeek *<http://www.mecklerweb.com/mags/ww/wwhome.htm>*	This free, controlled-subscription weekly is Mecklermedia's newspaper for Web developers. It is available both online and in print.

Table 4–1 *(continued)*

Usenet Newsgroups	
comp.infosystems.www.announce	A newsgroup in which new Web-related resources can be announced. Read the guidelines before posting.
comp.infosystems.www.advocacy	This newsgroup is for comparisons of different Web browsers, servers, and external viewer programs.
comp.infosystems.www.browsers.mac **comp.infosystems.www.browsers.misc** **comp.infosystems.www.browsers.ms-windows** **comp.infosystems.www.browsers.x**	These newsgroups are for discussions of World-Wide Web browsers on various computer platforms. Subjects might include configuration problems, helper applications, and bug reports. Browsers.x stands for X-Windows systems.
comp.infosystems.www.servers.mac **comp.infosystems.www.servers.misc** **comp.infosystems.www.servers.ms-windows** **comp.infosystems.www.servers.unix**	These newsgroups are for discussions of World-Wide Web servers on various computer platforms. Subjects might include configuration problems, security issues, directory structure, and bug reports.
comp.infosystems.www.authoring.cgi **comp.infosystems.www.authoring.html** **comp.infosystems.www.authoring.images** **comp.infosystems.www.authoring.misc**	These newsgroups discuss aspects of Web page authoring: CGI, or Common Getaway Interface scripts and programs; HTML features, formatting tricks, and proposed standards; image handling; and miscellaneous items like the use of video and audio.
comp.infosystems.www.misc	Check here for issues that don't fit clearly in one of the other comp.infosystems.www groups listed here.
bit.listserv.www-vm	This is a mirror of the BITNET mailing list WWW-VM for administrators of WWW systems running on the VM operating system.
comp.text.sgml	This newsgroup discusses Standard Generalized Markup Language.
comp.infosystems.users	This newsgroup is for those looking to browse or explore the Internet with a variety of tools.

Table 4–1 *(continued)*

Usenet Newsgroups	
W3O list of related newsgroups *<http://www.w3.org/hypertext/WWW/Newsgroups.html>*	Check here for WWW-related newsgroups.
WWW FAQ—What Newsgroups Discuss the Web? *<http://sunsite.unc.edu/boutell/faq/newsgroups.html>*	Check here for WWW-related newsgroups.
Electronic Mailing Lists	
WWW-announce. Send to *listserv@www.w3.org* Message: subscribe www-announce [your name]	This mailing list sends out announcements of new WWW sites.
WWW-html. Send to *listserv@www.w3.org* Message: subscribe www-html [your name]	This mailing list discusses HyperText Markup Language.
WWW-proxy. Send to *listserv@www.w3.org* Message: subscribe www-proxy [your name]	This mailing list discusses issues in proxy WWW servers. Proxy servers allow access to the Web through firewalls.
WWW-talk. Send to *listserv@www.w3.org* Message: subscribe www-talk [your name]	General issues in managing WWW servers. Very useful.
WWW-security. Send to *www-security-request@nsmx.rutgers.edu* Message: subscribe	Security issues in managing WWW servers.
Working group on HTML. Send to *html-wg-request@oclc.org* Message: subscribe html-wg [your name]	This group is for people who want to work seriously on updating the HTML standard.
WWW-buyinfo. Send to *www-buyinfo-request@allegra.att.com* Message: subscribe www-buyinfo	Discussion of different electronic commerce techniques, software, and issues.
Web4Lib. Send to *listserv@library.berkeley.edu* Message: subscribe web4lib [your name]	This discussion list is concerned with the creation and management of library-based World-Wide Web servers and clients. It is aimed specifically at librarians and library staff, but everyone is welcome.
Netscape. Send to: *listserv@irlearn.ucd.ie* Message: subscribe netscape [your name]	For announcements from Netscape Communications Corp. They make Web browsers and servers.

Table 4–1 *(continued)*

Electronic Mailing Lists	
ATM and the WWW. Send to: *listserv@ CMUVM.CSV.CMICH.EDU* Message: Subscribe atmwww-l [your name]	For discussion of the impact of Asynchronous Transfer Mode (ATM) technology and networking on WWW.
WN-MAINT. Send to *listserv@listserv. acns.nwu.edu* with the message: subscribe wn-maint [Your Name]	This discussion list is for the WN Web server by John Franks, "for those who think the Web should be more than a user-friendly version of FTP."
W30 list of related mailing lists *<http://www.w3.org/hypertext/ WWW/Mail/>*	Check here for WWW-related mailing lists.
WWW FAQ – What mailing lists discuss the Web? *<http://sunsite.unc. edu/boutell/faq/mailinglists.html>*	Check here for WWW-related mailing lists.
Books	
HTML Manual of Style by Larry Aronson, 1994	A detailed examination of HyperText Markup Language 2.0. Look for an update to 3.0.
Teach Yourself Web Publishing with HTML in a Week by Laura Lemay, 1995	A good resource for learning HyperText Markup Language.
The Internet for Everyone—A Guide for Users and Providers by Richard W. Wiggins, 1995	A good book for publishing on the Internet.
The World Wide Web Unleashed by John December and Neil Randall, 1994	Massive and thorough.
Managing Internet Information Services by Cricket Liu, Jerry Peek, Russ Jones, Bryan Buus, and Adrian Nye, 1994	Essential if you plan to run UNIX-based Gopher, WWW, or WAIS servers.
Internet Servers: A Step-by-Step Guide on How to Build Them by Greg Bean, 1994	Gives details on setting up FTP, Gopher, and WWW server software for Macintosh, PowerMac, Microsoft Windows NT, Microsoft Windows, and DOS systems.
Spinning the Web by Andrew Ford, 1995	A good book on WWW publishing.

Any WWW client should be able to interpret the HTML you write, so long as you conform to the HTML standard. HTML is a specific application of SGML, a more detailed markup language.

SGML

Standard Generalized Markup Language, or **SGML**, may become a popular language for WWW documents. It produces platform-independent (portable) documents and provides a consistent scheme for describing a wide variety of documents. Many large organizations have used SGML extensively, and there is a movement to create for it viewers that can be hooked up as helper applications added to WWW browsers. One advantage seems to be SGML's ability to fully define every structural element in a body of text, a useful feature when automated programs are designed to go out and retrieve for you specific sections of documents, such as a table of contents. But SGML can only define a document structure. To be useful it has to work with a viewer program or something that takes advantage of its document-structuring capabilities.

PDF

Portable Document Format, or **PDF**, is the name for Adobe Systems' method of representing documents in a manner independent of the original application, software, hardware, and operating system used to create those documents. In other words, it doesn't matter what type of machine or program created the document—it will show up virtually the same on any type of machine with a PDF viewer.

Gopher

Because WWW was designed to pull all existing Internet services together in a "web," it should be able to connect to Gopher servers. The problem is that most Gopher servers have evolved to the Gopher+ standard, and WWW clients haven't. Gopher+ forms, especially ASK blocks, bomb with WWW clients. At this point it's not clear that anyone is working to solve this problem.

WAIS

WAIS, or **Wide Area Information Server**, is another Internet resource that WWW was designed to work with. Chapter 5 details the advantages and disadvantages of WAIS.

GIF

GIF, or **Graphical Interchange Format**, is a method of storing graphics made popular by CompuServe, a commercial bulletin board service. It's notable here because GIF is the graphics type supported by most WWW browsers for inline images. That is, if you publish your images in GIF format, most people using graphical Web browsers won't have to do anything special to see them. GIF does a good job with crisp sharp images (like icons), whereas JPEG is better for realistic images, such as scanned photographs. A controversy erupted in early 1995 when Unisys, the patent holder for LZW compression, a key element of GIF, decided to charge CompuServe and its developers for the right to use this part of GIF. End users did not have to pay anything, and although talk about creating a new image standard is flying, GIF is a mainstay on WWW for now because all graphical Web browsers can display inline GIF images.

TIFF

Tagged Image File Format (**TIFF**) is a widely used image format often associated with scanning software. Some would like WWW browsers to automatically display inline TIFF images, which is how the browsers handle GIF images now. One problem is that TIFF image files are huge in comparison to GIF images. Remember to transfer TIFF files in raw format to avoid problems.

CGI Scripts

Technically, **Common Gateway Interface** scripts, or CGI scripts, are not a data type. CGI is a way to write programs or shell scripts or Perl scripts to perform some action when this item is chosen. This can be as simple as accepting information from an online form and mailing it to the Web manager. CGI scripts are behind most of the interesting interactive effects on the Web.

Plain Text

Plain text files can be stored on Web servers, but they won't look as good as HTML text. This is the main disadvantage of Web servers. Once users get a look at nicely formatted HTML files, they're no longer satisfied with a plain text file, which is what they usually see on a Gopher or WAIS server.

PostScript

PostScript is a printer-independent language (that is, it doesn't matter which printer so long as it is PostScript compatible), also from Adobe Systems. PostScript printers can print the same document the same way, no matter what platform or program created the file. This is an excellent and common method for providing high-quality text printouts. Viewers that will display PostScript on screen also are available.

Sound Files

Several different sound file formats are available, and none works on all platforms. Ulaw compression of sound files is standard for Sun Microsystems workstations. Wav and au are two other common formats.

JPEG

JPEG (Joint Photographic Experts Group) is a system for compressing still images that is better than GIF for full-color photos. JPEG usually requires an external viewer before it can be downloaded and viewed, although some WWW browsers like Netscape handle inline JPEGs.

MPEG

MPEG (Motion Pictures Experts Group) is a method for compressing movie images. MPEG requires an external viewer (add-on program to display these images) to the Web client before they can be viewed.

HTML—HyperText Markup Language

HTML is the essential ingredient in building a Web server. It can be read on almost any computer system and is relatively easy to learn. However, as you'll see, it raises expectations that it is not designed to fulfill. That is, HTML is the first computer code to offer a broadly accepted method for creating and displaying hypertext with images and text (and sound and movie files) in the same document. This means that you can create a multimedia document that is easily transported across the Internet. Unfortunately, the very attractiveness of the hypertext leads many to the false conclusion that they can further control the appearance of these Web pages. HTML was not designed to do that, although strides are being taken in that direction. HTML 3.0 offers many more formatting options than HTML 2.0.

HTML assumes that different Web browsers display documents differently, according to the needs of the operating system and equipment for which they're designed. The most dramatic difference is between Lynx, a text mode WWW browser, and Mosaic or Netscape. Lynx cannot display images at all, and it can't handle different font sizes or even italics, because it was designed for plain VT100 terminals, a common dumb terminal. Lynx is a common way to connect to the Internet because it requires only a telnet connection, which is possible over even the slowest modems.

As with Gopher, HTML has been evolving into newer versions. This process can be slow, because even when everyone agrees that improvements are necessary, it is hard to get all parties concerned to agree on how the improvements should be made. HTML 2.0 was completed in the spring of 1995, and 3.0 and 3.1 are under discussion. Some improvements include the ability to display tables and mathematical equations.

What HTML Is and Is Not

The purpose of HTML is one of the most hotly discussed issues in the Web world. Technically speaking, HTML is a specific example of SGML, which was invented by the U.S. government to aid in electronic publishing and manipulation of text. The main goal of SGML is presentation independence for any given body of information. That means that the information might be displayed as text or a graphic outline of that text or transposed to audio output. Text and documents by themselves are amorphous objects. SGML would tightly bind them to a structure that could be manipulated in various ways.

SGML does not concern itself with the layout or final form in which the text will appear. According to SGML philosophy, that is more properly handled by the user or client viewing the program. Because different clients have different types of machines with different capabilities, SGML purists say that it is foolish (and just plain wrong) to try to specify in any way how the text will be displayed in the final form. Instead they concentrate on identifying every piece of a document.

On the other hand, many, if not most, publishers were drawn to the Web by its ability to present attractive mixes of graphics and text. They constitute the other side of the controversy. They are using the various elements of HTML to create the image or presentation they want. In fact, multimedia authors are pushing to enlarge these abilities of HTML, to add things like centering and tables. Unconcerned with the SGML history of HTML, multimedia authors simply want to publish in this new medium and have more control over the way things are displayed.

Naturally, SGML purists feel that HTML's use as a page layout language is completely inappropriate and in fact a perversion of the pure SGML concept. To give an example: <H1> is the top header element in HTML. To some Web authors this is a way to emphasize text—make it bold and big and stand out. (Not all Web clients display it that way, but most do.) However, SGML purists see <H1> as a structural marker for the document, the principal header at the head of the main section. It's only incidental that some browsers display it in big bold type. Its significance lies only in its identification of the main section—nothing else.

Although the SGML purists may sound overly restrictive, in the long run they are probably right in suggesting that strict adherence to these principles will make these documents more useful for future document retrieval techniques. Unfortunately, those techniques aren't here, or at least in common use, yet. And it's much easier to pay attention to how your document looks than to how it might be logically parsed.

Conforming to HTML Standards

You can get into some bad habits writing HTML. In the interest of improving the standard of Web pages, Mark Gaither of HaL Software Systems has created a free online HTML conformance-checking service <*http://www.halsoft.com/html-val-svc/*> on the Internet. A similar one, also free, is located at the Georgia Institute of Technology <*http://www.cc.gatech.edu/grads/j/Kipp.Jones/HaLidation/validation-form.html*>. You can either submit your HTML text to be checked or point to a URL that the HTML validation service will then check and send comments back. The key point here is that writing HTML that is clean and conforms to current HTML standards ensures that your documents will display correctly in all compliant browsers.

Gaither, author of "Why Validate Your HTML Documents" <*http://www.halsoft.com/html/whyvalidate.html*>, has commented that one reason to ensure HTML compliance is so that newer and better browsers can be written with the assurance that most HTML pages on the Web are correct. That makes the job of designing a new browser easier because they don't have to continually allow for variations and mistakes in HTML layout. The writers of browser programs will be able to add core functions and greater sophistication if they can be sure the browsers will encounter well-structured HTML. Correctly written HTML facilitates searches, reformatting, document portability, and extracting or excluding pieces of documents. A paper titled "Designing a Web of Intellectual Property," by Terje Norderhaug and Juliet M. Oberding, a San Diego lawyer, was presented at the Third International WWW Conference in Darmstadt, Germany, in April 1995. The article called for the ability to "inline" pieces of documents as a way to cite someone else's work without infringing on their copyright <*http://www.igd.fhg.de/www/www95/papers/95/webip.html*>. To use a piece of another document "inline" would require the ability to extract and retrieve specific sections of someone else's HTML to be used in your document.

Writing HTML Quickly

One of the best tools for learning to write HTML quickly is the capability of all Web browsers to view and capture the source HTML of any document you find on the Web. That means that if you see something you like, you can look at it to see how it was done, and save it for further reference. Unfortunately, there's no guarantee that the examples you find this way will be clear, documented, or even good examples. But as with learning a foreign language, look at a wide variety of examples and pay attention to how they are used in different situations.

Another quick way to get started is to convert an existing word-processing document into HTML, using some of the filters and converters discussed later in this chapter. LaTex, Word for Windows, and WordPerfect documents can be converted this way, although sometimes you have to use a two-step process (first saving them in RTF (Rich Text Format). Once you've done that, making changes in your original word-processing document and converting again is an easy way to create useful Web documents quickly. Eventually, you'll need to learn HTML codes to handle problems that the converters and filters don't handle, but you can accomplish a lot by going this route first.

EasyHTML is a program from NCSA (National Center for Supercomputing Applications—creator of NCSA Mosaic) that lets you create and save HTML pages interactively by filling out online forms on a Web server. Users can create HTML pages by filling out forms in a Web browser like Mosaic, Netscape, or Lynx. The user answers questions and creates an HTML page one step at a time, with immediate feedback after each step, to show what the HTML page will look like. You can even redo parts of the page. Finally, users are given two ways to save their files and are encouraged to use both. One is straight HTML and the other is as a form, so that EasyHTML can be used to re-edit the file. EasyHTML doesn't let you use the full set of HTML commands, but it lets your users create simple HTML documents quickly and easily. <***http://peachpit.ncsa.uiuc.edu/easyhtml/***>

Several good online tutorials and guides to HTML are listed in Table 4–1. Also, some books have come out on HTML, and many others are being written.

Guides to Writing HTML

An easy way to find out what mistakes others are making and avoid them is to search for sites that have gone to the trouble of compiling common errors and mistakes in writing HTML. I found these valuable links, and you will probably find more by searching on the words *learning HTML.*

"Composing Good HTML," by James "Eric" Tilton of Willamette University <***http://www.willamette.edu/html-composition/strict-html.html***>

"Elements of HTML Style," by Jonathan K. Cohen of the University of California at Irvine <*http://bookweb.cwis.uci.edu:8042/Staff/StyleGuide.html*>

"Style Guide for Online Hypertext," by Tim Berners-Lee <*http://www.w3.org/hypertext/WWW/Provider/Style/Overview.html*>

"*PC Week* Lab's Crash Course on Writing Documents for the Web" <*http://www.pcweek.ziff.com/~eamonn/crash_course.html*>

"World Wide Web and HTML Developers JumpStation" <*http://oneworld.wa.com/htmldev/ devpage/dev-page.html*>

The most common mistake in HTML is to believe that the way your documents appear on your browser is the way that they'll appear on every other Web-browsing program. It is quite tempting to try to stretch the limits of HTML and make your document look a certain way. Your efforts may not carry over to a different Web browser. Because HTML resembles a page layout language, it is often hard to resist trying to use it that way. A commonsense way to avoid this trap is to check your HTML documents with several different browsers.

Relative Versus Absolute Addressing

Not all URL links have to be absolute, or completely written out. It is often more useful to simply refer to other documents or files "relative" to the current server, directory, and document. For example, this link is explicit:

<*http://latino.sscnet.ucla.edu/murals/Sparc/SPARC.html*>

And this link is relative, because it assumes the file is in the same directory as the file that does the linking (this trick does not work when linking to another server, of course):

<*sparc2.html*>

Note how short the second URL is. Many documents have at least 10 to 20 links, which is why relative links are popular. Also, the link will still work if both are moved to a new directory for some reason. For example, if our server gets too popular and we're forced to move it to a new machine, or a different directory, the relative links won't need updating. Just move the whole directory of files and set it down in the new site.

SGML Instead of HTML?

Many Web sites are using SGML for the primary storage of their Web documents and then converting them to HTML. The advantages are that SGML is a fully established, commercially accepted method of defining text files.

Several commercial SGML editors are available:

Internet Publisher by WordPerfect Corporation (Novell Applications Group); 800-824-3323; fax 801-222-5077; $49 (DOS)

Author/Editor (V.3.1) by SoftQuad, Inc. (subsidiary of SoftQuad International); 800-387-2777; 416-239-4801; fax 416-239-7105; $995 (Windows), $995 (Mac), $1,995 (UNIX)

SGML Author for Word by Microsoft Corporation; 800-426-9400; 206-882-8080; fax 206-93-MSFAX; $595 (Windows)

OmniMark by Exoterica Corporation; 800-565-9465; 613-722-1700; fax 613-722-5706; $2,495 (PC), $6,495 (workstation), $14,995 (VAX/VMS)

HTML Editors, Filters, and Converters

Table 4–2 offers a partial list of HTML editors available for creating HTML documents. This is an extremely fast-growing field, so watch for new entrants. The first two items in Table 4–2 are sites that list HTML editors.

One common complaint while I was writing this was that many HTML editors (especially those for Windows) are limited to files

TABLE 4–2 HTML Editors

Program	Platform	Description
W3 and HTML Tools <*http://www.w3.org/hypertext/WWW/Tools/Overview.html*>	Multiple	This site is an excellent resource listing the latest in HTML editors and related tools.
Gabriel's HTML Editor List by Gabriel White <*http://luff.latrobe.edu.au/~medgjw/editors/index.html*>	Multiple	A good place to go look for HTML editors.
HTML Editor Reviews by Carl Davis <*http://www.interaccess.com/users/cdavis/edit_rev.html*>	Windows	Useful commentary and reviews on a growing list of Microsoft Windows and HTML editors.
BBEdit Extensions for HTML by Carles Bellver <*http://www.uji.es/bbedit-html-extensions.html*>	Macintosh	Adds the ability to create and edit HTML files to both the commercial and freeware versions of the Macintosh text editor BBEdit (free).
Cyberleaf by Interleaf <*http://www.ileaf.com/*>	UNIX & Windows	Not strictly an HTML editor, it converts word-processing documents in Microsoft Word, WordPerfect, Interleaf, and Frame formats into HTML. $795 for UNIX and $495 for PCs.
HoTMetaL by SoftQuad <*http://www.sq.com/*>	Macintosh, Windows, & UNIX	HoTMetaL is notable for not permitting you to write incorrect HTML. It also allows you to update to newer versions of HTML as it develops (free and commercial $99 versions).
HTML Assistant by Howard Harawitz <*http://fox.nstn.ca/~harawitz/index.html*>	Windows	HTML editor (free and commercial $99 versions).
HTML Editor by Rick Giles <*file://cs.dal.ca/giles/*>	Macintosh	HTML editor (shareware $25).
Internet Assistant by Microsoft <*http://www.microsoft.com*>	Windows	Add-in program that works for Word for Windows 6.0 to allow you to edit and create HMTL files using Word for Windows editing commands (free).
Internet Publisher by WordPerfect/Novell <*http://www.novell.com*> 801-225-5000	Windows	Add-in program that works for Word-Perfect 6.1 to allow you to edit and create HMTL files using WordPerfect 6.1 (free).

Table 4–2 *(continued)*

Program	Platform	Description
WebAuthor from Quarterdeck Corp. *<http://www.qdeck.com>*	Windows	Add-in HTML editor for Microsoft Word for Windows (intro price of $99.95).
WebForce from Silicon Graphics *<http://www.sgi.com>*	UNIX	This HTML authoring environment comes bundled with some Silicon Graphics computers.

that are smaller than 32K. Although that's sufficient for quite a few screenfuls, it often is not enough for large documents. (For example, my bookmark file is up to 95K right now.) One solution I've heard of is to split large HTML files into pieces and then edit those pieces separately. Newer editors will probably remove this limitation.

Another aspect of HTML editors that you should consider is whether they discourage or prevent you from making mistakes in HTML. SoftQuad's HoTMetaL (see Table 4–2) won't let you write incorrect HTML. Getting it to accept preexisting HTML that comes with errors can be quite frustrating, however. You can also use an HTML validation service (see Table 4–1) to check your HTML files for errors.

Web (HTTP) Servers

When choosing a Web server (technically they're called HTTP servers), the first place to check for online information is the WWW FAQ by Thomas Boutell at ***<http://sunsite.unc.edu/boutell/faq/www_faq.html>***. Another source is Paul Hoffman's WWW Servers Comparison Chart at ***<http://www.proper.com/www/servers-chart.html>***. This chart documents at least nine Web servers, both free and commercial, and compares their features.

As with Gopher servers, you'll need to address at least five concerns when choosing a Web server:

- *Function*—Look at the functions it supports, the extra capabilities the server provides, and its record of compatibility with add-on indexing programs.
- *Platform*—Check the platform (operating system and hardware) required, such as UNIX, Windows, Macintosh, and its relative stability. Be aware of the difficulty of supporting a platform you're not familiar with.
- *Load*—Investigate the load the server's platform can be reasonably expected to handle. Be sure it is high enough for two to three times the load you expect.
- *Support*—Verify the level of support and activity this software enjoys, including newsgroups and mailing lists, as well as more formal commercial support mechanisms. An active newsgroup of administrators can be better than many companies' tech support desks.
- *Price*—Determine the licensing policy. If it's freeware, check that it's not limited to educational organizations. Many free programs have a different policy for commercial uses.

Another concern is ease of operation. You may find it worthwhile to first set up a Web server on a PowerMac or Windows machine, learn what's involved, and try out your publishing ideas. Then, when you are more comfortable and usage warrants, you might move up to a more powerful machine.

Some servers can run as **proxy servers**. This means that if your organization has a firewall, you could have a proxy server sitting on the firewall, passing out requests to the rest of the WWW and saving the documents returned (called *caching*) so that they'll be ready for the next person who asks.

Security provisions might be important to your organization if you want to limit the access to some sections of your Web server. Some commercial servers now on the market provide a secure transaction-processing environment, but they require similar clients. This area will almost certainly expand in the near future. See Chapter 7.

The section that follows lists many existing WWW (HTTP) servers and describes some of their various features. Some aspects to check out include the load, or number of requests that can be handled in a day; how easy it is to add information; the ability to limit the number of connections depending on the load; and the general popularity of the server (assuming that the more popular servers tend to get better user support from the Web community).

As of May 1995, in my humble opinion, the CERN and NCSA servers are by far the most popular Web servers, with GN, MacHTTP, and Windows-based servers coming behind. Now that commercial vendors are starting to make servers available, I expect that these rankings will change drastically. I expect a great increase in the use of Macintosh, Windows NT, and OS/2 as platforms as more and more individuals start putting up Web sites on desktop machines.

UNIX

Until recently, most Web servers ran on UNIX, because most of the Internet was developed on UNIX, an extremely flexible and powerful operating system. Many Web servers and tools for Web management were developed first on UNIX and later rewritten (ported to) other operating systems. The drawbacks to using UNIX-based WWW servers are that you need to be sure you have good UNIX support, and it can be a complicated and arcane field. Some companies, notably Sun Microsystems and Silicon Graphics, are working to make this easier, because they are in the business of selling UNIX hardware. For a comparison of features of UNIX-based servers, see <***http://mistral.enst.fr/~pioch/httpd/***>.

CERN HyperText Transfer Protocol Daemon

The CERN HyperText Transfer Protocol Daemon (HTTPD) server is available at no charge for UNIX and VMS and provides the ability to run as a proxy server with document caching for faster access. <***http://www.w3.org/hypertext/WWW/Daemon/Status.html***>

NCSA HyperText Transfer Protocol Daemon

The NCSA UNIX server is available at no charge and runs on UNIX systems. Server administrators can decide whether they want to permit their machine's users (account holders) to write their own HTML files in their own directory (as opposed to the server's data directory). These can be referenced with a tilde in front of the user name. For example, <***http://someplace.com/~smith/***> would get you to Smith's home page directory. This makes Web file updating extremely easy for users. They don't need special rights in other places. <***http://hoohoo.ncsa.uiuc.edu/docs/***>

GN

The **GN** server is a free combination Gopher/WWW server by Professor John Franks of Northwestern University. It runs on UNIX and has a loyal group of users with an active support mailing list. He stopped development before Gopher+, and now he's moved on to a WWW-only server called WN, which you may want to consider if you don't need Gopher. Both of his servers make it easy to do indexing. <***http://hopf.math.nwu.edu:70/***>

Netscape

Netscape Communications Corporation offers two commercial UNIX-based Web servers, Netscape Communications ($1,500; free to nonprofit educational and charitable groups) and Netscape Commerce Server ($5,000). Commerce Server makes possible secure financial transactions (for example, paying with a credit card over the Internet) with clients using their Netscape browser. <***http://www/netscape.com/***>

Open Market WebServer and Secure WebServer

Open Market offers two commercial UNIX-based Web servers, one for information services ($1,495) and the other (Secure WebServer, $4,995) for electronic commerce. A support contract, which costs

$999 per year, is required for the commerce version. The Secure WebServer supports both Netscape's Secure Socket Layer (SSL) and Enterprise Integration Technologies' Secure HyperText Transfer Protocol (S-HTTP). They support 1,000 concurrent users and are extensible so you can add your own programs. <***http://www.openmarket.com/***>

Plexus

The Plexus Web server is UNIX based and written in Perl by Tony Sanders based on an earlier version by Marc Van Heyningen at Indiana University. It is in the public domain and has authorization and access control. <***http://www.bsdi.com/server/doc/plexus.html***>

WN

The WN server by Professor John Franks of Northwestern University is a free HTTP server with many features, including title and keyword searching. It can return a range of lines (portion of the text) in a text file. <***http://hopf.math.nwu.edu/***>

Apache

Apache is a public domain "patched" (improved) version of NCSA's 1.3 HTTPD Web server. It was created by a group of WWW providers and part-time HTTPD programmers to get HTTPD to behave the way they wanted it to. It is 100 percent compatible with the existing NCSA 1.3 HTTPD. <***http://www.apache.org/***>

EIT Webmaster's Starter Kit

Enterprise Integration Technologies (EIT) has put together the Webmaster's Starter Kit, which is based on the NCSA HTTPD server for UNIX. This free Web server installs itself and optional enhancements as you answer the questions it asks via online forms.

The enhancements extend NCSA's HTTPD in several ways, including virtual document configuration options, automatic server monitoring and restarting, request prioritization, polite errors, and polite down time. *Polite errors* means the server can be configured to return a custom document for error responses. *Polite down time* means that all requests can be redirected to another server during maintenance down time. The Starter Kit also provides assistance in installing shareware tools such as libcgi, webtest, hypermail, and getstats. ***<http://wsk.eit.com/wsk/doc/>***

VMS

VMS (Virtual Memory System) is Digital Equipment Corporation's multi-user, multitasking operating system. It runs on DEC's VAX series of computers, from its smallest minicomputer to its biggest mainframe.

CERN HTTPD

The CERN HTTPD server is available at no charge for VMS and provides the ability to run as a proxy server with document caching for faster access. ***<http://www.w3.org/hypertext/WWW/Daemon/Status.html>***

Region 6 HTTP Server

This WWW server for VMS, written by David L. Jones of Ohio State University, is said to offer a performance advantage over the CERN version, because it runs with DECthreads, which allows it to serve multiple users simultaneously. ***<http://kcgl1.eng.ohio-state.edu/www/doc/serverinfo.html>***

Macintosh

Macintoshes are user-friendly places to set up WWW servers, and they are gaining in popularity. Running a Web server on a Macintosh epitomizes the ease-of-publishing trend. It allows those who use Macintoshes to set up a Web server on the type of computer they're used to and conveniently make their information available worldwide. And for small and medium-sized Web sites, a Macintosh works as well as a more powerful (and expensive) UNIX machine, according to Joe Holmes of Sonoma State University in California. His comparison of Macintosh and UNIX performance as a Web server is available at <***http://www.sonoma.edu/btools/theTest.html***>; reactions and further commentary are available at <***http://www.sonic.net/net.dreams/word/current.html***>. One of his main points is that while UNIX workstations are generally much more powerful than Macintoshes, they come with a large cost in UNIX support staff. If you don't have that staff in-house, you should definitely consider using Macintoshes as Web servers, especially if you don't expect yours to be the largest site on the Internet.

By using AppleScript and MacPerl, you can manage quite a bit of customization. MacTCP (the underlying software that communicates with the Internet) is the factor that limits the Web load that Macintosh-based servers can handle, but Apple is working on a replacement. That should improve things considerably. For excellent resources and data on Macintosh WWW systems and servers, look at the "Macintosh WWW Development Guide" by Jon Wiederspan of the University of Washington <***http://www.uwtc.washington.edu/Computing/WWW/Mac/Directory.html***>.

Another alternative for mounting a Web server on a Macintosh or PowerMac is to run A/UX (Apple's UNIX) instead of the normal Macintosh operating system. Then you would choose Web server software listed in the section on UNIX Web servers.

WebSTAR (Formerly MacHTTP)

The WebSTAR/MacHTTP Web server for Macintosh was originally written by Chuck Shotton of BIAP Systems <***http://brain.biap.com***> and has some enthusiastic users. It apparently can run on every Mac from a Mac Plus through a PowerMacintosh. MacHTTP 3.0 has been renamed WebSTAR ($295 educational, $795 other, from StarNine Technologies; <***http://www.starnine.com/***>) and speeded up and enhanced considerably. WebSTAR allows for multiple simultaneous transfers; CGI scripts in AppleScript, MacPerl, or any other language; directory and page password security; and setting maximum simultaneous connections. It is available in both 68K and PowerMac native versions. (*Native* means it was written specifically to take full advantage of that model CPU.) It is comparable to commercial Web servers on other platforms. Commerce and security add-ons will be available in 1995. MacHTTP 2.2 is still available from StarNine Technologies ($75 educational, $95 other).

Netwings

Netwings is an HTTP server for Macintosh built on the 4D database system. More than just a Web (HTTP) server, it provides most functions you would want from an Internet server, such as e-mail, mailing list, and database services. It also provides systemwide security, interactive forms, Internet visitor tracking, built-in database management, and a report generator. A one-user license costs $1,495 and prices escalate from there: five-user license, $7,150; 25-user license, $33,650; 50-user license, $59,500; 100-user license, $104,650. Government, educational, and medical (nonprofit) customers may apply for a 25% discount. <***http://netwings.com/***>

HTTPD4Mac

HTTPD4Mac is a bare-bones Macintosh Web server written by Bill Melotti and is not a port of either the NCSA or CERN servers. It does not support maps or other CGI applications, but it is free. <***http://130.246.18.52/***>

MacCommon Lisp Server

You can now interface your Lisp programs to the world to show exactly what you can do better and faster in Lisp (a programming language). The server is a free, full-featured server (HTTP 1.0 and HTML 2.0) that comes complete with source code. <*http://www.ai.mit.edu/projects/iiip/doc/cl-http/home-page.html*>

Windows NT

Windows NT 3.5 is now a serious choice for many Web administrators primarily because of the ease of installation and administration. Windows NT also offers the ability (on some servers) to interact with Visual Basic and data in regular Windows applications, such as Microsoft Excel and Access.

EMWAC HTTPD for Windows NT

Both a freeware and a professional Web server for Windows NT ($1,995 in the United States; $2,490 on the international market) are available from the European Microsoft Windows NT Academic Centre (EMWAC) at the University of Edinburgh. The professional version adds authentication, access control, virtual paths, a proxy server, and redirection. (Virtual paths let you serve files from more than one tree, or directory, at a time. **Redirection** means automatically retrieving a file from its new location.) <*http://emwac.ed.ac.uk/html/internet_toolchest/https/contents.htm*>

SAIC-HTTP

A noncommercial license is available to use to the Web server for Windows NT developed by San Diego–based Science Applicaton International Corporation (SAIC). Among other features, the server allows multiple hosts on the same machine and on the same port. <*http//wwwserver.itl.saic.com/features.html*>

Netscape

Netscape offers a Windows NT version of its Communications server that has the same features as the UNIX version. It is free to nonprofit educational and charitable groups, but costs commercial users $1,500. See <***http://home.netscape.com/***> for details.

Folio Infobase Web Server

Folio Corporation is licensing the Edinburgh University Computing Service to provide an HTTP server that runs on Windows NT and generates HTML pages on the fly from Folio infobases. *Infobase* is Folio's term for its extremely fast and efficient full-text searchable database system that first appeared as the software behind Novell NetWare online manuals. Since then infobases have been created for everything from the U.S. Tax Code to WordPerfect manuals to the Bible, and this server will make it easy to put them onto the Internet. This product also solves a problem for Folio, whose customers long have sought a version that runs on UNIX. By adding this feature to Web server software, Folio will enable its UNIX users to browse the Folio infobases through their Web browsers. Those already producing Folio infobases will find this Web server appealing. It costs $6,995. <***http://www.folio.com/***>

WebSite

WebSite ($499) is a 32-bit WWW server for Windows NT 3.5 released in May 1995. It also runs on Windows 95, has features for restricting access to authorized users, and has access authorization. It was developed by O'Reilly and Associates in cooperation with Bob Denny and Enterprise Integration Technologies, Inc. (EIT). <***http://www.ora.com/gnn/bus/ora/item/website.html***>

InterNotes Web Publisher

Lotus Development Corporation has announced that it is selling a Web server ($7,500) that runs on Windows NT and acts as a gateway between its popular Lotus Notes system and the WWW. Lotus Notes is a proprietary client/server platform that allows businesses to share and organize information among all their computer sites. Lotus Notes works whether they are linked by network or only occasionally by modem. Lotus Notes includes data replication and synchronization (keeps versions of the database up to date on all machines), as well as full-text search, and has support for Macintosh, DOS, Windows, and OS/2 clients.

InterNotes Web Publisher translates Lotus Notes documents and databases into HTML and delivers them in response to WWW queries. It also automatically creates HTML pages of Lotus Notes views to create an easy way for browsers to navigate among documents on the Web site. Lotus Notes document links become hypertext links. Bitmaps in Lotus Notes documents are converted into inline GIF files. Attachments to Lotus Notes documents are preserved and can be downloaded from the server. <*http://www.lotus.com/inotes/*>

DOS and Windows

DOS runs on a minimal PC so it is ideal for extremely inexpensive servers. Windows has the advantage of being widely used (even if it's not always stable), and its user-friendly features make it an easy platform with which to start Web publishing.

Hype-It 1000

Hype-It 1000 ($549) and Hype-It 2000 ($1,995) are commercial Web servers that run on a 386 PC running DOS and support 30 simultaneous connections. The server provides full-text searching of the document database, as well as FTP, e-mail, and telnet services. Connections to the Web server are logged into a separate database. The company also offers Web administration training and advertising for your server at an extra charge. <*http://cykic.com/homepage.htm*>

KA9Q NOS HTTP

KA9Q NOS is a full-fledged Network Operating System (NOS) that runs under DOS and acts as a server for e-mail, FTP, Gopher, WWW, and CSO (Central Services Organization). It performs best on 386s but can be recompiled for 8088s. It is free to educational users; contact the program author for costs to other users. <*http://inorganic5.chem.ufl.edu/ka9q/ka9q.html*>

HTTPD for Windows by Robert Denny

This Windows version of HTPPD has most of the features of the popular UNIX version, including CGI scripts. It is free for personal, noncommercial use and $99 for commercial use. <*http://www.city.net/win-httpd/*>

Other Platforms

HTTPD for the Amiga

This is a port (or transfer) of the NCSA HTTPD server to the Amiga computer platform. It is available free with Amiga Mosaic. <*http://www.Omnipresence.com/amosaic/2.0/*>

GLACI HTTPD

The Great Lakes Area Commercial Internet (GLACI) HTTPD server runs on Novell Netware (3.x and up) as an NLM (Netware Loadable Module). It can be configured with IP access lists and also to allow users to store their personal HTML documents in their Novell home directory. It supports clickable image maps. <*http://www.glaci.com/info/glaci-httpd.html*>

Webshare CMS HTTPD

This free server by Rick Troth is written to run on the VM/CMS operating system. It supports CGI scripting, user-defined Web spaces, redirection, transaction logging, forms support, and image maps. <*http://ua1vm.ua.edu/~troth/rickvmsw/rickvmsw.html*>

Deciding Who Runs Your Web Server

This is a good time to remind you of the difference between a system administrator and a data librarian. A **system administrator** keeps track of the technical details of the operating system and of the computer on which your server runs. The **data librarian** organizes, updates, and maintains the integrity of the data files and Web links to other sites. Neither description may fit you exactly, but whereas the cooperation of a good system administrator is essential for the UNIX Web servers, much of the job of maintaining your Web server will fall to the data librarian. This duty often becomes a responsibility of system administrators by default, but that lamentable practice need not continue.

Take control of your data. You should know what makes your server special. You should know the working rules for your server. And you should know its weaknesses. I am not saying that you have to have a data librarian to run your server. But I am saying that you ought not leave it to your system administrator and other technical personnel. So get your system administrator to read the documentation and go over the documentation with you, so that you know what your server is doing. What follows describes in plain English how Web servers can be configured.

Installing a Web Server

You have three areas to consider, no matter which Web server you install:

Server configuration

Resource configuration (data and documents)

Access control (security)

Server Configuration. Configuring your server requires you to specify where the server will store its log files, what port it will answer (normally 80), an e-mail address for the server administrator, the root directory in which the server program files reside, the host name that the server should give out, how long the server should wait for a client once a transaction has started, and so on. None of these is inconsequential, but usually you'll leave them for your system administrator.

You'll come across another Web server configuration issue with UNIX Web servers. They have two options for start up: **inetd** (Internet Daemon, which handles requests from the Internet) and **standalone**. **Standalone** means that once started, the server sits waiting for questions from Web clients. With inetd the program doesn't run until the moment an Internet connection comes in to the Web server. Then it starts up, fulfills the request, and closes down. The extra startup time can be a disadvantage for heavily loaded servers. On the other hand, if you don't see much WWW traffic, it seems a shame to have the Web server daemon always running. Also, inetd has some security features that can be useful. However, both CERN and NCSA recommend standalone instead of inetd for their server software for the increased speed.

Resource Configuration. Resource configuration means specifying where your Web documents can be located. NCSA's HTTPD server has some interesting directives: UserDir gives the directory name for public HTML files in user directories. The default is public_html. UserDir is important because it determines whether your staff or others with accounts on your Web server can set up their own public HTML directory. Set UserDir to Disabled if you don't want to allow this. Otherwise, those with accounts on your system would be able to publish on the Internet simply by creating a subdirectory by that name in their directory and putting files into it. They would then refer to them by using your Web server's address with *~theirname/* at the end. For example, if the Web server's address is <*http://www.someplace.com/*>, Jack Todd (with an account under the name todd) could refer to his own Web directory as <*http://www.someplace.com/~todd/*>. He could put as much or as little as he wanted in that directory (including subdirectories) and it would all be available under that URL, which he might put on his business card. This is happening all over the place, and you'll need to decide how much freedom you want your system users to have. Remember, this applies only to people with accounts on your system (running NCSA HTTPD server), not people browsing your Web site from elsewhere.

The DirectoryIndex command lets you avoid showing the contents of a directory. If an HTML file called index.html (default name) exists in a given directory, it will not send the directory list or index but will instead send the index.html file to the Web browser. The beauty of this is that you can use a shortened URL. If a file with that name is not there, the Web server will create an index of the contents of that directory and send that to the Web browser. This is important, because often you will want to limit what Web browsers see in certain directories. By creating a simple index.html file, the contents of that directory are available only if someone links to them by name. If you have no links to that directory from elsewhere, users will have no way of knowing what the names of the other files are. You can add links to the index.html file when you're ready, but in the meantime it acts as a shield for that directory.

One other advantage is that you can shorten your home page URL. Instead of using <*http://latino.sscnet.ucla.edu/murals/murals.html*>, I can change the name of murals.html to index.html and leave it off the URL so it becomes <*http://latino.sscnet.ucla.edu/murals/*>, and the effect is the same. Given that URLs are long and complicated, anything we can do to shorten them is helpful.

The AddType directive allows you to set certain file extensions to be treated as certain types of data. A useful example would be to make .htm an equivalent of .html to ease editing of your HTML files in DOS systems that can have only three-character extensions. In that way you can edit your files in DOS with an .htm extention and then FTP them up to your Web server without changing their names. When you have hundreds of files on your server, you'll appreciate this.

Access Control (Security). As discussed in Chapter 3 in regard to Gopher, sometimes you need to think about security and restricting access. If anyone for any reason should not see what's on your server, you'll need to know how to keep that person out. Different options are available, depending on the version of Web server you use. You should learn the options your server provides and be sure you understand them. Don't trust that the server software out of the box will be secure on your system. More advanced techniques are discussed in Chapter 7, Internet Commerce.

Here are some simple techniques for restricting access to your server or sections of your server:

1. Restrict or allow access by domain name.
2. Hide your server.
3. Hide files or directories.
4. Require a password for connection.

When restricting access by Internet domain or subdomain, you can also restrict access to subdirectories or block someone from using the entire Web server. (Check your server software to make sure it can do this.) For more information about restricting by domain, see the section on Configuring Access and Security in Chapter 3 because the process is similar.

Restricting by domain works when you have a small number of local subdomains that can be listed easily; anything else can be said to be external and shouldn't be allowed to see your server. This is appropriate when your company or campus is licensed for certain types of things, and you don't want to publish them for the world.

Hiding your server means running it on a nonstandard port (other than port 80) and not advertising its host name and port number except to those who need access. Also, make sure that it's not indexed by or linked by any other publicly accessible server. Basically, this method keeps people from finding your Web server by accident.

Successfully hiding your files and directories depends on your ascertaining that a particular set of files or directories on your server has absolutely no links and that users can't browse and find them on their own. Usually, a server will give a listing, or index, of whatever contents are in a specified directory. But, as we discussed earlier, the NCSA server, for one, allows you to specify that if the file name index.html (the NCSA default) is present in that directory, the file will be used instead. This a technique usually used to present a home page for that directory with links to the contents of that directory. But if you deliberately don't make links for the files you want to hide, no one will be able to find them in that directory unless they already know the file names. So be sure to make up unguessable file names. One professor used a random number generator to create unique file names where students could look up their grades.

Several Web servers provide for password protection. Make sure you are clear about the level of security this offers. Ask whether the password is passed over the Internet in the clear or whether it's encoded in some manner that is relatively secure.

Again, for real security look to one of the security systems being developed, such as Netscape's SSL, S-HTTP from Enterprise Integration Technologies, and the combination from Terisa Systems. As of May 1995 the **W3 Organization** had not yet decided on a standard means of providing secure exchanges to Web servers across the Internet.

Designing Your Web Pages

As with Gopher servers, everyone has an opinion about the best way to lay out a Web server. It is much easier to create bad Web pages than it is to look at them. Here are some sites that talk about Web design guidelines and other factors to keep in mind:

<http://www.arcade.uiowa.edu/hardin-www/jaffeDesign2.html>

<http://info.med.yale.edu/caim/StyleManual_Top.HTML>

Keep Home Pages Small

Keep your home page (or any other entry points) small. Remember that many people will connect to your home page just to see what's there, not because they really want all the information you have to offer. So don't put everything on the first page. Because small size equals speed on the Internet, it's only courteous to have a small, quickly downloaded home page that summarizes the information available with links to the larger bodies of content.

Watch Total Size of Your Pages

The more images you have, and the larger they are, the longer your page will take to load. The inline images that go with an HTML page add to the total time it will take to display, so keep them small and have as few as possible. Shrinking the text in your home page doesn't help if you have 30 inline images on that same page. Even if they're tiny, they take time to download. However, if you use inline images (of green and red dots, for example) several times in a document, most Web browsers cache, or save, them locally, so they are downloaded just once and then displayed several times.

Use Thumbnail Images as Teasers

Offer "thumbnail" graphic images that link to larger images on a separate page. Putting several of these on one page gives a catalog effect. This allows your users to choose the images they really want to take the time to download and see. Again, this is in the interest of speed for the user. It will also pay off in a lighter load on your server.

Offer Text-Only Views

Providing an alternative on your home page for text-only viewers is essential for the many people who use a text-mode Web browser. In many cases they have no other option, because the equipment they're using or their connection to the Internet will not support graphics. If you don't plan for them, you are effectively making your site useless to this set of users.

Text-only views also help those who have graphical Web browsers but turn off image loading so that they can move through Web sites quickly and explore what is available. When they find something they want, they turn image loading back on. This is particularly important internationally, because Internet connections and throughput vary widely from country to country.

Text views of your site are important to another group of Web browsers: the blind or vision impaired. They often use text-to-speech software, which dictates the text on screen.

Have a Unifying Element or Graphic

Users can easily become confused as they move through link after link of your server. Repeating a small graphic or piece of text at the top of all your pages will remind them where they are. If you use a graphic, be sure it's small and that you give a text description for it using the ALT (alternate) tag on HTML. In this way your text-only browsers get your text descriptions of the image instead of just a line that says *image*.

Provide "Sets" of Pages for Downloading

Consider offering a way for users to download all the linked files and images pertaining to a certain subject or theme in your Web server, if you think they'll want the whole set. For example, finding an online manual for the NCSA Web server is nice, but sometimes it's more convenient for users to get it all at once so that they don't have to worry that the connection to NCSA will be down just when they need to look at the manual. (This happened to me for days while first trying to install the NCSA HTTPD Web server.) Group the relevant Web pages and images, and compress them into one file that users can download easily and view locally. If you do this, be sure that you post the information in a prominent place.

Provide Print Versions

Users find PostScript or PDF (Portable Document Format) documents useful alternatives to your Web pages. A PostScript, PDF, or Microsoft Word version of your information can provide even better document formatting than is possible with HTML. In certain cases considering your Web server as a distribution method for these print versions of your information may be advantageous. Referring to information online is not always practical. For example, printed versions of instruction manuals and documentation are often much more useful than screen versions. Also, remember that many people have less time online than they would like, and they may prefer to download the information you have to offer in order to read and study it at their leisure.

Divide Your Information into Chunks

Wherever possible, divide your information into chunks that can be conveyed in one- to two-screen pages. This allows people to get the gist of your offering and move on quickly. If you find your documents are taking more than a screen or two, you should think about splitting them into smaller sections.

Offer Alternatives (ALTS) for Inline Images

Take advantage of the HTML ALT code in your inline images to provide text descriptions of those images for the users who can't view them. Otherwise, text-only viewers see the word *image* in brackets wherever an inline image appears in your document. With the ALT HTML tag you can be much more descriptive: [flag], [arrow], [picture of Abraham Lincoln].

Explain Your Server on Your Front Page

Although not everyone will enter your Web server through your front page, many will. Make life easier for everyone by clearly and prominently explaining the purpose of your Web server. If your server is intended to accommodate only students on your campus, make this clear so that others won't waste their time.

Sign and Date Every Document

The World-Wide Web is new and exciting, but time does pass and people do need to know when documents were written and last updated. You should also sign them with an e-mail address so that people can contact you if they find errors.

Avoid "Click Here" Links

Make each link descriptive. Remember that your links may well be indexed by programs that wander the Web collecting links. If the text of your links uses the word *here* (as in "Click here for tip on investing"), the indexer will pick up a bunch of *here*s and nothing useful. You can easily write that link as "See tip on investing."

Map Your Server

Although it's not always possible or necessary to map every link or even every section of your server, users find maps useful. See Figure 4–1 for an example of how one company used a map of its Web site to provide access to any page on its Web server with three clicks, at most, of the mouse. The company also offers an organizational chart of its site that both text-only and graphics browsers can use.

Ask for Feedback

Make it easy for users to give you feedback. Build a comment form or supply a "Mail to" link, and be sure to list your e-mail address in case the first two don't work. First, it makes good sense to ask your users for comment. They'll often surprise you with their insights. Second, the Internet is an interactive medium. You'll accomplish much more if you take advantage of that.

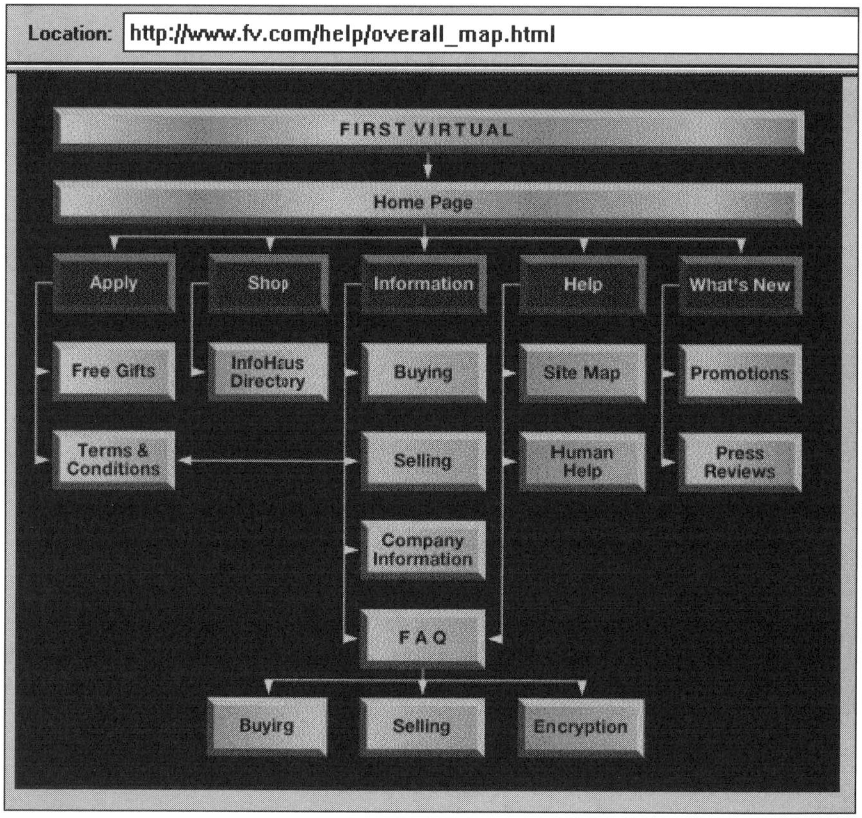

FIGURE 4–1 First Virtual Map (Reprinted with permission.)

Use Directional Links

Be sure that you put a link back to your home page on all your other pages. Remember that some users will land in the middle of your Web pages after doing an Internet search, and unless you give them a way to get to your home page, they may just give up.

Warn of Large Files

When your links hook up to large files (more than 50K), let your readers know in advance, ideally by specifying the file size. That way they'll think twice before downloading large files. When a user becomes frustrated and cancels because a download of a large file is slow, neither of you gains. Warnings keep users aware and might save a little of your server's workload.

Adding Information and Files

Several methods are available for adding items to your Web server. I'll list them and then discuss them in greater detail:

1. Type your text directly into an HTML editor or word-processing program that outputs HTML.
2. Convert existing text with filters or conversion programs.
3. Keep your data in a database and generate database reports in HTML format.
4. Add links from your reading and explorations.

Typing text directly into an HTML editor gives you control over every step of the process but can be quite time-consuming. Also, HTML may not be a long-term solution for data storage and management. SGML is often cited as a better document source language because of its flexibility and detailed structural labeling. Although you might not be able to imagine this now, eventually you may find that you need greater detail in accessing pieces of documents. Saving in SGML and converting to HTML is one way to be sure you're ready for that step. And if SGML is ever replaced, its structured format will allow for easy conversion.

Converting word-processing files to HTML is already possible for WordPerfect and Microsoft Word for Windows (versions 2.0 and 6.0). RTF-to-HTML converters as well as several others already are available. And Microsoft and Novell are both offering free add-in HTML editors for their word-processing programs (see Table 4–2). You can edit your text normally and have HTML too. Although these techniques appear to be ideal, be sure to check whether the conversion process is restricted in any way. What happens to images, tables, and equations? Are they converted correctly? Don't assume. Check the results. To quote an Arabic saying, "Trust in God, but tie your camel."

When you have a large amount of information, creating a database in which to store it may be a good idea. Or you might already have a database that you want to publish on the Internet. One scheme, used by Ian M. Sims, computing coordinator for the business faculty at Edith Cowan University in Australia, is to combine a naming convention with a database to create individual HTML documents for each record in the database. He does this for course offerings. The naming convention comes in when he decides to give each course a three-character code and a number. For example, Economics 101 might be eco1. The information record for that course is written to a file named eco1.html. Any summary report can look up each course's code and create hyperlinks for each one.

Finally, you will find as you explore the Internet and in your reading that you will come across links or URLs to all sorts of useful or interesting locations. Explore the bookmark capability of your browser so that you become proficient at organizing and copying the links that you save there, a relatively painless way to add to your server's resources. Your users will appreciate ancillary or related information, or links to services offering similar information. Internet policy isn't clear on this, but it's probably best to tell the administrator of any site to which you have provided a link. If nothing else, it's courteous, and it increases the likelihood that you'll be informed of any changes.

Be Careful of Embedded Codes

It is tempting to take your existing text files and online documents and add them directly to your Web server. But remember that HTML interprets certain normal text characters as special codes. I once came across a situation in which a vendor's Web site examples used the characters < and > in the text. HTML interpreted them as codes, and they did not display correctly on either Web browser to which I had access at the time (Lynx and Mosaic). The greater than and less than signs were being interpreted as HTML codes, but because they did not adhere to HTML coding requirements, they caused the loss of some text. Needless to say, the vendor's examples were mangled and highly confusing. I could see the full example only by looking at the HTML source. Taking the extra step of scanning all documents for all HTML special characters before loading them is important.

Web Tools

Many special tools, both free and commercial (even more than for Gopher—see Table 4–3), have been developed to help Web administrators manage their servers. Some tools are for dealing with graphic images—resizing, converting, or altering them in some way. Some tools are for server administration, to help analyze log files and check links. Other tools provide you with the capability of, for example, creating clickable maps or realtime GIF or HTML documents. *Realtime* in this case means a special image or document that might be always changing like the Southern California Traffic Report <***http://www.scubed.com/caltrans/***> or documents created on the fly or in reaction to input from a user. Look online for the latest tools, because they are always changing.

Advanced Web Techniques

Once you've got your Web server up and running, and you've tired of the thrill of seeing your HTML pages on screen, you'll want to try out some of the more advanced capabilities of your Web server. Some require you to configure your server in special ways. Others involve writing or using scripts to run with the server. Other techniques have more to do with image or document preparation. Eventually, you'll find them all useful.

Images

Images present a wealth of possibilities and problems. The main problem is to get an image that will show up well without being too large a file. Also, color quality varies considerably according to whether the image was scanned in 8-, 16-, or 24-bit color and viewed on Macintosh, Windows, or UNIX workstations.

TABLE 4–3 WWW Tools

Tool	Platform	Description
Web Developer's Virtual Library *<http://www.stars.com/>*	All	An excellent collection of resources for Web administrators. Check out the tools list, but you'll also find some tools in other sections.
Graphics Viewers, Editors, Utilities, and Info *<http://www2.ncsu.edu/bae/people/faculty/walker/hotlist/graphics.html>*	Windows, DOS, UNIX, & Macintosh	This site by Joseph C. Walker at North Carolina State University links a long list of graphics programs, converters, and tools.
Anchor Checker, by George Xie *<http://www.ugrad.cs.ubc.ca/spider/q7f192/branch/checker.html>*	UNIX	Program that checks the links in your Web document.
Link Verifier *<http://wsk.eit.com/wsk/dist/doc/admin/webtest/verify_links.html>*	UNIX	Link Verifier is intended for use by server administrators in maintaining links within the documents managed at their sites. The link verifier tool starts from a given URL and traverses links outward, producing a report on the state of all the links found.
WebMap, by Rowland Smith *<http://www.city.net/cnx/software/webmap.html>*	Macintosh	Tool to help create clickable image maps.
Mapedit, by Thomas Boutell *<ftp://sunsite.unc.edu/pub/packages/infosystems/WWW/tools/mapedit>*	Windows	Tool to help create clickable image maps.
WebStat, by Paul Sijben *<http://www.pegasus.esprit.ec.org/people/sijben/statistics/advertisment. html>*	UNIX, DOS, Windows, & Macintosh	WebStat is a program that gathers statistics on the usage of a WWW server. The tables and results it generates can be fed back as HTML pages on your WWW server.
ANIMATE, by Home Pages, Inc. *<http://www.homepages.com/tools/>*	DOS, Macintosh, & UNIX	This Perl script sets you up to do "pushed" Netscape animation.
Giftrans *<ftp://ftp.rz.uni-karlsruhe.de/pub/net/www/tools/>*	DOS & UNIX	This program can be used to make the background color of an image transparent and change background colors.
Transparency *<ftp://ftp.uwtc.washington.edu/pub/Mac/Graphics/Transparency1.0.sit.bin>*	Macintosh	Tool that lets you set the background of your GIF files to be transparent. It may not work with all browsers.

Table 4–3 *(continued)*

Tool	Platform	Description
GIFTOOL, by Home Pages, Inc. *<http://www.homepages.com/tools/>*	DOS & UNIX	GIFTOOL does everything from interlacing to transparency in batch mode. It also allows you to examine GIFs and add comments.
Netpbm *<http://hobbes.chem.uh.edu/news/netpbm.html>*	UNIX	Netpbm, based on pbmplus, is a tool kit for conversion of images between a variety of different formats. It also allows some basic image operations.
Weblint *<http://www.khoros.unm.edu:80/staff/neilb/weblint.html>*	DOS, Macintosh, & UNIX	Weblint is a Perl script for checking HTML for problems and inconsistencies. It even complains if you use *here* as a link.
GIF Construction Set *<http://www.north.net/alchemy/>*	Windows	Among other things you can make the background of GIF images transparent and add text to the image itself with this program from Alchemy Mindworks Inc.
Graphics Workshop (same site as GIF Construction Set)	Windows	This program from Alchemy Mindworks Inc. will let you view, print, convert, scale, rotate, color adjust, transform, crop, catalog, and generally fiddle with a large variety of image files.
Imagizer *<http://pc.inrird.com/imagizer.html>*	UNIX	This shareware program by Paul Colton can be run as a CGI script to allow creation of GIF images on the fly, or it can be used as an image-conversion utility. It can make images transparent or interlaced and scale both horizontally and vertically.
CGIRend *<http://pc.inrird.com/cgirend.html>*	Windows 3.11 & NT coming	CGIRend is a realtime, 3-D solid modeling engine for WWW servers. It renders objects in realtime, interlaced and transparent, and allows for complete user interactivity, specifying distance, x-rotation, y-rotation, and z-rotation by any graphical/web browser. Basically, it means users can interact with your images.

Table 4–3 *(continued)*

Tool	Platform	Description
Oracle World Wide Web Interface Kit *<http://dozer.us.oracle.com:8080/>*	UNIX	This free collection of tools and programs encourages the use of Oracle 7 database servers as back ends for WWW servers.
XV, by John Bradley *<ftp://ftp.cis.upenn.edu/pub/xv>*	UNIX	XV or X Viewer is a program that displays and converts images under the X Windows system. It is often used to find x-y coordinates in GIF files to create templates for clickable images.
FFW (Freetext Search for Web) *<http://www.nta.no/produkter/ffw/ffw.html>*	UNIX	FFW is a software package that can be used to build free-text search facilities on a World-Wide Web server similar to WAIS but claims to be easier to use, faster, and a better handler of HTML documents.
http_forward *<http://www.ph.tn.tudelft.nl/~klamer/http_forward.html>*	UNIX	Http_forward is a Perl script to forward HTTP requests to a different port on a different machine and include a message with the forwarded request.

Postage Stamp or Thumbnail Images

Large image files take time to transfer, so many sites make thumbnail or postage stamp–sized reductions of their image files to give users a taste of the images available. Most graphics programs can create these by shrinking images, although they often lose a lot of detail. Plan for the smaller versions to take up 2K to 10K instead of the 20K to 200K a larger image file might take. Although the postage stamp images are stored as GIF files so they can be used as inline images, the original full-size image could be in GIF or JPEG.

Transparent GIFs

Making the background of a GIF image transparent so that it takes the color of whatever background the browser uses can be a nice aesthetic touch. One site uses this technique to begin its files with a large initial in an archaic font. The giftrans program can do this on UNIX and DOS, and a program aptly called Transparency can do this on Macintoshes. See Table 4–3 for these and other such programs. Not all browsers display these images correctly, however, so test your images on many browsers.

Clickable Images

A clickable image is a graphic image on a Web page that has certain "sensitive" areas that, if clicked with a mouse, link to some other page or program. Basically, clickable images work in conjunction with CGI scripts on the server. When the user clicks on part of the image, its x-y coordinates are sent back to the WWW server, where a CGI script or program processes them and performs some specific action, depending on which section of the image the user selected. The uses of clickable images are limited only by your imagination.

Here's a short list of examples:

A clickable map of a city could lead to a list of the restaurants nearest the spot chosen.

An image could be enlarged by clicking on various sections, assuming you have larger versions of the image scanned and available.

Clicking a painting in different areas could lead to commentary on various aspects of the painting by art critics and historians.

A dissection of an animal, or even a human being, can be guided by clicking your way through pictures of the organs.

A common use is to use a clickable image as a sort of menu to the various areas of the Web site.

To create a clickable image decide first which areas of the image should lead to which actions. These actions could be as simple as displaying selected documents or images or running programs on your server. The NCSA version of clickable images gives you a choice of points, squares, rectangles, circles, and polygons with as many as 100 vertices. Points would be difficult for the user to click accurately, so they use a "closest to" rule—the point that is closest to the coordinates clicked will respond. Then mark these areas, and record in a map file the x-y coordinates and the URL to the appropriate image, document, or script for each area. The top left corner is 0,0—heading down increases the value of the y-axis, and moving to the right is positive for the x-axis. You also could use a default URL in case the users do not pick any of the zones you've defined. Then you make a link that points to your map file by using the IMG SRC code in HTML. The Macintosh and Windows HTTP servers are similiar, but CERN uses a different approach.

The major drawback of the current method of providing clickable images is that users get no immediate feedback as they move the mouse over the image. They have to wait until the x-y coordinates are sent to the server and it looks up the nearest zone. Because the Internet isn't instantaneous, clickable images delay an otherwise interesting process. In development are several alternatives for image mapping that allow the browser to do more of the work and provide immediate feedback. Because the browser program is considered a Web client, this is called *client-side image mapping.*

Interactive Image Format (IIF)

Interactive Image Format (IIF) is a form of client-side clickable image developed at the University of Michigan by the Weather Underground (a weather service, not the 1960s radicals). IIF originally was written to allow Gopher servers to provide special weather maps via the Blue Skies Gopher client (browser). As you moved your mouse across the map, text in a box at the top tells you which weather-reporting station is nearby. If you then click the mouse, you are connected to that server and you receive a weather report on screen. The University of Michigan is exploring this technology with a grant from the National Science Foundation. Blue Skies Gopher clients are available for Macintosh and Windows. <***http://cirrus.sprl.umich.edu/***>

Creating GIF Images on the Fly

"On the fly" means that your server creates the GIF image only after the user requests it. The image might be a special graphic representing flood damage in an area, a zoom-lens view of a map, a spinning globe, a graph of rising (or falling) profits, or the amount of coffee left in a pot. Imagizer is one software program that can do this (see Table 4–3).

CGI Scripts

CGI scripts are behind many of the most interesting applications on the Web. Whenever the Web server does something special (as opposed to simply providing a file), it does so because of a CGI script. CGI, or the Common Gateway Interface, is a standard way for external programs to interact with Web and other information servers. What this means is that CGI is your main tool for adding special functions to your Web server. Some functions, like gateways to Archie, Finger (a user information lookup command; see Chapter 6), and WAIS have already been added by CGI scripts or programs that come with your WWW server software. Others can be created by altering existing programs or writing new ones from scratch.

The Common Gateway Interface designates how programs will interact with Web servers behind the scenes. For example, a commonly used CGI script takes the information from an online comment form and e-mails it to the Web administrator. It does this by taking the information submitted on the form and using it to fill out a mail message, which it sends.

CGI programs can be UNIX shell scripts (a series of commands in a file, like DOS batch files), Perl scripts, or programs written in C, C++, or other programming languages. The important thing is that they interact with the Web server according to the rules of the CGI specification <*http://hoohoo.ncsa.uiuc.edu/cgi/interface.html*>. The link to NCSA's collection of CGI examples and overviews is

<http://hoohoo.ncsa.uiuc.edu/cgi/>; one link to a CGI primer is *<http://hoohoo.ncsa.uiuc.edu/cgi/primer.html>*.

NCSA-Supplied CGI Scripts

The simplest way to start using and writing CGI scripts is to look at the CGI scripts and example programs that came with your server or those mentioned here. For instance, the NCSA HTTPD Web server comes with the following sample CGI scripts and programs. Use or modify these to meet your needs, or write your own, using these as examples:

archie is a simple gateway to Archie servers.

calendar invokes the UNIX cal command to produce simple calendars.

date prints the current date.

fortune links to the UNIX fortune program, which gives a random fortune cookie message.

imagemap provides the background script for making image maps clickable.

jj is an example HTML form that Champaign, Illinois, residents use to order submarine sandwiches from a restaurant called Jimmy Johns.

phf sends queries to a PH (telephone book) server and returns the results to the user.

query is a demonstration script for a general online form that can be adapted for various purposes.

test-cgi is a script that echoes all the information that accompanies a CGI script request to test the design of your forms.

uptime runs the uptime command on the server, if it exists, and sends the response to the user. The uptime command tells the user how long the server has been running in case they want to know.

wais.pl is a CGI script written in Perl that passes queries on to a WAIS server, wraps the response in HTML, and sends it back to the user.

Other CGI script tricks include adding access counts to your documents, which allows your users to see how many times a particular document has been accessed. Chuck Musciano of Harris Corporation explains how to do this and gives away a C program for the NCSA HTTPD server that counts accesses and displays a message saying you are visitor number such and such. It keeps track of all efforts to access the documents to which it is linked. <***http://melmac.corp.harris.com/access_counts.html***>

Server-Side Includes

Server-side includes are a feature of NCSA's HTTPD server that permits a server to automatically include information from files and environment variables in an HTML file as it is being sent to the user. It can include other information, such as date and document size, if you wish. One useful application is to have your HTML documents automatically show the date they were last updated, without you or anyone else modifying the date in the file. This means you won't have to remember to change the date each time you change a file. Server-side includes have many other uses, but be sure that you look for any warnings or advisories about them, because in some situations they may pose a security threat. They also add a load to the serve and can slow it down. Each time a document goes out, it has to check and process any included scripts.

Forms

Online forms are among the most useful and appreciated features of Web servers. If the Web provided no way for users to give feedback, the Web would not be what it is today. Forms are used for everything from comments to subscriptions to entering HTML pages for validation to ordering pizzas.

Basically, forms consist of two parts, the HTML description of the form and the CGI program on the server that will do something with the answers to the form's questions. This might be as simple as taking the information and mailing it to the Web administrator. Or it might mean reporting the number of users since the server went online. Whatever the application, it's always a combination of a form written in HTML and a CGI script or program.

HTML 2.0 forms can be created from the following pieces:

INPUT specifies a field that the user fills out. You control the maximum length of the text the user can enter as well as the size of the onscreen space. You can also specify a default value to sit in the field for the user to see. (This lets you put standard answers in for the convenience of your users.) Input fields can be of the following types:

- CHECKBOX provides users with a list of values and allows them to check off the ones they want to use. For example, users might check off various categories of music or books they enjoy.
- HIDDEN sends the contents of this field along with the completed form to the user but doesn't show this field. The HIDDEN field can be used to send certain control information to the Web server. This is one way to carry over user information from one request to the next. For example, sites that let users build a running invoice as they shop on a Web site use this technique.
- IMAGE lets you specify an image that, when clicked, causes the form to be submitted with the x-y coordinates of the clicked spot. This is widely used for a variety of functions (see the discussion of clickable images earlier in this chapter).
- TEXT is a single-line entry field. Use TEXTAREA for multiple-line fields.
- PASSWORD is the same as TEXT (a single-line entry field), but what the user types does not show up on screen.
- RADIO allows users to select a single value from a set of alternatives.

- RESET is a button that resets the form to its initial default values when pressed. This option lets users start to fill out an online form and then reset and start again.
- SUBMIT is a button that submits the form when the user presses it. You can use the VALUE option to change what appears on the button. For example, you might want the button to read REGISTER instead of SUBMIT.

SELECT allows the user to select from a list of headings or options. If you set the button to read MULTIPLE, the user can make more than one selection. You can and should include a SIZE button when the list is longer than what a single screen can display. I've seen one Web server with a SELECT option of several hundred items, but because SIZE wasn't specified, users of some browsers could choose only those options that appeared on the first screen because the browser didn't scroll automatically. Once this server was set for SIZE (to 17 in this case), the browser started scrolling through the entire list, showing 17 items at a time.

TEXTAREA lets users enter more than one line of text. ROWS and COLS show the visible dimensions of the field in characters. Browsers are supposed to allow scrolling beyond these limits so that users can enter longer text as necessary.

Almost all the fields also have a name attached to them so that your CGI script can easily distinguish between them. The user doesn't see these field names, but they are essential nonetheless. Each answer the user gives is paired with its variable name, and these sets are sent back to the Web server. Without the NAME attribute, the CGI script that the server uses would not know which answer went with which variable.

Several books on HTML and many online resources, including one from NCSA, <*http://www.ncsa.uiuc.edu/SDG/Software/Mosaic/Docs/fill-out-forms/overview.html*>, provide, among other things, examples of forms, complete with explanations. At the end of its document NCSA is kind enough to offer a test server that you can use to test any forms that you develop. The script simply echoes back to you any of the fields that it receives, so you can see whether they work as you expected.

Don't forget that you can always look at the source (HTML) of any form you come across on the World-Wide Web. This is one way to learn new form techniques. Some examples of forms in use on the Web include a form for adding home pages and a form that forwards e-mail.

Figure 4–2 shows part of a form used by the Web site HUMnet (Humanities Computing) at UCLA to allow students, staff, and faculty to add their own home pages to the humanities Web server.

Figure 4–3 shows a portion of the HTML that created the form that appears in Figure 4–2. Note all the departments listed as options and how Art History is listed as the default option by using <option selected> (see Figure 4–3).

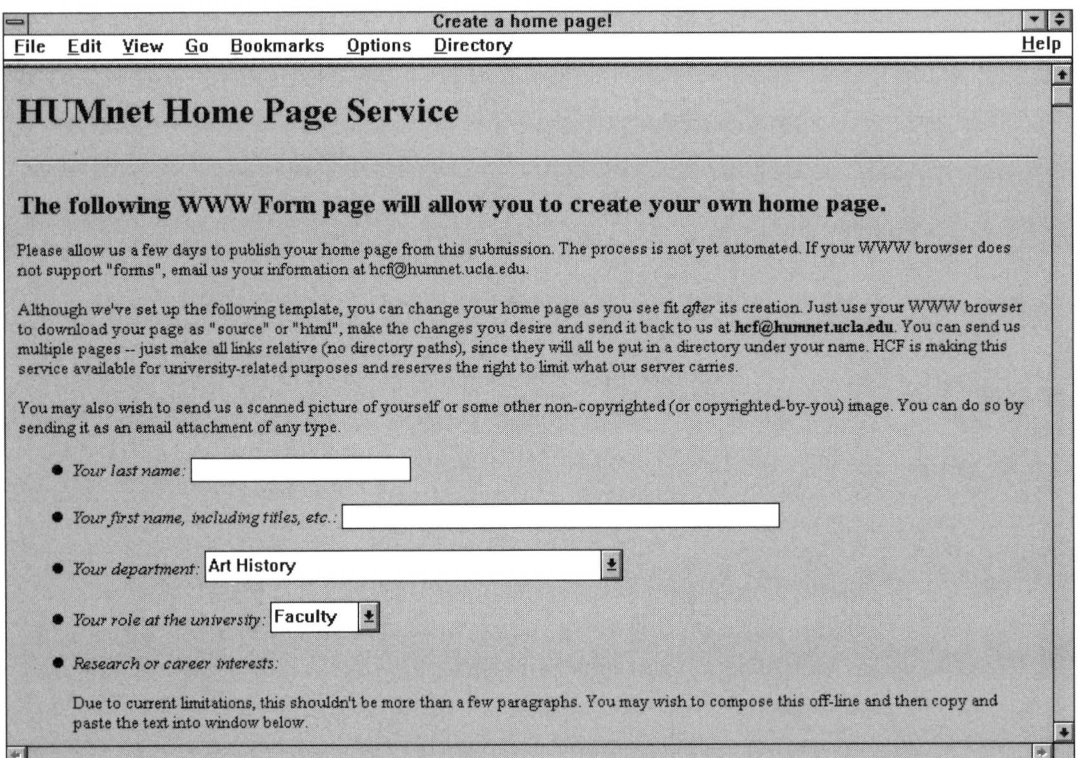

FIGURE 4–2 HUMnet (Reprinted with permission.)

FIGURE 4–3 HTML for Adding Home Pages Forms—Humanities Computing, UCLA

```
<FORM METHOD="GET" ACTION="http:/feedbacktest.script">
<UL>
<LI><em>Your last name: </em>
<INPUT TYPE="text" NAME="lastname" SIZE="20" MAXLENGTH="30">
<P>
<LI><em>Your first name, including titles, etc.: </em>
<INPUT TYPE="text" NAME="firstname" SIZE="40" MAXLENGTH="40">
<P>
<LI><em>Your department:</em>
<select name="department">
<option selected>Art History
<option>Classics
<option>Comparative Literature
...........
<option>Center for Medieval & Renaissance Studies
<option>Center for 17th & 18th Century Studies
</select>
<P>
<LI><em>Your role at the university:</em>
<select name="position">
<option>Faculty
<option>Student
<option>Staff
</select>
<P>
<LI><em>Research or career interests:</em>
<P>
```

The E-mail Forwarding Request Form in Figure 4–4 also was designed and is used by HUMnet at UCLA. It takes information that enables it to forward e-mail from users. Note that HUMnet also uses this form to communicate the rules and establish the information required for e-mail forwarding on its system. The portion shown here uses checkboxes and radio buttons as well as the TEXTAREA field for a long text entry. Figure 4–5 shows how that form was written in HTML.

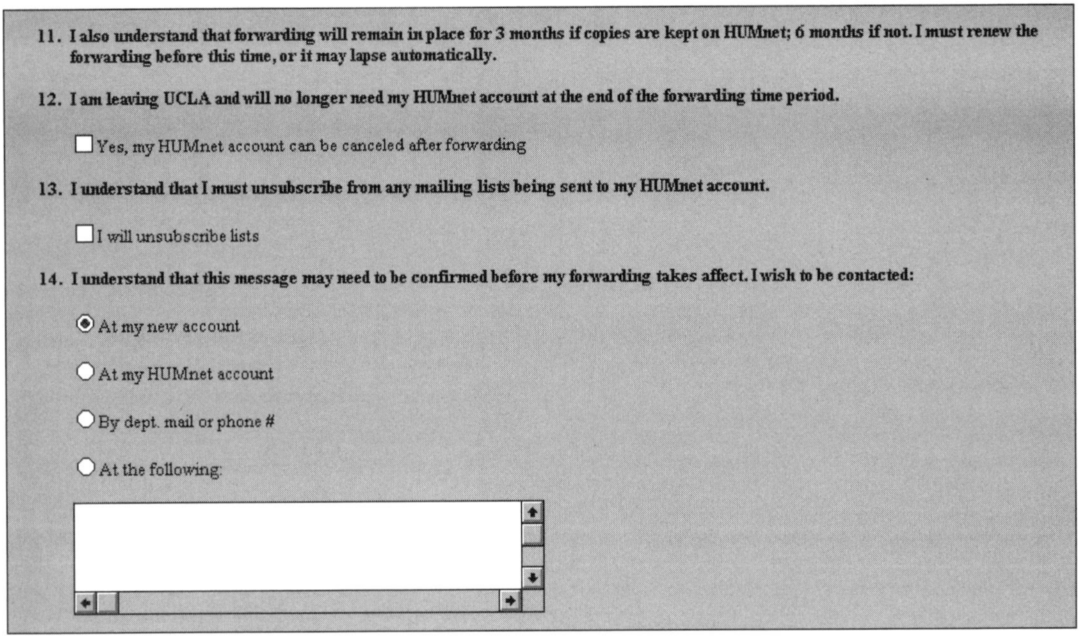

11. I also understand that forwarding will remain in place for 3 months if copies are kept on HUMnet; 6 months if not. I must renew the forwarding before this time, or it may lapse automatically.

12. I am leaving UCLA and will no longer need my HUMnet account at the end of the forwarding time period.

☐ Yes, my HUMnet account can be canceled after forwarding

13. I understand that I must unsubscribe from any mailing lists being sent to my HUMnet account.

☐ I will unsubscribe lists

14. I understand that this message may need to be confirmed before my forwarding takes affect. I wish to be contacted:

◉ At my new account

○ At my HUMnet account

○ By dept. mail or phone #

○ At the following:

FIGURE 4–4 E-mail Forwarding Request Form (partial)—Humanities Computing, UCLA
(Reprinted with permission.)

Web Indexing

One criticism of the WWW is that it is not nearly as easy to index as Gopher servers. If you want to index all documents and links in a Web server, you have to actually scan through all the HTML documents, looking for the title of that document, as well as all the HTML links. And when you do find a link, what do you index—the link's URL or the link's descriptive text (see Figure 4–6)?

The link URL is great for getting you somewhere, but isn't always useful for describing what it's linking to. The descriptive text is the logical thing to index, but it might not always be available. Servers commonly use graphic images as links instead of descriptive text. And as we just saw, clickable images can link to many different files or locations, without having any text attached.

Nonetheless, the reasons for indexing Web servers are the same as for Gopher servers: so your users can find out what you have (and don't

FIGURE 4–5 HTML for E-mail Forwarding Request Form (excerpt)—Humanities Computing, UCLA

```
<strong><LI>I also understand that forwarding will remain in place for
<strong>3 months</strong> if copies are kept on HUMnet; <strong>6
months</strong> if not.  I must renew the forwarding before this
time, or it may lapse automatically.</strong>
<P>
<strong><LI>I am leaving UCLA and will no longer need my HUMnet account
at the end of the forwarding time period.</strong>
<P>
<INPUT TYPE="checkbox" NAME="terminate" VALUE="yes">Yes, my HUMnet account
can be canceled after forwarding
<P>
<strong><LI>I understand that I must unsubscribe from any mailing lists
being sent to my HUMnet account.</strong>
<P>
<INPUT TYPE="checkbox" NAME="unsubscribe" VALUE="yes">I will unsubscribe
lists
<P>
<strong><LI>I understand that this message may need to be confirmed before
my forwarding takes affect.  I wish to be contacted:</strong>
<P>
<INPUT TYPE="radio" NAME="contact" VALUE="new_account" Checked>At my new
account
<P>
<INPUT TYPE="radio" NAME="contact" VALUE="humnet_account">At my HUMnet
account
<P>
<INPUT TYPE="radio" NAME="contact" VALUE="phone">By dept. mail or phone #
<P>
<INPUT TYPE="radio" NAME="contact" VALUE="other">At the following:
<P>
<TEXTAREA NAME="contact_info" ROWS=4 COLS=40>
</TEXTAREA>
```

have) quickly and with minimal frustration and so your server is efficient in providing its information. Next I'll describe several different indexing systems, some of which are built into particular WWW servers. The important thing to keep track of is what is being indexed—file names and links, document titles, the full text of all

FIGURE 4–6 Hypertext Anchor

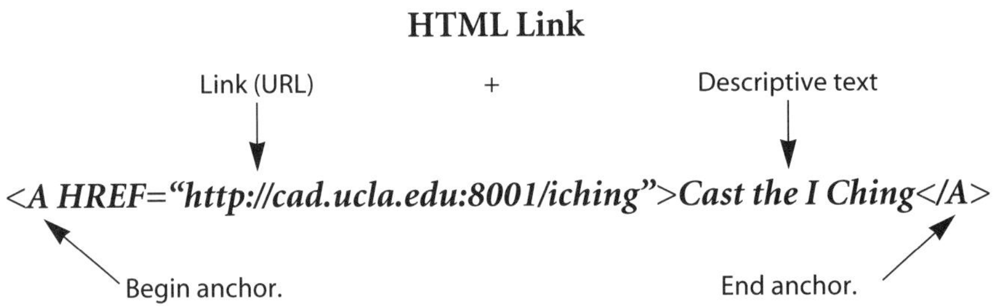

documents, or an abstract written by the Web administrator. Different indexing programs or systems have different philosophies. Look at them all, but be sure that when you choose one, you know exactly what it is designed to index and what its advantages (and disadvantages) are.

Internal Indexers

I call do-it-yourself indexing *internal indexing.* Servers and add-on programs that are available for indexing your Web server yourself include:

- GN and WN, both of which provide built-in internal indexing. Both are described earlier in this chapter under the heading Web (HTTP) Servers.
- ICE is an indexing extension for WWW servers by Christian Neuss. It is a lightweight, easy-to-install alternative to WAIS gateways, and it allows free-text searches of an indexed World-Wide Web server. *<http://www.igd.fhg.de/~neuss/>*
- GlimpseHTTP is a powerful full-text indexing and query system that allows approximate matching, Boolean searching, and limited **regular expression** (UNIX-style) searching. Glimpse directly supports WWW (HTTP) servers through the gateway program GlimpseHTTP. This means that users can search your Web server directly if you've indexed it with

Glimpse. It does not rank the results the way WAIS does, but it does allow misspellings. <***http://glimpse.cs.arizona.edu:1994/ghttp/***>

- WAIS is detailed in Chapter 5.

External Indexers (Web Crawlers, Spiders, and Worms)

External indexers are programs that reside on someone else's machine but index all servers. Often called *Web crawlers, spiders, worms,* and *robots,* they are programs that attempt to traverse all the known menus or links in Gopher and Web servers in order to build comprehensive indexes of Gopher or Web space. Gopher is simpler to index, and Veronica and Jughead take care of that. Because WWW is much harder to index, there are many approaches to indexing or cataloging the exploding World-Wide Web. It is important that you understand the distinctions between each one so that you can make sure that your server and its documents are indexed in the way that's most appropriate for them. If you want to advertise your Web server, register it with every external index, or subject server, you can find. This is where your notes from your own searches will come in handy.

These programs require your cooperation to avoid excessive efforts on their part and to limit the load on your server. Basically, some information on your server may not be of interest to outside users. Or you may not want it indexed for some reason, either to limit access or because the information (such as Usenet News links) changes too quickly. Some protocols have been developed for dealing with information that should not be indexed. Certain hidden files can be placed in specified locations on your server that tell the indexing programs which sections to index and which to ignore.

The link to Martijn Koster's list of Web Wanderers, a good list of Web robots and spiders, is <***http://web.nexor.co.uk/mak/doc/robots/active.html***>. Check it out, and look at some other places that can index your Web site.

ALIWEB

ALIWEB asks Webmasters to summarize in an index file the various themes or subjects covered in their WWW server. When you register with ALIWEB <***http://web.nexor.co.uk/aliweb/doc/aliweb.html***>, it looks for this file and checks its structure; this index file is picked up by the ALIWEB harvester at regular intervals. The index file is a plain ASCII file in a special format left in a special place on the Web server. The protocol even allows Web administrators to specify how often their server should be checked for changes. The ALIWEB database is also incorporated in the CUI W3 catalog.

GENBBB

GENBBB allows you to add WWW titles, reports, and links to other virtual libraries via an online WWW form. <***http://www.cs.colorado.edu/homes/mcbryan/public_html/bb/summary.html***>

EINet Galaxy

EINet Galaxy lets you add your own annotations and links to its catalog. <***http://www.einet.net/galaxy.html***>

Lycos

Register your Gopher, WWW, or FTP site with Lycos at <***http://lycos.cs.cmu.edu/lycos-register.html***>. It takes a few days to a week for newly registered items to be added to the index. Lycos ignores redirected pages, so you must register the actual server name and path.

World-Wide Web Virtual Library

This is a directory or catalog of the Internet by subject. Mail information about your Web server to the maintainers of the specified subject or to www-request@mail.w3.org. You might also offer to contribute to administration of a subject area to share your expertise. *<http://www.w3.org/hypertext/DataSources/bySubject/Overview.html>*

Advertising and Registering Your Web Server

Putting something on the Web doesn't necessarily publicize it. Unless you want to have a little-known Web server, you'll want to register it and advertise it as much as possible. I'll give you some ways to do that, but check online for additional services and sites. One drawback to the Internet is that there is no guaranteed way to intensively advertise your site among the tens of thousands of other Web sites available for browsing.

Try these techniques:

1. Register your server with W3O by following the instructions given at *<http://www.w3.org/hypertext/DataSources/www/Geographical_generation/hew-servers.html/>*.
2. Post information about your server to the Usenet newsgroup comp.infosystems.www.announce.
3. Send e-mail to the list server www-request@www.w3.org, which should get your server on the W3O World-Wide Web servers' list. This list is sorted alphabetically by continent, country, and state.
4. Send an announcement to whats-new@ncsa.uiuc.edu in HTML format and third person to get your announcement on the NCSA Mosaic's "What's New" page.
5. Put information about your server in your .signature file (an e-mail feature on many systems that lets you automatically place your organization, title, and other data at the end of every message), on your business cards, brochures, and such, and spread the news via word of mouth and e-mail.
6. Find the relevant subject lists and guides and make sure they know about your server.

Summary

WWW is a method of publishing on the Internet that is generating tremendous interest and enthusiasm among users. It combines text, graphics, and hypertext links using HTML in a way that is appealing and easy to navigate. The capacity for formatting documents is deceptive, however, because different WWW browser programs display the same HTML document differently. A certain percentage of users is limited to text-only browsers (Lynx) that do not show images. Web designers have to take these variations into account. Meanwhile, HTML is being improved, with new features added constantly.

WWW (technically, HTTPD) servers are available in both commercial and free versions for most types of computer systems. Although UNIX has been the operating system of choice for development and for most WWW servers, that is changing as more and more individuals set up servers on their desktop computers—PCs running Windows, Windows NT, or Macintoshes. Web managers find the PCs friendlier than UNIX, and they perform well for small and medium sites. Another option is to take a 486 or Macintosh and run it with a UNIX operating system, which can make it perform much faster and more efficiently as a Web (or Gopher) server.

Writing HTML is getting easier with the new tools (both HTML editors and word-processing add-ons) that are being developed. Be sure to check your HTML for conformance to HTML rules and standards; several online sites do this for free.

Design your Web site so that its contents and purpose are clear to even the most casual user. Organize your material and be consistent. Where possible, index the contents with WAIS, Glimpse, ICE, or some other indexing program to allow users to quickly search for material. Keep the sizes of pages and graphics down, particularly in your most frequently used pages. When you can't avoid having large documents or files, label the links with the size of the file so that users are forewarned.

Considerable programming effort and creativity are being applied to making Web servers do more than just provide documents and files on demand. CGI scripts are programs that can be added to most Web servers to perform special functions such as searches, updating databases, performing commercial transactions, and providing interactive online forms. Sun's Hot Java is adding an actual programming language that will be "understood" by any Hot Java–compatible Web browser (see Chapter 11).

With more than 25,000 WWW servers on the Internet and increasing all the time, it is extremely important to register and advertise your Web site in as many places as possible. Indexing the contents of Web servers was originally thought to be one of the weak points of the WWW. Now, with robots and spiders (like Lycos from Carnegie Mellon University) that traverse Webspace to add to their indexes of Web documents, the situation has improved dramatically.

CHAPTER 5

WAIS and Indexing Alternatives

WAIS, pronounced *ways,* stands for Wide Area Information Server, an animal quite different from Gopher or WWW. Whereas Gopher and WWW are systems that help users to look at documents on various servers with ease, and indexing was added as an afterthought, WAIS was designed from the beginning to retrieve information from multiple indexed document sources. Its designers recognized that those documents might well be stored in many different places. The emphasis on searching and the ability to query many different data sources simultaneously are why WAIS is often the indexer (or search engine) running in the background for Gopher and WWW.

A key point about WAIS is that your users do not have to use special WAIS clients, because you can use WAIS indexes with a Gopher server or a WWW-to-WAIS gateway. Most WAIS indexes are accessed via Gopher or WWW clients.

To a greater extent than the various versions of Gopher and WWW, WAIS is split between a commercial version, offered by WAIS, Inc., and freeware versions supported by various organizations and individuals. The commercial version, WAISserver from WAIS, Inc., costs $15,000, and there has been no intermediate version available at a lower price. That's why alternative indexing systems (such as Glimpse and ICE) have gained popularity.

WAIS: Pros and Cons

WAIS is one approach to indexed searching. It has the advantage of being written to work with both text and nontext files so that you can use a WAIS server for a collection of photographic images, word definitions, book reviews, video or audio clips, and almost anything else you can imagine. It does full-text indexing when text is available. It can index nontext files by file name or index descriptions of each nontext file.

However, one major drawback of WAIS is that the organization that had supported the noncommercial version (called **freeWAIS**) has dropped it in favor of a model based on the international standard Z39.50 v.2 (or v.1992). The University of Dortmundt in Germany has modified and improved the free version to allow for structured fields. This version is called **freeWAIS-sf. Structured fields** are containers for certain types of information, such as title, author, date, and other data. For example, if you index all your e-mail with the structured fields version of WAIS, you might designate fields for the sender, the subject, and the date. Then you could retrieve any message sent by your boss between certain dates pertaining to a specific subject. This kind of structured field searching offers much more flexibility to the user.

ADVANTAGES

- Provides full-text indexing.
- Can serve up images, sound, and other nontext files. WAIS indexes by filename or associated text file.
- Structured-field searching available from some servers.

DISADVANTAGES

- Little development for noncommercial WAIS servers.
- Users need some training to take advantage of all features.
- Technically complicated to administer.

How WAIS Works

WAIS does its work by transmitting a **natural language query**—a question in plain English—to a select number of information servers previously chosen by the user. Each of those servers compares the request with documents it has on file and sends back the headlines, or document titles, of their closest matches, ranked by how many words they had in common with the query. The user sees the list of headlines (each of which is a link to the original) alongside a number that gives each headline's relative ranking against the query. One thousand is best and it's downhill from there. The user then selects one or more documents to view and the full text shows up.

With **relevance feedback** a user can take one document and use it as a basis for a new search in an effort to find more documents that closely match the subject matter of the first one. The new search looks for documents that contain the same words as the user-selected document. In effect, it now has a much more specific search query to work from, with many more example words to try to match.

When WAIS Is Useful

When you have a large amount of text that you want to be completely searchable, you need an indexed server tool like WAIS. The text could consist of many different files, or it could be one or more large files, with blocks of information divided in some standard way. For example, a card catalog might have title, author, publication date, and such with a blank line between each record (a record is a set of fields). WAIS would return only the individual record (book in this case) that matches your search query.

For example, you might profitably use WAIS to search the

Congressional Record
U.S. Library of Congress card catalog
Encyclopaedia Britannica
Back issues of a set of computer magazines

WAIS and Z39.50

WAIS and Z39.50 are both protocols for retrieving information from computer to computer. The assumption is that one computer acts as a client and the other, with indexed databases, acts as a server. They are different from WWW and Gopher protocols in that they aren't "stateless." That is, they are designed to carry on an extended conversation between the client and server until the search session is complete. Stateless protocols, on the other hand, do all their work in one short interaction. Their conversations consists of "Give me this" and "Okay here it is." Z39.50 and WAIS allow for a longer interaction, building on previous responses.

Z39.50 (which was started in the United States) has gone through several versions, beginning with the largely unimplemented 1988 version (Z39.50-1988). The WAIS protocol was developed as an enlargement of Z39.50-1988 and built into a productive working system. The development of the Z39.50 standard continued, however, and not in the same direction as the WAIS enhancements. Z39.50-1992 (also called Z39.50-V2) improved the standard, among other things by bringing it closer to a similar international standard that also was being developed. WAIS, Inc., the principal holder of the WAIS torch, has altered its product to conform to the newer standard. CNIDR (Clearinghouse for Networked Information Discovery and Retrieval at *<http://cnidr.org/>*), which had been the developer and guardian of the freeWAIS (noncommercial) version, decided to switch its development efforts to the newer Z39.50 standard. **ZDist** is CNIDR's Z39.50 implementation and includes a UNIX client, server, HTTP-to-Z39.50 gateway, and an e-mail-to-Z39.50 gateway. Unfortunately, WAIS clients won't work with ZDist servers and vice versa.

FreeWAIS is a single indexer, single search engine, which means that it supports only one method of indexing documents and one search engine for searching those documents. A search engine is the program that actually does the searches. In contrast, ZDist allows more than one indexer and more than one search engine to be used at one time. This is useful when you want to search information stored at different sites and indexed in different ways. Ideally, users would be able to search many different databases without needing to learn the ins and outs of each one. That learning time was a significant barrier to using indexing systems.

WAIS fits in with Z39.50 in that the WAIS protocol has become what is called a ***Z39.50 profile,*** or a specific application of Z39.50. Profiles are formal implementation agreements within the context of the Z39.50 standard. They define which portions of the basic Z39.50 protocol are used in a given system and how the system should interpret these portions. WAIS is one of several publicly available Z39.50 profiles. The U.S. Government Information Locator Service (GILS), started by the Office of Management and Budget in concert with the Information Policy Committee of the Information Infrastructure Task Force, is another Z39.50 profile. The purpose of GILS is to make accessible the tremendous quantity of economic data, environmental data, and technical information collected and processed by various agencies of the U.S. government. GILS uses Z39.50 so that the information can be retrieved in a variety of ways. For more information on GILS see <***http://www.usgs.gov:80/gils/***>.

The single biggest use of Z39.50 might be the bib-1 profile developed for the library OPAC (Online Public-Access Catalog) market. This profile was developed by the library technology community for bibliographic applications of Z39.50. It has numerous commercial implementations in addition to free ones, like ISite from CNIDR. It is hoped that as bib-1 proves successful, profiles for other applications may be developed, such as geographic and medical information systems. Table 5–1 provides links for more information on Z39.50 and WAIS resources available online, as well as WWW-to-Z39.50 gateways.

Searching Capabilities and Limitations

Some WAIS servers support **stemming**, which reduces every word in a query to its word stem. For example, stemming would treat *computer, computing,* and *computers* identically, with the stem *comput.*

TABLE 5–1 WAIS Resources

Documents and Sites	
Example of WAIS Searching telnet to sunsite.unc.edu	You'll see several different anonymous login options that let you try out WAIS. Among databases provided are a collection of White House documents and Sun Inc. documentation.
WAIS Inc. *<gopher://wais.com>* or *<http://www.wais.com/>*	The site for the commercial version of WAIS, founded by Brewster Kahle.
WAIS Bibliography *<ftp://ftp.wais.com/pub/wais-inc-doc/>*	Bibliography of WAIS-related articles.
CNIDR *<http://cnidr.org/welcome.html>*	Site for freeWAIS, ZDist, and other information-searching–related files.
CNIDR Projects *<http://www.cnidr.org/cnidr_projects/cndir_projects.html.>*	Check out ZDist. CNIDR stopped freeWAIS development and moved to ZDist, which is a Z39.50 distribution server and client.
freeWAIS-sf FAQ *<ftp://ls6-www.informatik.uni-dortmund.de/pub/wais/FAQ>*	This is the originating site for the structured fields enhancement of freeWAIS.
Z39.50 Resources—A Pointer Page *<http://ds.internic.net/z3950/z3950.html>*	This is a useful collection of links to Z39.50 resources and points to explanations of the Z39.50 update process.
U.S. Library of Congress Web Page for the Z39.50 Maintenance Agency *<http://lcweb.loc.gov/z3950/agency/agency. html>*	The Library of Congress has been shepherding the Z39.50 standards process.
WWW to Z39.50 Gateways *<http://is.rice.edu/~riddle/ webZ39.50.html>*	This collection of Z39.50-to-WWW gateways demonstrates some of the power of Z39.50.
Usenet Newsgroups	
comp.infosystems.wais	This is the more "official" WAIS newsgroup and hosts discussions and questions, usually from those trying to install one of the freeWAIS versions.
alt.wais	This is the alternate or less "official" WAIS newsgroup, and it sees much less traffic.

Table 5–1 *(continued)*

Electronic Mailing Lists	
wais-interest contact wais-interest-request@think.com	This is a moderated list used to announce new releases.
wais-discussion contact wais-discussion-request@think.com	This is a moderated list on electronic publishing issues in general and Wide Area Information Servers in particular.
wais-talk contact wais-talk-request @think.com	This an open list (not moderated) for implementers and developers. This is a technical list that is not meant to be used as a support list.
Z3950IW contact LISTSERV@nervm.nerdc.ufl.edu	Z39.50 Implementers' list for low-level discussions of protocol details.
SIG-WAIS contact sig-wais-info@cnidr.org	This is a list for announcements of meetings and presentations of the WAIS Special Interest Group. These face-to-face conferences provide useful demonstrations and talks on WAIS and Z39.50.
WAISCUST To subscribe, send e-mail to listserv@rice.edu with the following in the body of your message: subscribe waiscust firstname lastname	This list is for discussion among customers of WAIS Inc. It is not sponsored by WAIS Inc.
Books	
Managing Internet Information Services by Cricket Liu, Jerry Peek, Russ Jones, Bryan Buus, and Adrian Nye, 1994	This is an excellent guide for the UNIX administrator and includes chapters on WAIS, Gopher, and WWW.
The Internet for Everyone—A Guide for Users and Providers by Richard W. Wiggins, 1995	Good description of WAIS.

It is important to understand that the rankings or scores that WAIS generates for documents are just approximations or guesses at what you really want. Technically, they may match on a certain number of words, but those words might be used in different contexts, so that the document with the highest score might not be useful at all. For example, searching on a question like Why is the sky blue? might bring poetry with those words in one stanza or information about the University of Michigan's Blue Skies Gopher project but nothing that answers the question. Basically, computers still can't think like a human being can. But using indexes is still better than going out and looking for each document. To use a sports analogy, think of computer searching as getting you into the ballpark but not playing the game for you.

The key to WAIS is that by using a powerful search algorithm, it locates and orders documents that match your query, but it doesn't guarantee their utility to your needs.

Fielded Searching

Fielded searching gives you the ability to search for certain information, such as author or publisher or company. So if you are looking for information about publishing on the Internet, you would prefer to find the words *publishing on the Internet* in the title of a document instead of scattered throughout the text. When you use fielded searching, a document does not receive a high ranking because it has each of those words individually in its text but because it has those words in its title. Obviously, a better choice.

WAIS Servers

The selection among WAIS servers is not nearly as ample as it is for Gopher and WWW.

FreeWAIS (CNIDR)

Thinking Machines gave the original WAIS program to the public domain. It was supported for a while by the Clearinghouse for Networked Information Discovery and Retrieval (CNIDR) <***http://cnidr.org/welcome.cnidr.html***>. The CNIDR version (freeWAIS 0.3) has Boolean searching and stemming, and the source code is available for other programmers to modify, but it does not offer structured fields and has many bugs that haven't been fixed. CNIDR has switched its development efforts to ZDist, which is based directly on the newer Z39.50-1992 standard. FreeWAIS 0.3 is available at <***ftp://ftp.cnidr.org/pub/NIDR.tools/freewais/***>.

FreeWAIS-sf

The *sf* in freeWais-sf stands for structured fields. **FreeWAIS-sf** is a UNIX-based WAIS server that builds on the freeWAIS code to provide the ability to search structured fields (including text, date, and numbers) as well as full text. This means that you can search traditional bibliographic citations, which include title, author, and publisher, by those fields. Such a search for *James Bond* in the title would turn up only those titles in which the words *James Bond* appears, not all articles or martini recipes that mention James Bond. Or you could restrict your search to only those items published after a particular date.

FreeWAIS-sf can be used as a plain WAIS server and is compatible with existing WAIS clients. In addition, it improves on freeWAIS by allowing the user to define document format and headline layout without having to be a C language programmer. It supports country-specific character sets (8-bit only), which means that server operators will have fewer problems indexing data, at least in European languages.

Development is continuing, but this is not a commercial product. FreeWAIS-sf comes from Ulrich Pfeifer of Dortmund University, Germany. <***http://charly.informatik.uni-dortmund.de/freeWAIS-sf/***>

Two other programs are available. SFgate is a CGI script that connects with WWW and freeWAIS servers. <*http://charly.informatik.uni-dortmund.de/SFgate/SFgate*> And SFproxy lets you index your personal WWW hotlist (or bookmark file—the collection of Web links you've saved) and easily add URLs. <*http://ls6-www.informatik.uni-dortmund.de/SFgate/SFproxy.html*>

WAISserver by WAIS, Inc.

WAISserver 2.0 by WAIS, Inc., is the top-of-the-line commercial WAIS server ($15,000). The company was founded by Brewster Kahle, who also created WAIS while at Thinking Machines. WAIS, Inc.'s customers include Britannica Online and CMP's TechWeb, among others. Its Web site includes links to freeware WAIS clients and servers. <*http://www.wais.com/*>

WAISserver for VMS

WAISserver for VMS is noncommercial software by Jim Fullton (formerly of the University of North Carolina, now at CNIDR) and runs on VAX VMS systems (contact Fullton if you want to use the software for commercial purposes). The files you need in order to compile it are located at <*ftp://sunsite.unc.edu/pub/packages/infosystems/wais/servers/vms/vms-server/*>.

WAISserver for Windows NT (EMWAC)

The European Microsoft Windows NT Academic Centre (EMWAC) is an integral part of Computing Services of the University of Edinburgh and has been set up to support and act as a focus for Windows NT within academia. It is sponsored by Datalink Computers, Digital, Microsoft, Research Machines, Sequent, and the University of Edinburgh. <*http://emwac.ed.ac.uk/html/internet_toolchest/top.html*>

WAISserver for Windows

There is an older, free, pre-WinSockets (a program that allows Windows to talk TCP/IP) version of a WAIS server that will run on Windows. It was written by Tony Addyman and is noncommercial, and he provides no support but will help someone who wants to take it over. FTP from ftp.salford.ac.uk in pub/wserver.zip.

Indexing Alternatives to WAIS

Some alternatives to WAIS don't use the WAIS protocol but do provide full-text indexing.

ISite: ZDist Under a New Name

ISite, a server for the protocol Z39.50.92, is based directly on the latest version of Z39.50 protocol. Read the document "Why We Changed the Name freeWAIS to Zdist" by Kevin Gamiel of CNIDR for background <*http://cnidr.org/talks/whyzdist.html*>. The client and server software for UNIX (including an HTTP gateway) are available at <*http://vinca.cnidr.org/software/zdist/zdist.html*>. The main advantages of ISite over freeWAIS are that

1. It conforms to the U.S. and international standards for search and retrieval.
2. Its development is continuing, whereas freeWAIS's is not. (Development continues for freeWAIS-sf.)

INQUERY

The INQUERY system, from the Center for Intelligent Information Retrieval (CIIR) at the University of Massachusetts, is not intended to be an off-the-shelf information retrieval system. CIIR's focus is on collaborating with industry and government to address challenging and important problems associated with text databases. INQUERY is often used to solve those problems. Additional features are being developed, but it currently incorporates relevance feedback techniques (the user's picks help refine the search). A Japanese version is available, and Spanish and Chinese versions are under development. INQUERY has a WWW gateway. <***http://ciir.cs.umass.edu/inquery homepage.html***>

Glimpse

Glimpse is a powerful indexing and query system that allows fast file searches (free for nonprofit use; for licensing information contact the authors at glimpse@cs.colorado.edu). Glimpse can be used by individuals for their personal filing systems as well as by organizations for large data collections. Glimpse is the main searching mechanism behind Harvest, an information discovery and access system that is also worth checking into. <***http://harvest.cs.colorado.edu/***>

The GlimpseHTTP gateway allows WWW searching of Glimpse indexes. <***http://glimpse.cs.arizona.edu:1994/***>

ICE

ICE, an indexing program for WWW servers by Christian Neuss, is a lightweight, easy to install alternative to WAIS gateways. It allows free-text searches on a World-Wide Web archive. It is free for use in any noncommercial product. According to the author, ICE is beerware—if you decide that you like it, send him a can, or case, of your favorite beer. <***http://www.igd.fhg.de/~neuss/***>

Open Text

Open Text Corporation offers a commercial alternative to WAIS, also called Open Text, that is best known for its use with large tagged structures such as SGML databases. It can be used with many other data formats, however, including free-text, word-processing formats, and nontextual data. For example, Open Text has been used to do as complete an index of the WWW as possible. Right now the project is at 574 million words of text with more than 11 million hyperlinks indexed. Try searching—it's extremely impressive, particularly because it lets you search specific sections of HTML documents as well as do proximity and occurrence count searches. (The latter means that the searcher will send back only those documents in which your search term appears a specific number of times.)

Open Text would like to run its Open Text Web Index as a charged service, but it is available for free while the company tries to convince people to buy its Open Text indexing products. <*http://opentext.uunet.ca:8080/*>

WAIS Resources

WAIS resources are much less prevalent than Gopher and WWW resources, although they are sorely needed. Managing a WAIS server is an inherently more complicated task, so you may find the news-groups and mailing lists to be fairly technical. But monitor them nonetheless (see Table 5–1).

Estimating Computer Requirements

WAIS servers can run on UNIX systems, Windows NT, and Windows. Remember that a UNIX system doesn't have to be a large machine. Linux is one version of UNIX that runs on 386 PCs, and Macintoshes can also run a form of UNIX as their operating system. These can give you a relatively inexpensive platform from which to run a UNIX-based WAIS server.

Installing a WAIS Server

Like Gopher and WWW servers, setting up a WAIS server is a two-part process, installing the server and adding the data, documents, or images it will serve. With Gopher servers data preparation is a simple matter of putting the data, document, and image files into the data directory. Web servers require the additional task of writing HTML code to format the documents you want to go out. Indexing for both Gopher and WWW servers is optional.

But indexing is what WAIS servers are all about. WAIS servers don't deal with documents—they deal with the indexes to those documents. If they aren't indexed, they aren't available. And unfortunately, indexing is not always a simple matter, as we'll see. But first let's get the various pieces installed.

We'll use freeWAIS-sf 1.1 as an example. It is a free WAIS server for UNIX machines, and it has some advanced features, including the ability to search structured fields. It is an enhancement of the original version of freeWAIS and was written by Ulrich Pfeifer and Tung Huynh of the University of Dortmund, Germany.

The installation process consists of running a configuration script that checks out the kind of UNIX system you have. Then you run the UNIX make utility to build the WAIS programs: waisserver, waisindex, waissearch, and waisq. Installation also provides for storing UNIX online documentation files (called *man pages*) in appropriate directories. Here's what the various programs that are part of freeWAIS-sf 1.1 do:

- *waisserver* is the program that sits and listens at port 210 (that's the default, but you can name another port). When it receives a query, it looks at the index files specified, searches, and returns the results.
- *waisindex* is the program that indexes your document and data files in preparation for making them available to waisserver. You usually run waisindex once for files that don't change and every so often for files that do.
- *waissearch* is a script that allows you to search what you put on your WAIS server. Actually, it can search whatever index files you point it at.
- *waisq* is a program that stores questions or queries and lets you rerun them. That way, as the WAIS database is updated, you can ask the same questions again. This might be particu-

larly useful for regularly searching electronic magazines, journals, or list server archives.

- *ws* is a shell script that calls waissearch to perform local index file searching.

After you have tested your server and pronounced it ready for use, you set it up to be ready and waiting at all times. You can do this either by using inetd or by running it as a stand-alone program. See the discussion on inetd versus local in Chapter 4, because the same concerns apply here (inetd applies only to UNIX). Basically, inetd starts up only when a request comes through; it doesn't waste system resources by waiting, but its startup is slower. Running the WAIS server in standalone mode gives the quickest response because the software is always running. Check the WAIS server documentation for further considerations.

WAIS Fundamentals

Because WAIS is based on indexing, the most important part of setting a WAIS server up is to index your data, whether it's a collection of text files, images, sound files, or programs. A WAIS server can deliver all of these, but you first need to understand a few of its restrictions:

1. WAIS indexes must be created before the WAIS server program can deliver any files.
2. If the file changes, you need to run the indexing program again to replace or append the new indexes. For files that change often, you can build new indexes separately and then use a shell script or a timer to swap them with the older indexes every day or every hour, whenever necessary. The commercial WAIS server from WAIS, Inc., allows for incremental indexing, which means no swapping is necessary. As new material is added, it is indexed, and that index is added incrementally to the original index.

3. The WAIS indexer has to know the type of files it's indexing. It then passes this information on to the WAIS client when it retrieves these files. Although it "understands" 30 different types or formats of files (see Table 5–2 on WAIS data types), you can also specify other types explicitly. This capability is particularly important because it allows you to include newer types of files and multimedia formats as they are developed.
4. WAIS indexes only text. If you want to index image or sound files, or other nontext files, you have two options. You can index them by their file name, or you can relate them to a text file with descriptive information and index that.
5. A WAIS index has two parts, the headline or title line, and the contents. The headline is what the user sees if the record matches. The contents are what users receive if they request a specific title. What the user receives might be text, images, or sounds.

WAIS File Types

When you use waisindex to index your files, you need to specify what type they are. The word *type* is used to describe the different formats of files. A picture in GIF or JPEG format is obviously different than a text file. But text files also come in different types. One type of text file might have each entry on its own line. Another might have several items of information on various lines for each item. WAIS file types try to recognize and take advantage of these differences. See Table 5–2 for a list of data types from the freeWAIS-sf documentation.

As you can see there are many special purpose file formats on the list. Whenever a pattern is consistent throughout a file, waisindex can take advantage of those differences. What follows are some examples from the list in Table 5–2.

TABLE 5–2 WAIS Data Types

Type	Description
text	Simple text files; this is the default
bibtex	BibTeX/LaTeX format
bio	Biology abstract format
cmapp	CM applications from Hypercard
dash	Entries separated by a row of dashes
dvi	dvi format
emacsinfo	The GNU documentation system
essence	CU-Boulder Essence Summaries
first_line	First line of file is headline
filename	Uses only the file name part of the path name for the title
ftp	Special type for FTP files. First line of file is headline
gif	GIF files, indexes only the file name
irg	Internet resource guide
jargon	Jargon File 2.9.8 format
mail_digest	Standard Internet mail digest format
mail_or_rmail	Mail or rmail or both
medline	Medline format
mh_bboard	MH bulletin board format
netnews	Netnews format
nhyp	?:? hypertext format, Polytechnic of Central London
one_line	Each line is a document
para	Paragraphs separated by blank lines
pict	Picture files, indexed by file name only
ps	PostScript format
refer	Refer format

Table 5–2 *(continued)*

Type	Description
irlist	irlist mail or rmail or both
formfeed	Entries separated by a formfeed
bibdb	Steve file entries separated by a formfeed
bibinf	bibinf entries separated by an empty line
rn	Netnews saved by the [rt]?rn news reader
server	Server structures for the dir of servers
tiff	TIFF files, indexed by file name only
URL	What-to-trim what-to-add—URL
oneline_phonix	Phonebooks PHONIX
oneline_soundex	Phonebooks SOUNDEX
listserv_digest	Standard Internet mail digest format
fields	Document format given in <database>.fmt

Source: Excerpted from freeWAIS-sf documentation. *<http://charly.informatik.uni-dortmund.de/freeWAIS-sf/>*

Text

Text files are anything that contain text and are stored in ASCII. They could be a collection of résumés, or papers from a conference, or recipes for margaritas. The rule here is that when the server finds a match, it returns the entire file to the client, whether that file is a single résumé or 1,500 résumés, a conference paper or 12 papers from the one conference, or a margarita recipe or a collection of recipes. This can be a problem when all you want a user to see is a single résumé or a single recipe or a single conference report. For example, you have a file that contains the names and addresses of all members of your organization. If that file were indexed as a simple text file, every search would return all the names. But you can use other WAIS file types to gain more control over what your users receive.

Para

Say your file of names and addresses has a blank line between each name, as in Figure 5–1. If you use the para (short for *paragraph*) type, each name and address combination is treated as a separate document, because a blank line separates each address into "paragraphs." The headline would be the first line of each paragraph, which would work fine for this example. So if *Brazil* were the search item, the server would return only Rosa Mello's name and address.

One_Line

If you want every line of a file to be treated separately, you would specify the file as the one_line type. For example, you have a collection of one-liners (jokes) that you want to index, as in Figure 5–2. The waisindex program will treat each line as a separate document to be indexed and retrieved separately.

FIGURE 5–1 Examples of Para Type

```
Jane Doe
4950 Lake Drive
Mudville, Florida

Joe Shmoe
2312 Anywhere St.
Someplace Interesting, Illinois
U.S.A.

Rosa Mello
Rua Cardoso Junior
Rio de Janeiro
Brazil
```

FIGURE 5–2 Examples of One_Line Type

```
Bad joke #1 goes here.
Bad joke #2 goes here.
Bad joke #3 goes here.
Bad joke #4 goes here.
Bad joke #5 goes here.
```

Dash

With the dash type you can have several paragraphs grouped together, so long as they are separated by a row of dashes. This is useful when the text is longer than a paragraph but not long enough to be in a file by itself. This also allows for some entries to be much longer than others. Just separate them with the row of dashes and they'll be indexed and retrieved separately. In Figure 5–3 student 1 wrote an essay of several paragraphs, student 2 wrote only one paragraph, and student 3 wrote three paragraphs. Because of the dashes between them, they'll be searched and retrieved separately.

Mail_or_Rmail

Large amounts of text often accumulate in mail files. These could be personal messages, the archives of a list server, or the record of your company's e-mail correspondence. Use the mail_or_rmail type, and WAIS can index each message as a separate item, with the subject line of the message acting as the headline. Mail_or_rmail will search and retrieve separately the two mail messages in Figure 5–4. The system will treat the subject line for each as its headline, even though it is not the first line in the section.

Netnews or RN

Similarly, you can use waisindex to specify Usenet News (Netnews) files or those saved by the rn news reader as a type. That way individ-

FIGURE 5–3 Examples of Dash Type

```
Essay by Student #1
First paragraph of wonderful prose.
First paragraph of wonderful prose.
First paragraph of wonderful prose.

Second paragraph of wonderful prose.
Second paragraph of wonderful prose.
Second paragraph of wonderful prose.
-----------------------------------------------------------------
Essay by Student #2
First paragraph by someone who should have studied harder.
First paragraph by someone who should have studied harder.
First paragraph by someone who should have studied harder.
-----------------------------------------------------------------
Essay by Student #3
First paragraph of deathless prose.
First paragraph of deathless prose.
First paragraph of deathless prose.

Second paragraph of deathless prose.
Second paragraph of deathless prose.
Second paragraph of deathless prose.

Third paragraph of deathless prose.
Third paragraph of deathless prose.
Third paragraph of deathless prose.
```

ual Usenet News postings can be retrieved separately. Logically, the subject line will be used as the headline.

GIF, TIFF, and PICT (Image Files)

If it seems strange that WAIS can index image files, don't be fooled. WAIS is not magically ferreting out the contents of the images and indexing them. All it is indexing is the file names of these nontext files.

FIGURE 5–4 Example of Mail_or_Rmail Type

```
Date: Fri, 17 Mar 1995 00:37:53 -0800
Message-Id: <9503170837.AA28492@library.berkeley.edu>
From: listserv@library.berkeley.edu (Listserv v3.0.3)
Subject: Welcome to list 'web4lib'
To: franks@nicco.sscnet.ucla.edu (Mike Franks)
Web4Lib Overview
*** Please save this message ***
PURPOSE
The Web4Lib electronic discussion exists to foster discussion
of issues relating to the creation and management of library-
based World-Wide Web servers and clients.
<rest of message deleted>
Date: Wed, 8 Feb 1995 10:12:36 -0500
Message-Id: <199502081512.KAA02769@relay.openmarket.com>
To: franks@nicco.sscnet.ucla.edu
From: Majordomo@OpenMarket.com
Subject: Welcome to internet-index
Reply-To: Majordomo@OpenMarket.com
Welcome to the internet-index mailing list!
If you ever want to remove yourself from this mailing list,
send the following command in email to
"internet-index-request@OpenMarket.com":
<rest of message deleted>
```

Another technique is to match an explanatory text file with a nontext file, one with the extension .text, the other with an extension suitable to the type of file it is, such as .gif, .au, .mpeg, and so on. For example, lincoln.text and lincoln.gif would both turn up during a search for *Lincoln*. WAIS indexes the text in the description file and it can be set up to return the titles of both the nontext and text files when it finds a match. You can use this method to link multiple files, such as video, image, and sound relating to the same topic.

More Information on Types

Most of the data types listed in Table 5–2 are probably unfamiliar to you. Even when they are familiar, it can be helpful to have a model against which to check to ensure you and WAIS really are speaking the same language. For that reason the nice folks at Dortmund University in Germany put a set of example files on the Net: *<ftp://ls6-www.informatik.uni-dortmund.de/pub/wais/fmt-examples>*.

Indexing with WAIS

Once you've identified the type of file format you have and know where you'll store the indexes, you're ready to run the waisindex program to create all the indexes that waisserver will need. The indexes created will take up as much space as the original files. For a file full of one-line records, you would type waisindex -d QUOTES -export -t one_line quotes.txt. The parameter -d QUOTES creates a WAIS database called QUOTES. The -t one_line means treat it as a type one_line where every line is indexed separately. The -export parameter means to send the information on your WAIS server to the master directory of WAIS servers at WAIS, Inc. *<http://www.wais.com>*

Figure 5–5 shows an index from a file of mural artists' biographies that fit the para (paragraph) type. Unfortunately, as you can see in Figure 5–5, the name of the artist leads right into the first line of the biography. Because the para type uses what it finds on the first line to create the headline presented in query results, this is messier than we want. Each headline will show up with the artist's name, date of birth, and a few words from the first sentence. In this case we have a simple solution—there is a consistent pattern that helps differentiate the title information. Note that in Figure 5–5 the artist's name and date information ends with a colon.

After checking that the colon usage is consistent throughout the file, we can write a simple Perl script to find everything up to the colon

FIGURE 5–5 Artist Biography (Before Doctoring)

```
BARTLETT, IVAN (born 1908): Bartlett was active in the New Deal art
projects, working on murals in Redondo Beach, Huntington Park, and Long
Beach. After the 1930's Bartlett moved to New York City.
```

(Used with permission from *Street Gallery: Guide to 1000 Los Angeles Murals* © Robin J. Dunitz, 1993)

FIGURE 5–6 Artist Biography (After Doctoring)

```
BARTLETT, IVAN (born 1908):
Bartlett was active in the New Deal art projects, working on murals in
Redondo Beach, Huntington Park, and Long Beach. After the 1930's Bartlett
moved to New York City.
```

(Used with permission from *Street Gallery: Guide to 1000 Los Angeles Murals* © Robin J. Dunitz, 1993)

and put a carriage return character afterward it. The resulting file looks like Figure 5–6.

Now when waisindex takes the first line of each paragraph to be the title for that record, the artist's name and birthdate show up alone for a clean title. As in this case, you may often find yourself cleaning up text file formats for better indexing.

Indexing HTML files is a common occurrence with the tremendous increase in WWW servers. The freeWAIS-sf FAQ describes how to do this using the freeWAIS-sf server. See <***http://www.cis.ohio-state.edu/hypertext/faq/usenet/wais-faq/freeWAIS-sf/faq.html***>.

WAIS Tools

The key to indexing documents is to clearly separate and identify each piece that you might want to treat separately. In the case of a book breaking it into chapters probably is not sufficient. If a WAIS search finds a match in a 20-page chapter, the person who requested the material still will have to plow through 20 pages to find the section that matches. Dividing the book's chapters into sections or even one- or two-page parts might make more sense. That way a search response returns a much smaller and more manageable piece of text for the user to view. However, you'll want to make sure that you don't break it down so much that viewers will lose the context.

Parsers and Filters

Parsers and **filters** are tools that can split up your text or rearrange it for you. Basically, you can program parsers and filters to take advantage of any built-in patterns in the text to break it the way you want it. Say you have a file of mail messages that is separated by a row of equal signs (Microsoft Mail for DOS can produce files like this), and you want to index each message individually. The dash type would work, except that it wants a row of dashes instead of a row of equal signs. No problem. Convert each row of equal signs to a row of dashes. That's easy to do with any program that can do searches and replaces. Stream editor (sed) and Perl in UNIX can easily do this. Similar tools are available for almost every computer platform.

Create Your Own Filters

It may be possible to create your own filters by using a language such as Perl, C, or even shell scripts. In Figure 5–5, I wanted the artist's name to show up as the headline, or title, for each record. The easiest way to do that was to use Perl to convert the text to fit an existing format type. You can make the server make such changes automatically when you have a regular supply of files that need exactly the same alteration. But the problem often is that each file is different, and someone has to find the easiest way to convert it to a form that will work. If you know your tools, you're halfway there.

Advertising Your WAIS Sources

Once you have installed your WAIS server and set up some databases for public searching, you can use the Register parameter in Waisindex to register with the central WAIS directories. This is not necessary if you are going to access WAIS databases only from your Gopher or WWW servers.

Summary

WAIS is a very different animal from Gopher or WWW. Gopher and WWW provide information over the Internet, but for the most part any indexing that is done is hired out, that is, done by other programs. (The GN Gopher/WWW server and the WN WWW server are exceptions.) WAIS and Z39.50, to which it's related, are specifically about indexing text databases and providing for online searches of those databases. This is a large and growing area of Internet publishing, but it is often hidden behind Gopher and WWW front ends.

The commercial version of WAIS servers is available only from WAIS, Inc., and is expensive ($15,000), although the company is considering a free version (see Chapter 11). The freeWAIS version is no longer supported by CNIDR. The improved freeWAIS-sf version adds the ability to do structured field searches, which adds quite a bit more flexibility for the user. Many alternative indexing systems are available, including Glimpse, ICE, and Open Text. For the most part these focus strictly on indexing. Most have some sort of gateway to WWW so that they can be searched by WWW browsers.

Z39.50 is a U.S. standard that complies with a similar international standard for information indexing and retrieval. Large-scale information publishers and libraries have developed some interesting applications using Z39.50. See <***http://www.lib.ncsu.edu/staff/morgan/alcuin/wwwed-catalogs.html***> for Library Catalogs with WWW-to-Z39.50 Interfaces. The U.S. Office of Management and Budget has helped to set up the Z39.50-based program called GILS to make available the vast amount of information and data collected by various U.S. government agencies.

CHAPTER 6

Other Tools of the Trade

Although this book focuses on Gopher, WWW, and WAIS as the three most popular and effective tools for publishing on the Internet, there are others. This chapter explores some of them with examples and pointers about where you can learn more about them.

Perl

Imagine a programming language written specifically for dealing with text. Instead of being designed for square roots and numerical calculations, this language is designed for finding and manipulating text in large or small files. Now suppose that it's free and available in UNIX, DOS, and Macintosh versions. And further suppose that it is so trustworthy that UNIX administrators often use it for system administration tasks. This is Perl, and you or your Web administrator should become familiar with it, because much of what you'll be dealing with is text—transforming it, rearranging it, and filtering it. The more you can do this automatically, the more time you'll have to call your own.

Many utilities for Web and Gopher servers are written in Perl. Perl has some features that are particularly useful for manipulating text. One such feature is the associative array, which allows you to store data in an array (sort of a table) subscripted (referenced or addressed) by text instead of just by number. With most programming languages programmers have to keep track of text in some numerical way, such as State(50)='Alaska'. But with Perl you can use the text itself as a locator inside your array. For example, you might make an array of countries in which the two-character country code is stored under the full country name $country{'Singapore'} = 'SG' or $country{'BR'} = 'Brazil'. Your UNIX administrator will find other uses for Perl. <***http://www.cs.cmu.edu:8001/Web/People/rgs/perl.html***>

Python

Python is an extremely powerful programming language that has text-handling features and is object oriented. It interfaces to many systems and is extendable with C or C++. Python runs on UNIX, Macintoshes, OS/2, DOS, Windows 3.1, and Windows NT, so Python programs are portable between all these platforms. Best of all, although it is copyrighted, it is free and may be distributed, even for commercial use. The commercial Internet indexing service InfoSeek claims that it set up shop quickly because of the power of Python. Check it out at <***http://www.python.org/***>.

Glimpse

Glimpse, which stands for Global Implicit Search, is a powerful tool for indexing the contents of a file system. Some people have started using it as an alternative to WAIS because of problems and bugs in the freeWAIS version. Glimpse was originally designed to index everything in a directory. It can create three sizes of indexes; the biggest index is the fastest at finding what you are searching for. Glimpse supports Boolean searches and has a feature called *approximate matching,* which allows it to find misspelled words. <***http://glimpse.cs.arizona.edu:1994/***>

Harvest

Harvest is a different approach to collecting, organizing, searching, and replicating relevant information across the Internet. Harvest can be tailored to digest information in many different formats and to offer custom search services. Harvest makes efficient use of network traffic, remote servers, and disk space. Harvest was developed by the Internet Research Task Force Research Group on Resource Discovery (IRTF-RD) in a project funded by ARPA (the Advanced Research Projects Agency, the founder of the Internet). <*http://harvest.cs.colorado.edu/*>

Harvest may have solved three primary problems of Internet publishing:

- How to collect and collate information from many sources automatically
- How to make it easier for users to find what they want
- How to distribute (replicate) information to many servers to ease server load

In the bargain Harvest's developers created an extremely powerful set of tools that are available for commercial licensing or free educational and government use. Check out their link, if only to see their example sites, like the searchable index of AT&T's 800 numbers.

FTP Daemons

FTP daemons (daemons are programs that run by themselves) are an easy way to make files available publicly. Recall from Chapter 1 that Internet publishing began with FTP (File Transfer Protocol). Well, it's still around, and although it's not as friendly or easy to use as Gopher, WWW, and WAIS, it does work. You might choose to run an FTP daemon when you know that your users will have no trouble using FTP and you don't want to bother with anything extra. FTP daemons wait for FTP requests to come in and then service them. FTP is available as part of the UNIX system. For Windows, Macintosh, and mainframes you'll have to run special software—consult your network administrator.

Finger

Finger is a UNIX utility that was designed to give current information about a particular person, usually whether they are currently logged in, how they spell their names, and the like. A UNIX account holder can also put information into two files, .plan and .project, which will be displayed with their login information when they are fingered (queried with the Finger program).

One creative idea was to use this utility to quickly make available simple company sales or contact information. Just create a pseudo UNIX account name, such as sales or products, and put the appropriate company marketing information in the .plan and .project files for these accounts. When prospective customers give the command finger sales@company.name.com or finger products@company.name.com on their computer, they'll receive that company's sales or product information. It is also used to provide earthquake reports (finger quake@geophys.washington.edu). This system has the advantage of being easy for a UNIX system administrator to set up, and it can provide a small amount of information quickly.

CSO

CSO is a computer resident phone book, or a sort of White Pages for the e-mail and telephone directory system used at many universities. According to Ed Krol's *Whole Internet User's Guide and Catalog,* CSO (sometimes also called a QI server) got its name from the Computing Services Office of the University of Illinois at

Champagne-Urbana. What's important for us is that with a client program called PH, or with Gopher and from Web browsers, looking information up in these computerized White Pages is simple.

The server software for CSO can be found at <*ftp://vixen.cso.uiuc.edu/pub/qi.tar.gz*>. The client software is at <*ftp://vixen.cso.uiuc.edu/pub/phitarigz/*>. You may join the QI/PH mailing list by sending e-mail to majordomo@listserv.cso.uiuc.edu with subscribe info-ph in the body of the message.

List Servers

Electronic mailing lists, commonly called list servers, are so common on the Internet that it's hard to think of them as a form of publishing, but they are. List servers are a means of distributing information to a controlled circulation list. Some list servers are open and anyone can join and send messages. Others are called moderated lists, and the moderator edits the contributions for what is appropriate and what is not. Finally, some list servers are one-way and consist entirely of announcements from a central source with no mechanism for sending replies or comments. People subscribe to such a list to get the most current information from that source. The three types of list servers are

- *Open lists,* which promote discussion between any and all subscribers of the mailing list, whether they know each other or not. Usually, subscribing to such a list means nothing more than sending a subscription request via e-mail. No one guarantees that the content of the messages will be restricted to the theme of the list. If you don't like a message, you are free to ignore it.
- *Moderated lists,* which are edited by a moderator who decides which messages will get "published" and which will not. These lists tend to stay on subject more, but an active list can create a great deal of work for the moderator.

- *One-way lists,* which do not provide for participation by subscribers. These are used for announcements from the sponsoring organization, association, company, and the like.

Although most of the thousands of list servers are free, at least one group has figured out how to make money publishing this way. WEBster publishes two electronic magazines on the Internet entirely via e-mail. WEBster began with the *Journal of High Performance Computing* and, as it developed its customized list server software, added *WEBster* and is considering offering others.

You can find out more about WEBster by sending e-mail to sos@webster.tgc.com. If you prefer to correspond with a living breathing WEBster staffer, send e-mail to human@webster.tgc.com or call 800-795-4472 (from outside the U.S., call 619-625-0070). <***http://www.tgc.com/webster.html***>

MUDs and MOOs

MUD stands for (take your pick) Multiple-User Dimension, Dungeon, or Dialogue. MOO stands for Multiple-user system, Object Oriented. Basically, both are computer programs (usually text based) that you can login to and explore. Each user takes the role of a character that can walk around, chat with other characters, explore monster-infested areas, solve puzzles, and even create rooms, descriptions, and items. Some are similar to the Dungeons and Dragons game, others are more social groups. Basically, they allow a group of people to join together to play in (and create) the illusion of an artificial world. With MOO you can create objects that other players/users can build on or use.

If you think these are just games and have nothing to do with Internet publishing, here are some possibilities to make you change your mind:

- The games could be educational. You could simulate labor negotiations or a game of international or community diplomacy. For example, you could use MUD or MOO to help people negotiate a mutually acceptable site for a sewage treatment plant.

- MUD and MOO could be used to take students (or customers) through the various steps of a computer program, lab experiment, or engineering project.
- MOO could be used to create a library for historians, so they can edit and annotate bibliographies online.

MOO and MUD are not typical Internet publishing tools, but they have some interesting capabilities for those who want to give their users an imaginative experience. John December, co-author of *World Wide Web Unleashed,* maintains an excellent online guide to Internet tools that contains this section on MUDs and MOOs:

> <*http://www.rpi.edu/Internet/Guides/decemj/itools/cmc-group-mu*.html*>

Also check out Francis Litterio's Web site on MUDs and MOOs at <*http://draco.centerline.com:8080/~franl/mud.html*>.

Hyper-G

The Institute for Information Processing and Computer-Supported New Media (IICM) at Graz University of Technology in Austria is developing Hyper-G to replace WWW. The Web and Hyper-G have some basic differences in philosophy, primarily that Hyper-G maintains the connection between the user and the server throughout the session. Although maintaining the connection imposes a greater load on the server, it allows the server to know who the user is and what he has been doing. When combined with several different layers of user access rights, Hyper-G could enable the server to interact with the user in a very different way than WWW servers can. Hyper-G also supports multilingual hypertext and compiles an ongoing context reference to keep users from getting lost. Free client (browser) programs are available for Windows and UNIX. A paper about using Hyper-G to publish on the Web was presented at the

April 1995 World-Wide Web Conference in Darmstadt, Germany. <*http://www.igd.fhg.de/www/www95/papers/105/hgw3.html*>

For more information see <*ftp://ftp.iicm.tu-graz.ac.at/pub/Hyper-G*>, <*http://hgiicm.tu-graz.ac.at*>. To try it in plain terminal mode, telnet -l info info.tu-graz.ac.at or telnet info.tu-graz.ac.at and login as *info*.

HyperNews

HyperNews is a conferencing system that is a cross between WWW and Usenet News (although it doesn't rely on Usenet News) that lets people add comments or responses to items posted to a HyperNews Web server. The comments are stored hierarchically (with sections divided into subsections that are in turn divided into more subsections), and users can add new areas on their own. Unlike Usenet News, the postings don't disappear after a few days, so the record of discussions is more permanent.

You might find this a useful tool, particularly if you want to create a discussion group for a subject and make the feedback immediately available publicly. This might be useful in an educational situation in which you want students to learn from each other's questions. <*http://union.ncsa.uiuc.edu/HyperNews/get/hypernews.html*>

Internet Relay Chat (IRC)

Internet Relay Chat is a sort of free party line on the Internet for fast typists. It was designed in Finland as a replacement for the UNIX talk command, but it has since grown into an enormously popular (and addictive) Internet resource. IRC is divided into hundreds of channels on all sorts of subjects in many different languages (primarily English but also German, Japanese, French, Finnish, Spanish, and others). Because IRC is an Internet protocol, it is available wherever the Internet is, which means more than 50 countries.

Users connect to IRC servers using free IRC client software and check the list of channels for one that looks interesting. Once users enter a channel, whatever they type appears immediately on the screens of all others connected to that channel. Such immediate interaction without regard for geography proved its utility during the Persian Gulf War and the attempted coup against Boris Yeltsin when live reports came from IRC in those areas out to the rest of the world. <***http://www.rpi.edu/Internet/Guides/decemj/itools/cmc-mass-irc.html***>

WebChat

WebChat is a realtime, fully multimedia chatting application that is available as an add-on for most WWW servers. It is available in free and commercial versions from <***http://www.irsociety.com/webchat.html***>. What's nice is that it doesn't require special software on the browser side. It should work with any standard browser.

This might be something you could use to schedule an online discussion with your company president or just for discussions on topics related to your Web site.

Summary

Gopher, WWW, and WAIS together provide a wide variety of Internet publishing capabilities (especially when enhanced with CGI scripts). You may want to use other tools as well, both to enhance your existing servers and to provide different services.

Perl and Python are computer languages that are available on many types of computers for free. They are particularly useful in Internet publishing because of their text-handling capabilities.

Glimpse is an indexing alternative to WAIS (see Chapter 5 for other indexing alternatives), and Harvest tackles the whole problem of collecting, organizing, searching, and replicating information across the Internet. It can solve problems you didn't know you had, such as conserving network traffic and speeding up delivery by replicating portions of your data on various servers automatically.

FTP daemons and Finger are traditional UNIX services (available on other platforms as well) that can be useful in Internet publishing. List servers (electronic mailing lists) are another old standby that are useful for widening your audience because may people find that e-mail is easier to get than full Internet access.

MUDs and MOOs are multiple user systems that permit many people to build a "virtual world" together. Don't knock them unless you've tried them. Because of their unique capabilities they may provide exactly the kind of interactive experience that you want to add to your site.

Hyper-G may be the replacement for WWW because it maintains the connection between the user and the server and has several different layers of user access rights. It also supports multilingual hypertext and helps users keep track of where they are in their online travels.

HyperNews, Internet Relay Chat, and WebChat provide an interactive set of tools. You may want to use them to have online discussions with your site users. Kaleidospace, profiled in Chapter 10, uses WebChat for scheduled chats with its artist in residence.

As you can see, some creative software is already available, and more is being developed. It will behoove you to stay abreast of what's being developed on the Internet and how it might complement what you're doing.

CHAPTER 7

Internet Commerce

Commerce shows up on the Internet in two forms: the technology of commerce on the Internet and the psychology, philosophy, and economics of commerce. Let's talk about the latter first.

Advertisers: You're Not in Kansas Anymore

First, the Internet is not a mass of consumers waiting to buy what you want to sell. It may become that someday, but for now it is the closest thing to mass communication that the world has. Television, radio, newspapers, and magazines are almost entirely one way, allowing little or no feedback or interaction between the readers and the writers, whereas the Internet comes from a tradition of intense discussion of almost every issue imaginable.

Don't go onto the Internet with old ideas about marketing and sales—they won't work, and they'll do you great damage. Irate customers can easily make their views known to thousands of people. On the other hand, on the Internet word-of-mouth praise can spread faster than you thought possible.

Imagine a world in which Question Authority is a way of life, not a motto on a bumper sticker. And remember that much of your audience is in a position to evaluate, analyze, test, and comment on any exaggerated claims you might make for your product. Internet users are interested in solid information and technical responses to their problems, not hot air from public relations people. This is the culture of the Internet—it looks nothing like a Nielsen family.

Demographics

The demographics of the Internet are changing. Users of the Internet are not just the young, white (nerdy) male computer students that many people assume is the Net population. For the last few years, partly because of Gopher, WWW and WAIS, the Net has seen a huge influx of new faces. First, more and more university faculty, staff, and students are seeing the Internet as important to their research and communication needs. History and anthropology students and faculty are on mailing lists and run Gopher and Web sites. Many who once thought computers were only useful as word processors are now browsing the WWW and doing Veronica searches. In addition, the number of commercial hookups to the Internet has increased tremendously. Many companies want their employees to have access to the databases and information on the Internet. Finally, the major commercial online services, like America Online, CompuServe, and Prodigy, are racing to provide full graphical browsing of the Internet along with their commercial databases. Their users are even more varied.

For all these reasons the quantity and variety of potential users of your Internet publishing efforts have changed. But because the Internet is expanding so rapidly and is controlled by no one, it is impossible to say with any precision exactly what the demographics are. The Graphics, Visualization, and Usability Center of the College of Computing at Georgia Institute of Technology in Atlanta has made some valiant and sophisticated attempts to find out, however, at least for the WWW. The center ran its third WWW User Survey on April 10, 1995, and plans to resurvey every six months. (For results see <***http://www.cc.gatech.edu/gvu/user_surveys/***>.)

Georgia Tech received 13,000 responses to the April 1995 demographics questionnaire, which also had separate sections on WWW browser usage, consumer attitudes and preferences, and questions for Web service providers. The survey runs for a month, during which the center posts notices about it all over the Net. In addition, Prodigy placed a link to the surveys from Prodigy's entrance to the Web. Because the survey is voluntary, the center makes no claims about the representativeness of the data for the entire Web population. The center provides the data and results free of charge to the Internet community.

Opportunities

The Internet offers many opportunities in addition to direct sales. The opportunities consist of using the Internet's amazing interactive communications possibilities to complement other aspects of your business or organization. For example, you might

- Decrease your user-support costs by putting your technical support database on the Internet
- Enhance your company's reputation by responding quickly and publicly to users' complaints
- Educate your potential market by providing sample products, demonstrations, or detailed online brochures
- Improve your products by monitoring and participating in related list servers and Usenet newsgroups

If you are thinking about making people pay for access to your Gopher, WWW, or WAIS servers, several factors make this more complicated than you might suspect. The solutions are being worked out, but each approach is different. This chapter attempts to describe some charging schemes that are in development or use and to explain how they are different. You must decide which, if any, you want to use.

Is Anyone Making Money on the Net?

Don't expect to get rich, but yes, some are making money on the Internet.

The officers of First Virtual Holding Company, one of the first transaction systems on the Internet (see Survey of Charging Techniques later in this chapter), say that thousands of dollars are coming in daily through its InfoHaus online "store." Author Stu Sjouwerman said that in 10 weeks he sold 200 copies of his book *Make Money on the Internet . . . The Right Way* at $10 per copy through InfoHaus.

In the sprig of 1994 Laura Fillmore, president of the Online BookStore, told attendees at a Texas conference on making money on the Internet that they should expect to use imagination and creativity to come up with new approaches to publishing. Her speech, "Slaves of a New Machine: Exploring the For-Free/For-Pay Conundrum," is worth reading. <***http://cism.bus.utexas.edu/ravi/laura_talk.html***> Her point is that the Net remains a learning experience for everyone, and it's not always possible to predict what you'll learn or whether you'll make money in the process. Check out the archive at <***http://marketplace.com/obs/english/papers/top.htm***> for some of her other talks and papers.

Economic Models

There are several different economic models for making money on the Internet. The first thing to think about is what exactly you are selling. Even something as seemingly simple as selling the text of a book or an article may present many different alternatives.

Here are some ways to approach online sales:

- *Per copy*—You sell the text (or item) to one user at a time, charging for each copy downloaded.

- *Site license*—You require a site, or collection of sites, to pay a fee for the right to download an infinite number of copies of the text. Site licensing often is used in combination with subscriptions to limit the right to download to a certain period of time.
- *Subscription*—You sell the right to download the text for a certain period of time. This can work well with timely or large amounts of material. Examples would be Britannica Online and Clarinet News Service.
- *Free sample*—You allow browsers to download a sample, for free, of something that you are selling as a form of marketing.
- *For free* in its entirety—You allow downloading of the entire text in one format (such as ASCII) for free but charge for it in other formats, such as print. The hope here is that the Net version will boost sales of the print version.
- *Sponsorship*—You sponsor a site on the Net much as you might sponsor a Little League team or a broadcast on PBS. Usually, there is no charge to the user, although sponsors often require users to register so they know who is getting their message. The text is available for free but comes with a small notice that it arrives courtesy of Such-and-Such Corporation. In some cases the sponsorship is for extremely short periods of time, in others months or years. Some organizations have sponsored entire sites in order to advertise their products or in support of the Internet.
- *Advertising*—You set up shop on the Net to advertise your business or product. This is similar to sponsorship, but you make it clear that you are advertising. Some Net advertisers believe that if they do not offer browsers content with some quality, browsers won't drop in to see their ads.

Table 7–1 lists several Net sites and resources where people are dealing with issues related to commerce on the Internet.

TABLE 7–1 Internet Commerce Resources

Documents and Sites	
www-buyinfo Mailing List Home *<http://www.research.att.com/www-buyinfo>*	An excellent starting point for links to most of charging methods planned or in use. It also archives the www-buyinfo e-mail list.
Economic FAQs About the Internet *<http://gopher.econ.lsa.umich.edu/FAQs/FAQs.html>*	This site contains papers by two University of Michigan economics professors, Jeff MacKie-Mason and Hal Varian.
Print Publications Related to Business Use of the Internet *<http://arganet.tenagra.com/Tenagra/books.html>*	Useful for links to reviews, announcements, and comparisons of books and periodicals on business use of the Internet.
Internet Marketing Successes of 1994 *<http://arganet.tenagra.com/Tenagra/awards94.html>*	Tenagra Corporation's first annual awards for best use of the Internet for marketing.
Internet Marketing Archives *<http://galaxy.einet.net/hypermail/inet-marketing/>*	Holds the searchable archives of the Internet marketing mailing list as well as useful links on Internet marketing.
"**Achieving Electronic Privacy**" *<http://www.digicash.com/publish/sciam.html>* *Scientific American,* August 1992, pp. 96–101	Article is by David Chaum, managing director of DigiCash.
Cryptography: The Study of Encryption *<http://draco.centerline.com:8080/~franl/crypto/>*	This site by Francis Litterio links to a large collection of materials and resources on encryption technology and policy.
RSA's FAQ About Today's Cryptography *<http://www.rsa.com/faq/faq_toc.html>*	Good introduction to cryptography and its applications from a major commercial vendor of cryptographic software.
Electronic Mailing Lists	
www-buyinfo Mailing List To subscribe send e-mail to: *www-buyinfo-request@allegra.att.com* and in the body of the message put: *subscribe www-buyinfo*	For those interested in pursuing the vision of buying and selling easily, transparently, and securely via WWW. Techniques and alternatives are discussed.
Internet Marketing List - To subscribe send e-mail to: *listproc@einet.net;* in the body of the message put *subscribe inet-marketing <your name or organization>*	Focuses entirely on Internet marketing. An active list with a point of view different from that of many programming groups.

Charging Issues and Concepts

Once you get into the world of online commerce, you have to pay attention to a range of issues and concepts that could affect the security of any system you put in place. Some concepts and questions will prepare you to understand and evaluate the charging techniques that follow. Other questions constitute the beginning of a check list for developing a charging system that will meet your needs.

1. If you are considering a system that involves electronic money, checks, or tickets, can the buyer get away with reusing them (in effect, double spending)?
2. Does the system you're installing require realtime (immediate) online confirmation of the buyer's account balance? This may seem essential, but some systems don't or won't have this requirement. The Internet today is plagued with slow connections and sometimes unstable servers and clients. A system that requires realtime balance checking will be dependent on the speed and stability of the Internet. And if the verification server is down, no one can buy anything from your online service.
3. Does the system that you'd like to use depend on technology and cooperation that do not yet exist? Some sophisticated charging systems may depend on equipment, banking participation, international exchange agreements, and such, that may take time to establish or invent. Remember that much of the Internet is based on experimentation. Many techniques, protocols, and software tools are experimental. Sometimes people agree on the merits of these tools and they are widely adopted, which is what happened with Gopher and WWW. But experiments frequently provoke discussion, which someone—often the author—uses to devise a better version or a completely different approach. So don't forget that plans described, discussed, or even prototyped on the Internet may never become reality. Plan accordingly.

4. Is your charging system scalable? Something that is **scalable** will operate just as well when millions of people are using it as when a few hundred are. Given the size of the Internet and its amazing growth, you want a program or system that can grow past one machine or site.
5. Will the system be flexible, or does it force every buyer and every seller to interact in exactly the same way, with the same equipment? Obviously, flexible is better. What if your business expands, and you start getting orders from Japan, Brazil, or India? Is your system flexible enough to handle currency conversions or different languages? (The latter capability is called *language localization*, which means that the software will run in the language of the country in which it is being used.)
6. Will the system be adaptable to changes in hardware or software technology? If someone comes up with a new and improved authentication protocol (way to ensure the right person is using your system), will you be unable to use it because your charging system isn't adaptable?
7. How much will each online transaction cost you? If the usual credit card transaction charges apply (20 cents or more per transaction), you need a different approach for selling things (such as screens of text) at a half-cent each.
8. Does the charging system guarantee secure transmission? You shouldn't send credit card information in the clear over the Internet—you wouldn't send it on a postcard. Information sent across the Internet traverses many different systems, any one of which might be insecure. Someone could lay an electronic trap to capture all messages that look like they contain credit card numbers. Then they could use them without your knowledge.
9. Does the system offer any way to verify the identity of a customer and make a record of the transaction? How confident are you that the user is who she says she is? Does your system provide a way to prove that the transaction took place, if the buyer later denies it? Do you need to?

10. Does the system preserve your buyers' anonymity? Many developers of charging systems are concerned about the Big Brother aspect of computers and the potential for abuse. Anonymity for buyers is a reasonable goal, and many of the charging techniques described here ensure it. You ignore this concern at your peril.
11. If the system you are considering does not offer your customers anonymity, does it at least protect their confidentiality? Whereas buyers might concede the seller's need to know their identity, they might very much resent (and boycott the seller because of) a charging system that allows outsiders to track their purchases.

Digital Cash

Digital cash is the electronic equivalent of cash money. Like cash it would be anonymous and come in different denominations. Various electronic commerce schemes are being developed to offer this capability over the Internet. Usually, they rely on some form of public key encryption or digital signature to determine the value and validity of this electronic currency.

Digital Signatures

Originally proposed in 1976 by Whitfield Diffie, a digital signature is a way to ensure that something composed entirely of electrons is actually a message sent to you by a certain person. Digital signatures usually use public key encryption techniques.

Heavy Duty and Lightweight Security

Lightweight security schemes are considered to have certain fundamental flaws that leave them open to attack by sophisticated programmers. But they can be useful when the value or security of what you need to protect is not likely to inspire sophisticated attacks. Heavy-duty security systems are considered safe from all manner of attack. **Kerberos** is one example of a heavy-duty security system. You can find out more about Kerberos at <*http://www.contrib.andrew.cmu.edu/usr/db74/kerberos.html*> or <*http://nii.isi.edu/info/kerberos/documentation.html*>.

Private Key Encryption

Private key encryption is the type described in most spy novels. Someone uses a key or cipher to encrypt a document, and only those who have a copy of that key can decode the message. This is a powerful method, but it requires the safe transmission of the key between the people who need to see the message. Obviously, e-mail is not a safe means of transmission so this can be a problem over the Internet. One technique is to send it using public key encryption.

Public Key Encryption

Public key encryption, the brainchild of Diffie, is based on the difficulty of finding the prime factors of extremely large numbers. This makes it possible to generate linked encryption keys, one is kept private, the other made available publicly. They both do one-way encryption, that is, whatever is encrypted using one key can only be decoded by using the other. If someone encrypts a message to you with your public key, only the owner of the matching private key (presumably you) can decrypt the message. To exchange encrypted messages both parties must have their own private key as well as the other's public key.

Survey of Charging Techniques

This section reviews some efforts to develop online charging. I'll attempt to explain how each works, as well as its advantages and disadvantages. Think of this as a survey of a growing field and inquire online for more information about any that catch your interest. This is a fast-growing field and changes come rapidly.

Anonymous Credit Cards

A series of papers at the AT&T Research site describes an anonymous credit card system that preserves the anonymity of the parties and the security of the transaction while arranging for payment for goods and services. *<http://www.research.att.com/#acc>*

CyberCash

CyberCash can be used to buy and sell information as well as hard goods. The CyberCash approach to Internet commerce is to establish a trustworthy link between the Internet and the traditional banking world (see Figure 7–1). A Reston, Virginia, company called CyberCash, Inc., has teamed up with Wells Fargo, the seventh largest

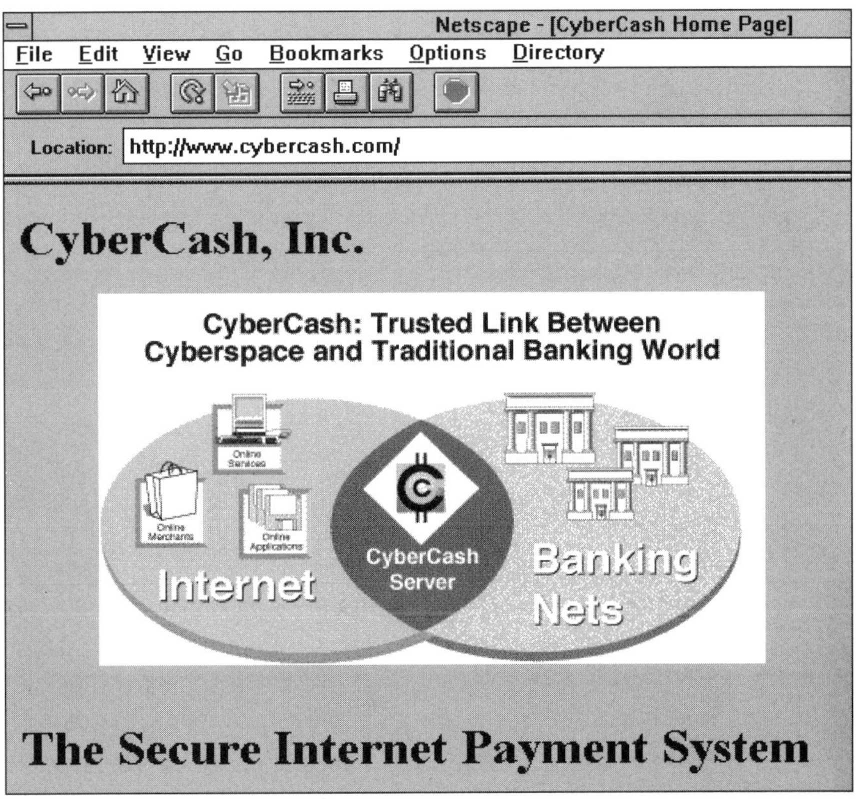

FIGURE 7–1 CyberCash Web Site (Reprinted with permission.)

bank in the United States, and Check Free Corporation, the leading electronic commerce company in the United States. CyberCash offers credit and debit card transactions and eventually plans to offer true digital cash that can be transferred among friends and strangers and not just merchants.

CyberCash allows credit card holders to encrypt their personal credit card data in a way that only CyberCash can decrypt. It goes like this:

1. Buyer downloads free CyberCash software.
2. Buyer finds an Internet site or merchant that accepts CyberCash.
3. Buyer selects Pay option on a CyberCash form on seller's site.
4. The merchant sends an online invoice detailing purchase information and a statement that confirms total charges.
5. The buyer adds her credit card number, name, and expiration date to the statement. If the buyer is using a debit card, she adds a personal identification number (PIN).
6. The statement and credit or debit card information are encrypted by the buyer's CyberCash software and sent to the merchant.
7. Merchants add their own identification information to the encrypted statement and forward it to the CyberCash server.
8. The CyberCash server initiates a standard credit or debit card authorization request to the merchant's bank or designee.
9. When the authorization request has been processed, the CyberCash server forwards the response to the merchant.
10. The merchant completes the sale.

CyberCash can handle charges, voids, and returns, as well as peer-to-peer transactions (direct exchanges between two equal parties) and transactions too small to handle through normal credit card channels. CyberCash will charge banks a fee for the consumer-to-merchant transactions, but the fee structure will be competitive with traditional systems. CyberCash fees for transfers between individuals are expected to cost about as much as a postage stamp. <***http://www.cybercash.com/***>

Ecash by DigiCash Corporation

The DigiCash Corporation's ecash™ system (see Figure 7–2) provides an electronic equivalent for most functions of cash, especially anonymity. Ecash enables users to withdraw "digital coins" from their ecash bank and spend them across the Internet anonymously. This ability to cut the chain of interlocking information that invades privacy is one of the main goals of ecash and DigiCash's related plans for echecks.

Ecash was announced in May 1994 at the First International WWW Conference in Geneva; a $1 million open-ended trial run began in

FIGURE 7–2 DigiCash™ Web Site (Reprinted with permission from DigiCash bv, Amsterdam, The Netherlands.)

October 1994 during the Second International WWW Conference in Chicago. The trial uses a currency called cyberdollars or cyberbucks, which have no relation to any currency, living or dead. During the trial period (which has no set end date) DigiCash gives $100 in cyberbucks to every participant to spend in participating cybershops. More than 11,000 people have registered, and 5,000 have "spent" their cyberbucks.

Ecash, short for electronic cash (which is the same as digital cash), <*http://www.digicash.com/ecash/ecash-home.html*>, relies on public key cryptography to create digital signatures that are then used with random-number "blinding" to ensure the privacy of all parties. Ecash is a product of DigiCash, <*http://www.digicash.com*>, which has offices in Amsterdam and Palo Alto, California. DigiCash was founded in 1990 by cryptographic experts and has been involved in smart cards, security, and electronic payments systems.

The client software for ecash is available for Macintosh, Windows, and UNIX platforms after registration. The server software is available for UNIX WWW servers (both NCSA and CERN), Windows (but only for testing), and is under development for Macintosh WWW servers. Although DigiCash is running an ecash bank for the trial, it has no plans to link cyberdollars to any real currency. Instead, the company is discussing licensing arrangements with banks, financial institutions, and other organizations (possibly governments) that are interested in issuing ecash.

There are ecash shops, ecash customers, and ecash banks (although the cyberbucks have no value, the items and services being sold do). One of the main goals of ecash is to provide security, confidentiality, and auditability. Although it is not possible for the bank or government authorities to link the buyer to a specific transaction, it is possible for buyers to prove definitively (if they wish) that they have made a particular payment. But if they try to spend the coins more than once, they effectively leave a trail. The system is designed in such a way that anonymity is assured for only one transaction per coin. See DigiCash's Web site for additional details.

The ecash system works as follows:

1. Buyer downloads free software for Macintosh, Windows, or UNIX.
2. Seller downloads free scripts and software for WWW servers.
3. Buyer establishes account with ecash bank and deposits money.
4. Buyer withdraws "digital coins" from ecash bank. (Digital coins are encrypted with digital signature from ecash bank verifying their value. They also have a serial number to prevent double spending. The serial number is "blinded" however, so that purchases can't be linked to the buyer.)
5. Buyer finds WWW ecash shop displaying "we accept ecash" logo (see Figure 7–3).
6. Buyer's ecash software, running in background, pops up and sends the appropriate combination of digital coins to the seller.
7. Seller verifies the digital signature of the ecash bank and provides merchandise or service to buyer.
8. Seller sends the digital coins to the ecash bank, and amount is credited to seller's account.

FIGURE 7–3 DigiCash's "we accept ecash" logo
(Reprinted with permission from DigiCash bv, Amsterdam, The Netherlands.)

First Virtual

First Virtual Holdings, Inc. (see Figure 7–4), which began providing services in late 1994, has a different slant on the electronic commerce problem. <*http://www.fv.com/*> Instead of developing complicated

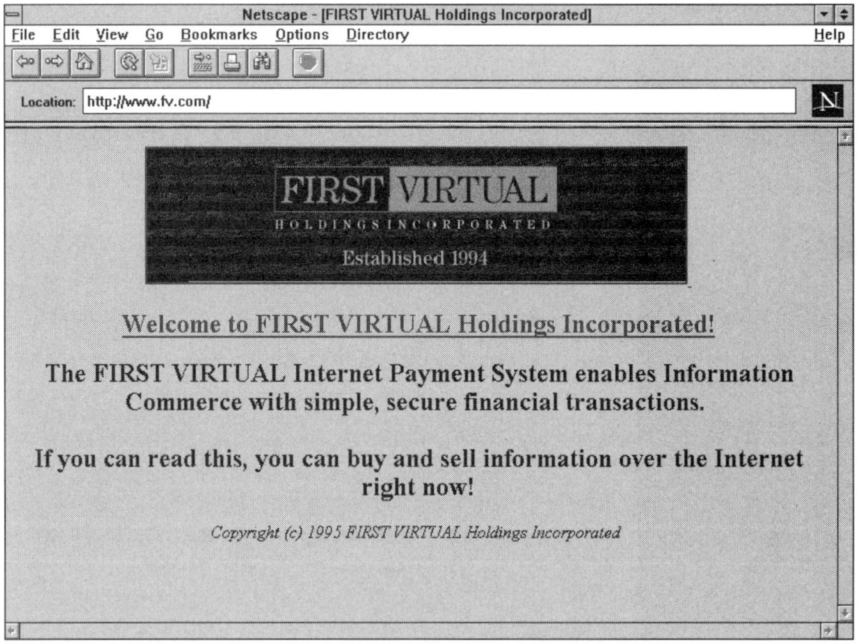

FIGURE 7–4 First Virtual Web Site (Reprinted with permission.)

password and encryption schemes, First Virtual set out to design a system that does not need to send any confidential information over the Internet and does not depend on particular hardware or software.

First Virtual's solution is to replace your credit card number (which you provide by voice when you first sign up) with a First Virtual account that you use for all transactions. You might ask why First Virtual's account number doesn't run the same risks as a credit card number when passing over the Internet. But the account number alone is not enough to complete a transaction. No purchases are final until they are confirmed by e-mail with the purchaser. Although someone could lie and deny making a purchase, someone who does that often is going to lose their account. The system was designed to work from any country but initially requires a credit card (and for merchants a checking account) from a financial institution in the United States or Canada. Follow this link to reach First Virtual's FAQ: <*http://www.fv.com/faq/index.html*>.

First Virtual offers a software addition to Web servers that allows them to accept First Virtual payments. Buyers pay a $2 registration fee and no transaction charges. Sellers have a $10 registration fee and a transaction fee of 29 cents plus 2% of the value of the transaction, which is deducted from the amount paid by the buyer. Sellers also pay a $1 fee whenever a deposit is made to the seller's checking account. For those without servers of their own First Virtual offers InfoHaus, <***http://www.infohaus.com***>, an electronic go-between that will sell your items for you, for a commission, of course, and a monthly charge of $1.50 per megabyte of storage. According to Tom Gable, spokesman for First Virtual, InfoHaus merchants were doing thousands of dollars in sales per day in April 1995.

A transaction on the First Virtual system would proceed as follows:

1. Buyer with a First Virtual account number browses the Internet.
2. Buyer finds something he wants to buy from a First Virtual seller.
3. Seller asks for buyer's First Virtual account number.
4. Buyer sends his account number in the clear (no encryption necessary).
5. Seller allows buyer to download his purchase.
6. Seller sends purchase information to First Virtual.
7. First Virtual sends buyer e-mail to confirm purchase.
8. Buyer replies with *yes, no,* or *fraud*. (*Yes* means First Virtual should charge his credit card for that amount; *no* means the product was in some way unsatisfactory—don't charge. Too many *nos* mean the buyer is abusing the system and his account will be deactivated. *Fraud* means buyer did not make the purchase. If a buyer responds with *fraud,* First Virtual immediately deactivates the buyer's account and contacts him about establishing a new one.)
9. First Virtual debits buyers' credit card accounts and deposits money in sellers' checking accounts within 90 days of transactions.

First Virtual's system requires the sellers to be willing to allow buyers to download their product with no absolute guarantee of getting paid each time. But First Virtual does guarantee it will eliminate abusers from the system. Except for requiring a certain amount of trust, First Virtual's is an elegant system for certain types of sales and appears to be growing. It's main advantage is that all it takes to be a seller is an e-mail address and a checking account.

Mondex

Mondex is an electronic cash smart card (a plastic card with a microcomputer chip embedded in it) that allows the safe movement of money over the Internet. Each time a Mondex card is used, the chip on the card generates a unique digital signature that is recognized by the other Mondex card involved in the transaction. The digital signature is the guarantee that the cards involved are genuine and that they are dealing with genuine Mondex signals. This recognition process also identifies the card for which the cash is intended, which means that a third party cannot intercept funds. Mondex is being launched in England by NatWest and Midland Banks in conjunction with BT (British Telecom). A test was started in Swindon, England, in July 1995. For additional information, see <*http://www.mondex.com/mondex/home.htm*>.

NetBill Electronic Commerce Project

Carnegie Mellon University's Information Networking Institute is designing the protocols that will allow users with NetBill accounts to buy from merchants whose servers run NetBill software. The system would use a debit approach like a bank ATM card. The institute is designing the system so that it is possible to bill for 1-cent transactions (credit cards usually charge 25 to 50 cents per transaction); its focus will be network-delivered (downloaded) goods with a certified delivery protocol to guarantee delivery. The protocols will be open so that others can build on this technology. In February 1995

Carnegie Mellon and Visa formed a partnership to develop and conduct a precommercial trial of NetBill by the end of the year. For further information, see <***http://www.ini.cmu.edu/netbill/***>.

The constraints are that the system assumes realtime communication between three parties and it uses encryption (which limits its exportability). NetBill does not prevent redistribution of downloaded goods, although another project of the institute's involves encoding serial numbers in documents.

NetCheque/NetCash

NetCheque/NetCash at <***http://nii-server.isi.edu/info/NetCheque***>, which is being developed at the University of Southern California's Institute for Scientific Information, works much like paper checks. It will require an electronic signature, and the payee will have to endorse with another electronic signature. Based on the Kerberos security software system and **Prospero** file system, users registered with NetCheque servers can write checks to other users. The other users or merchants then deposit these checks via an electronic clearing house.

NetCheque software was released in December 1994 for testing and development. It runs on SunOS. Its developers say it meets the following criteria:

Security—works on open networks but protects all parties to the transaction

Flexibility—allows different kinds of payments: personal checks, cashier's checks, credit cards, and eventually electronic cash

Scalability—can handle extremely large numbers of transactions

Efficiency—a per-transaction cost of a fraction of a cent

Unobtrusiveness—does not interrupt other computing activities and is expected to integrate easily with existing network and online software, such as CompuServe, America Online, and Prodigy

NetChex

NetChex is a virtual checking account system for online transactions in development by Net 1, Inc., based in Phoenix. The client software runs on DOS or Windows machines and permits authorized users (members) to gain access to and transmit electronic checks for free. NetChex processes those electronic checks and generates an actual check that is sent to the merchant's bank. Without the client software the member cannot generate signature keys and access encryption algorithms. The software is copy protected so that it cannot be copied surreptitiously to another machine for fraudulent purposes. According to the June 26, 1995, edition of *PC Week*, NetChex is ready to unveil its system but is waiting to ally with a bank or larger partner. <***http://www.netchex.com/***>

Open Market

Open Market's payment system, as embodied in its $4,995 WebServer, allows for the purchase of both hard goods and information. Open Market <***http://www.openmarket.com/***> uses existing Internet and World-Wide Web protocols, but it comes in separate parts, or modules, each performing a specific function. The modular design means that when improvements in **authentication** or security schemes (or some other part of the process) come along, the newer version can replace the appropriate module, and the server need not replace the entire system.

The Open Market purchase process goes like this:

1. Buyer finds something to buy on seller's WWW server.
2. Buyer follows the payment link for that item. The payment link is a URL with item information, price, and other information encoded and stamped with a digital signature.
3. The payment link takes the buyer to the Open Market authentication server.
4. The Open Market server verifies the buyer's identity.

5. The Open Market server ascertains that the buyer has sufficient funds for this purchase. For credit cards this is done through realtime connection to the credit card clearing network.
6. The Open Market server debits the buyer's credit card account and gives the buyer an access link, which is a link back to the seller's server that also serves as confirmation of the sale, complete with a digital signature.
7. The seller then sends the buyer the merchandise, either hard goods or information that the buyer can download.

Open Market has some advantages:

- No modifications to existing HTTP/WWW servers are necessary.
- Authentication and payment methods are separate from the seller.
- The risk of fraud is reduced because sellers do not have access to the buyer's confidential information.
- The system is modular for replacement of individual pieces as the technology improves.
- Different authentication methods can be designated by transaction to provide an appropriate level of security. Authentication methods can range from asking for name and password to challenging (asking questions only the legitimate buyer can answer) to requiring the buyer to have a hand-held authenticator.

PayNet

PayNet Corporation is working with the Thompson Publishing Group to develop a system that focuses specifically on business-to-business information. PayNet provides a service for niche business publications (such as *Management of Aboveground Storage Tanks*) that are distributed as newsletters and inserts to looseleaf notebooks. Most consumers don't pay $500 a year to subscribe to a newsletter, but many companies do.

PayNet is a three-party payment system; providers and customers register with PayNet and the customer gains access to any publication in the system. Companies can get reports similar to long-distance phone bills. Employees can allocate purchases to particular job codes and subscribe to publications or pay by access.

The billing approach is a hybrid of telephone and credit card billing systems. Like telephones, PayNet is designed to handle many small charges. PayNet's goal is to process 10-cent transactions economically, with the smallest transaction costing 1 cent. That would increase for larger transactions. PayNet relies on encryption for messaging. It can provide encryption for content, but that's not the focus. PayNet does not depend on a particular brand of encryption. Initially, PayNet will be for U.S. companies only because of the complexities of international payments.

PayNet is expected to work like this:

1. Customer finds a PayNet publisher with a publication she needs to read.
2. Customer registers with PayNet at that moment, or her company is already registered.
3. Customer downloads software.
4. Customer requests an item.
5. Provider says to PayNet, "Customer X is asking for something costing Y dollars."
6. PayNet contacts customer to verify request.
7. Customer okays charge (signs request electronically).
8. PayNet notifies provider, who allows download.
9. PayNet confirms customer's receipt of goods using an electronic fingerprint of the goods before and after. (This method gives PayNet a record of the accurate delivery of the merchandise.)

The PayNet server has to be online to complete the transaction, but there will be multiple servers so that one will always be available. For further information send e-mail to info@paynet.com.

Secure HTTP

Secure HTTP <***http://www.commerce.net/information/standards/drafts/shttp.txt***> is being developed by Enterprise Integration Technologies (EIT) as an extension of the HyperText Transfer Protocol to provide a secure means of transporting information across the Internet. Secure HTTP can be used in a wide variety of WWW contexts because it is concerned only with the way messages are formatted and the protocol by which they are exchanged. Secure HTTP is available to software developers through Terisa's SecureWeb client and server tool kits (see section on Terisa).

Secure Sockets Layer (SSL)

Netscape calls its solution to security problems SSL (Secure Sockets Layer) <***http://home.mcom.com/info/SSL.html***>. Netscape has proposed that the W3O working group on security consider SSL for "part of a general security approach for the Web." Netscape is also working with W3O and others to establish open security standards for the Net. Open standards mean that the details are openly available and not proprietary to any one company. Note that open protocols are what the Internet was built on. Netscape has joined with Terisa to develop a common security standard that incorporates both Secure HTTP and SSL.

Netscape's system works at a low level, below the application level, but above **TCP/IP**, to secure transmission privacy between a client and server, no matter what application they're running—FTP, Telnet, Gopher, Usenet News, e-mail, WWW, or anything else that comes along. Application messages between client and server are sent in encrypted form, using RSA's patented encryption algorithms.

Netscape's SSL provides three types of protection:

- Server authentication so that the client, or user, can be sure they are dealing with the server they expected
- Privacy using encryption for messages so that prying eyes can't read them

- Data integrity to ensure that the messages sent cannot be edited or changed in any way

The key feature of Netscape's security scheme is that it would underlie the actual application you are using without interfering with it. So you could layer another security system atop SSL, flexibility that could prove useful.

Shen Plan

Shen <*http://www.w3.org/hypertext/WWW/Shen/ref/shen.html*> is a security scheme being developed under the sponsorship of CERN and the European Union. The philosophy is to build as much as possible on existing RFCs, especially the Privacy Enhanced Mail (PEM) standard in order to encourage integration of e-mail, Usenet News, and Web systems. PEM is defined in a set of four RFCs (1421—1424) available at <*ftp://ds.internic.net/rfc/*> that define message encryption and authentication techniques for electronic mail over the Internet.

The Shen security scheme provides for three levels of security:

Weak authentication with low maintenance overhead and without patent or export restrictions

Strong authentication via public key exchange

Strong encryption of message content

Terisa Systems SecureWeb Toolkit

Terisa Systems was founded as a joint venture of Enterprise Integration Technologies (EIT) and RSA Data Security to formulate a security system for the WWW. The company did that with S-HTTP, but competitor Netscape Communications proposed its own scheme for network security. Both systems have advantages (detailed later), but it looked like they were going to fight for customers. For users and those wishing to sell on the Internet, such competition promised confusion, because some sites would require one security system and others would use another. An elegant solution was reached, however, when America Online, CompuServe, Prodigy, IBM, and Netscape Communications announced their intent to join Terisa as equity holders in the effort to develop Terisa's SecureWeb client and server tool kits, incorporating both S-HTTP and SSL by late 1995 (see Figure 7–5). These tool kits are aimed at software developers instead of end users or merchants.

The inclusion of America Online, CompuServe, and Prodigy in this venture is particularly important, because they are the three largest commercial alternatives to the Internet. This signifies how important they consider the Internet and Internet commerce to their future business. The move also bodes well for the rapid development of uniform standards for Internet commerce.
<*http://www.terisa.com/*>

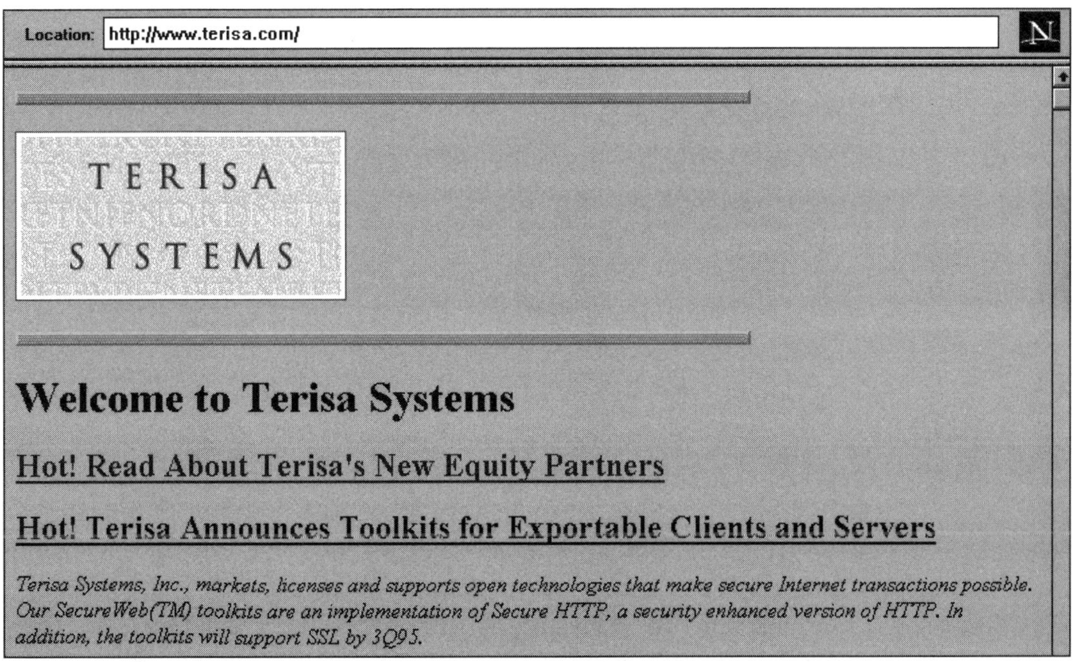

FIGURE 7–5 Terisa Systems Web Site (Reprinted with permission.)

Offline Payment

Some companies have avoided the wait for secure Internet commerce to develop by collecting money and credit card information offline. Voicemail systems or human telephone operators are often used to take credit card numbers over the phone and then activate the requested service online or supply the user with an authorization code that can be used safely via e-mail or online forms. Although the authorization code might be stolen via the Internet, it is not widely useful like a credit card number, so it is much less vulnerable.

WEBster Electronic Magazine via E-mail

An electronic magazine called *WEBster* came up with an ingenious method for selling its electronic text over the Internet (see Figure 7–6). For $29 you subscribe to one of its electronic magazines. Every two weeks you receive an e-mail table of contents. If you like some or all items on the list, you send an e-mail message requesting the articles. *WEBster*'s specially modified list server accepts such requests only from registered subscribers. The payment for the subscription is handled entirely offline. The system enables *WEBster* to market to a much larger population—all those who have e-mail access, as opposed to those who have a WWW or Gopher browser. <***http://www.tgc.com/webster.html***>

Summary

Internet Publishing is not just about selling things, but this chapter is. Commerce is becoming part of the Internet, although the new forms of communication between companies and their customers may be more important than direct transfers of electronic cash or checks. The Internet isn't advertising as usual. Marketing on the Internet has a different flavor, because Internet users have the same ability to disseminate their message worldwide as do the corpora-

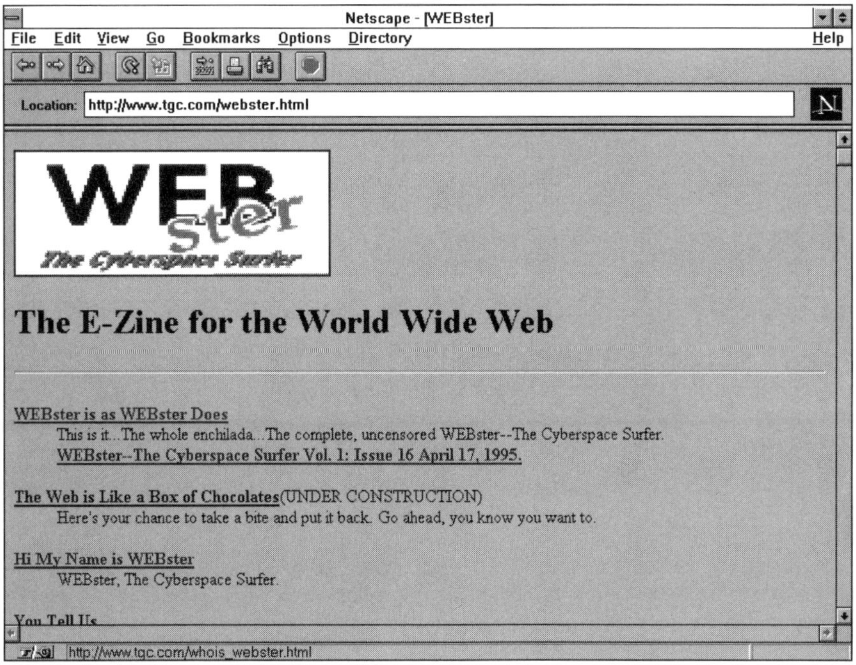

FIGURE 7–6 Webster Electronic Magazine Web Site (Reprinted with permission.)

tions and organizations doing the marketing. Fitting into the changing Internet culture is a requirement for a company that wants to come off well. This is done by active participation in relevant newsgroups and mailing lists with an emphasis on solid technical information rather than marketing hype. Servers should provide free tools and information that are valuable, not just public relations hype.

Different economic models exist for making money on the Internet, which has room for many more. It's not clear yet whether Gopher, Web, or WAIS servers can directly pay for themselves through sales on the Internet. Many companies are experimenting with the technology. Some are using the experience to position themselves for the future and learn about related technologies (like multimedia CD-ROMs). Others are exploring different relationships with their customers and between different sections of their companies.

Some charging techniques are already in place (First Virtual and CyberCash) and others are in testing or coming online (DigiCash and CyberCash). The technology is being built into Web browsers and servers now and may come to FTP, Gopher, and others in the near future.

CHAPTER 8

Hiring Out the Work

If you still have not recovered from the travails of setting up your own PC and the very idea of establishing a server yourself is giving you nightmares, you can have someone else set up and run your Gopher, WWW, or WAIS server—and it can be quite inexpensive. This chapter goes over the reasons to hire out and tells you what to expect in such a situation. You'll also find profiles of a cross-section of consultants and companies that provide Internet publishing services. These are by no means the only companies offering these services. This is a fast-growing field, and the options are expanding daily. Read the sidebar to this chapter, Finding and Selecting an Internet Service Provider, if you need a better connection to the Internet or just to learn about some of the network connection issues that will affect you.

Reasons to Hire Out

There are a lot of reasons not to do the work of publishing on the Internet yourself. You might not be at all sure of what you're doing (despite reading this book), and you don't want to risk your company or organization's reputation while you experiment. Or perhaps placing your Web pages on someone else's server for a few dollars a month is the quickest and easiest method to get your material online. This chapter discusses other reasons for not doing all the work yourself.

Finding and Selecting an Internet Service Provider

The bandwidth of your connection to the Internet is a key element in your success as an Internet publisher. Bandwidth is the speed at which you can transmit information and has a much greater effect on your server's performance (whether it's Gopher, WWW, or WAIS) than computer speed. This section is divided into three parts: concepts you'll need to understand, questions you'll need to ask, and places to look for an Internet service provider that will keep you and your users satisfied.

Concepts

You need a full-time connection to publish on the Internet. You have to arrange this with an Internet service provider (ISP) and the telephone company, which will connect your location to that of the Internet service provider. Sometimes you can pay the ISP to take care of everything for you. This will be more expensive but might be worth the savings in aggravation. Also, if you are going to rent space on the ISP's server, or house your computer at its location, you don't need to deal with the telephone company. The discussion that follows assumes you need some sort of connection between your site and the Internet service provider. Connections to the Internet come in several flavors—analog, digital, cable, and wireless—and each has different charging schemes. We'll talk about only analog and digital; cable and wireless are in development.

An analog connection is the familiar business or residential telephone line. It's the least expensive but has a maximum speed of 14.4 or 28.8Kbps (thousand bits per second—the higher the number the better for speed). This is okay for dial-in browsing but the absolute minimum for publishing on the Internet. The advantages are easy set-up and minimal hardware (just a 28.8Kbps modem). The disadvantages are the limited bandwidth, which will make your server very slow. And the cost of using your phone line 24 hours a day will add up quickly. A business line usually costs more than residential. If your server is not for business use, you might be able to run your server at residential phone rates. Check with your telephone company.

Businesses that are in the same telephone switching area as their Internet service provider can sometimes use a Centrex service. This is not faster, just less expensive, because there's no charge per minute. It's a regular line but prearranged for 24-hour connection to a particular number. Contact your telephone company for more details and pricing.

A digital connection uses a different, newer, faster (and more expensive) technology for transmitting phone calls. It comes in various forms (ISDN, 56K, fractional T-1, T-1, and T-3), not all of which are available in all locations. When checking for prices, be sure to check on whether there are different pricing schemes for different levels of support. If you do the technical set-up yourself, you may be able to pay less.

A 56K leased line will transfer data at 56Kbps (or twice the speed of a regular phone line). It requires special equipment (a CSU/DSU and a router), so there will be equipment costs and an installation fee as well as the monthly charge. Many small Internet servers have 56K connections to the Internet.

A T-1 leased line will transfer data at 1.54Mbps (megabits, or million bits per second). This is roughly 28 times as fast as a 56K line. For this reason fractional T-1 is often available in different fractions as an intermediate option. The monthly line charges are less for fractional T-1, but the set-up is the same because it requires the full T-1 version of the CSU/DSU and router. The equipment alone costs about $4,000.

A T-3 leased line is the top of the line at 45Mbps, or almost 30 times faster than T-1. Few organizations get into T-3, and those that do usually are national network providers or major universities that support thousands of subnets.

ISDN (Integrated Services Digital Network) is only starting to become available, depending on where you are located. It runs 64Kbps or 128Kbps. It is a tariff service, which means you pay by the minute, with different rates for different times of the day. If you can do Centrex ISDN, your bill can go from hundreds of dollars per month to $30 to $40 per month.

Questions for Your Internet Service Provider

What is your guarantee of bandwidth? Everybody oversells because nobody needs all of their bandwidth all the time—does your ISP have any procedures for monitoring bandwidth? Or does the ISP just wait for complaints about overloading?

Will you have to pay more if you overload your ISP's system? What's the ISP's definition of overload and how is it measured? Compare what the competition says.

How many lines to the Internet does your ISP have? Are the lines to single or multiple national Internet providers? You'll want them to have multiple lines to different national providers to handle major outages.

Are there any restrictions on what you can use your connection for? Is commercial use acceptable? Check the ISP's acceptable use policy and see how your plans fit. Some ISPs don't enforce their acceptable use policy, but don't count on such laxity continuing forever. Make sure that what you plan to do is acceptable.

Can you resell your bandwidth? Say, for example, that you're in an office park, you buy a T-1, and then you get only 20 hits a day. If you want to bring your cost down, you might want to consider reselling some of your bandwidth. Some ISPs offer this as a selling point; others absolutely refuse.

How long has your ISP been in business? Talk to other clients, get references, and talk to them.

Post to Usenet newsgroups (particularly newsgroups in your area and alt.internet.access.wanted) asking for experiences with a particular provider. You are probably going to hear more horror stories than success stories, so take them with a grain of salt.

Are there any time constraints in the contract your ISP wants you to sign—is it month to month, six-month, or year-long?

Ask as many questions about delivery time as you can (the phone company and ISP both have to do installations). Get reasonable due dates and talk to both former clients and those who are satisfied.

How does the ISP handle domain name service (DNS)? Do they offer a secondary name server on a completely different network? Some ISPs will take care of that for you. Sometimes you have to give something up for that. The ISP may agree to manage DNS for you, but you may have to put up with delays. If you have the technical skills, you could run it yourself.

Does your ISP recommend any local line providers that they work with instead of the phone company? Who do they like to work with?

Does the ISP have 24-hour technical support? These are often called NOCs or (Network Operations Centers). If the ISP has a technical support staff, how do you get through? Do you page the techs? Are real people available 'round the clock?Or do they work only from 8 to 5, Island Pacific Time?

Does the ISP have any kind of general communication with its users, such as a mailing list or newsgoups dedicated to different subjects such as scheduled outages and other recurring problems?

How many subscribers does your ISP have, and how many of each type (dial-in, 56K, T-1)? This information gives you some idea of who you are sharing the ISP's Internet connections with and how much attention the ISP may pay to your problems.

Places to Go

The following sites have either advice or lists of Internet service providers. Particularly important is to read the white paper "How to Select an Internet Service Provider."

"The Internet Society's Guide—How to Find Internet Service Providers" *<http://www.isoc.org/~bgreene/nsp-c.html>*

"How to Select an Internet Service Provider" *<http://tlg.org/how-to-select-ISP.html>*

"Internet Access Providers—List, Links, and Advice from St. Joseph County Public Library, South Bend, Indiana" *<http://sjcpl.lib.in.us/homepage/Reference/InternetProviders/InternetProviders.html>*

"The List—1,119 Internet Service Providers, by Country" *<http://thelist.com/>*

"U.S. Internet Service Providers List" *<http://www.primus.com/staff/peggy/provider.html>*

Twenty-Four-Hour Internet Connection

Providing a part-time Internet publishing service doesn't make any sense because this is truly an international medium that requires 24-hour access. A site available during only certain hours would provoke a great deal of frustration among potential users. If you don't have an Internet connection 24 hours a day, you will want to weigh the costs of running such a connection yourself against the costs of hiring out the service. Internet connection rates differ considerably, so you'll have to shop around the Internet providers in your area.

Fast Internet Connections

You may already have a 24-hour Internet connection, but Internet publishing can add quite a bit to the load on your computer. It's essential to think about the load your Internet connection can tolerate. Connections can handle only a certain quantity of material at any given time. A Gopher, Web, or WAIS server that becomes popular might quickly overwhelm all the other traffic you send via that link. Upgrading the link might be too expensive for you. That's when it might make more sense to use someone else's service, and let the provider worry about handling the load.

Computer Power

One good reason to hire out your Internet publishing is to make sure that the computing power available on your Gopher, Web, or WAIS server matches the demand you expect. If the load you expect will overburden your computer, it might make a great deal of sense to hire out your Internet publishing venture to some place with a much more powerful computer.

An Inexpensive Alternative

At the very least you need a computer and an Internet connection to run your own Gopher, WWW, or WAIS server. But you can become an Internet publisher for as little as a $10 set-up fee and an e-mail account if you use First Virtual's InfoHaus service. Other Internet providers offer similarly inexpensive plans. These options might be ideal for an artist, writer, computer programmer, or small business or organization that wants to establish an Internet presence with minimal upfront costs. This allows you to have your own home page without owning a computer. But shop around, because the amount of material you can store on the server without incurring additional charges varies considerably.

Expertise

Obtaining expertise is one of the most popular reasons to hire out the work of establishing and running a server. Paying the right consultants to do the work can be a safe and efficient method of ensuring a professional looking result. In addition to the design issues is the matter of running the system. UNIX servers are among the most powerful machines for running a Net site, but they demand a great deal of attention and experience to manage. It's safe to say that you'll spend more time managing the UNIX operating system than the Gopher, Web, or WAIS servers.

Security

If security concerns are paramount in your organization, the safest way to limit your vulnerability is to run your service on someone else's machine. Your computers can stay entirely out of the loop, with no link back for hackers to follow.

What You Pay For

Publishing on the Internet is a new field, and it's tempting to hand the responsibility to a consulting firm or marketing agency that sounds or looks good. But charges vary widely, and the impression you make on the Internet can have little correlation to the amount of money invested. Know what you're paying for, and decide what is really best done in-house. Because Internet publishing is such a new area, you'll find it's fairly flexible. But it's important to know what you're paying for so you don't get overcharged.

First and foremost, you are paying for someone else's 24-hour Internet connection. However, connections provide various capacities, so learn what type of connection your provider has, and get the provider to estimate how many users and how much data its computers can support comfortably. Ask about guarantees so that you don't get stuck. Pity the folks who shared *Penthouse Magazine*'s Internet provider. Their services came to a stop because the traffic for *Penthouse*'s Web server overloaded the service provider's connection.

Paying for an Internet consultant or service provider's expertise is reasonable. But ask the consultants or providers to describe that expertise and experience, and be sure it's appropriate for you. Be sure to determine whether they have graphic designers on staff, and ask for samples of their work. Marketing is an especially big field these days, but be wary of promises of tremendous financial gains. Whether the Internet will become the shopping center of the future is not at all certain. What is certain is that it provides an unprecedented level of interactive communication on an international level. Your money is best spent on people who can find creative ways to use that communication to support your goals.

Obviously, you'll be paying for a portion of whatever computer system and server software your outside provider is running. Know the limitations of that hardware and software. What is its capacity in terms of connections per second? Is it mirrored? If it is not mirrored, how is it backed up? Is there any regular downtime or maintenance period during which your server would be unavailable? What kinds of software tools does the provider make available to help you load your data? How much backup support does the provider have for its hardware and software?

One way to spend more money is to have someone else prepare all your documents and data for you. And in the beginning that might be exactly what you want to do, if only to get started right and get your staff trained and up to speed. But don't lock yourself into a situation in which you must continue to pay for consulting in addition to the server and storage costs.

Also, find out what kind of tools the experts provide to help you assemble and publish your data. Can you upload the files to the server yourself? Can you write your own scripts, or do your experts provide scripts and programs for most common functions, such as online forms and collecting users' comments?

How much storage space are you getting for your money? What happens if your needs exceed that amount? Is there a charge for how much is actually delivered to users as well as for storing your documents and data? Although you may not expect large amounts of data to accumulate, it's always wise to leave room for expansion.

If at all possible, make sure that your site's link is short, easy to remember, and contains the name of your company or organization. Until recently, companies that wanted their name in their URL were told by their Internet providers that it wasn't possible. But now at least one commercial Web server has the ability to respond as if it were multiple servers (as many as 256), each with a different name and IP address. The advantages are clear. It is much easier to remember a short URL than a long one, and why not advertise your company or organization's name instead of the Internet provider's?

When you are told that your Web site has had 1,000 connections per day, don't be too impressed. That number may have no relation to the number of people who came for a visit. Each inline (embedded) image in an HTML page counts for one connection. So if your organization's home page has nine inline images plus the home page text itself, each user will show up as 10 connections in the logs. Much more useful is monitoring key documents and asking for statistics on how often they are downloaded.

Services and Consultants

If you're convinced you need to hire out your Internet publishing, and you know what to look for and watch out for, it's time to consider what's available. Remember that geography isn't an issue on the Internet. Assuming you are comfortable with communicating via e-mail, fax, and phone, your Internet consultant or service could be on the other side of the world as easily as right next door. In fact, when dealing with localization to different languages or cultures, contracting with someone in the country you wish to reach might be only sensible.

How to Find Services and Consultants

Because this field is expanding so rapidly, it makes sense to search the Internet itself for information about services and consultants. One excellent resource is Open Market's Commercial Sites Index <***http://www.directory.net/***>. Open Market lists companies that offer Web (and other) services. In May 1995 Open Market listed more than 370 companies that are in the business of creating a presence on the Internet for other organizations. Also check <***http://union.ncsa.uinc.edu/HyperNews/get/www/leasing.html***>.

Another way to find services and consultants is to look at the Internet sites you like. Web sites in particular usually provide a link to the company or person responsible for that site. If the site is maintained by an Internet publishing service or consultant, it almost always will have a link to its own site or information on how to contact it.

Internet publishing consultants are increasingly a cottage industry. Their one- and two-person shops offer services ranging from planning your Internet strategy to writing HTML pages and CGI scripts to installing software and hardware at your site. They might have a site of their own with enough capacity to rent space, but often they don't.

Internet publishing services on the other hand, are usually large organizations with a dedicated Internet connection and powerful computer of their own. In addition to helping you plan your Internet strategy and develop your content, they offer a site with storage (and sometimes usage) fees. Some services specialize in certain markets with certain prescribed services. For example, an Internet shopping center might offer "storefronts" with leasing costs pegged to the amount of material or "space" provided. Other services are more oriented to the marketing or advertising segments of Internet publishing. They will advise you on publicizing your site to reach the most people possible. Still other services offer traditional book- and magazine-publishing services in an online context.

The next section briefly profiles eight companies that offer some form of Internet publishing service. There are hundreds more to pick from, but these will give you some idea of what is available.

Cyber Publishing, Inc.

Cyber Publishing, Inc., <***http://www.travelweb.com/thisco/cyber/cyber.html***> (see Figure 8–1), based in Phoenix, specializes in consulting and constructing World-Wide Web pages and sites. Cyber Publishing did all the pages for the TravelWeb site <***http://www.travelweb.com/***>, including electronic brochures for Hyatt Resorts and Best Western International. Bruce Covill, president of Cyber Publishing, Inc., e-mails that

> The biggest danger is companies or individuals spending time or money building Web pages or Web sites with little or no real idea of to whom they are talking nor what real business those people can or will do with these pages. The mad rush to build pages—and the mad rush of individuals and companies to sop up the money they perceive is out there waiting for someone to offer to build these pages—is creating a glut of sometimes colorful but mainly useless Web pages and sites that really serve no larger purpose than the vanity of a decision-maker in the sponsoring company.

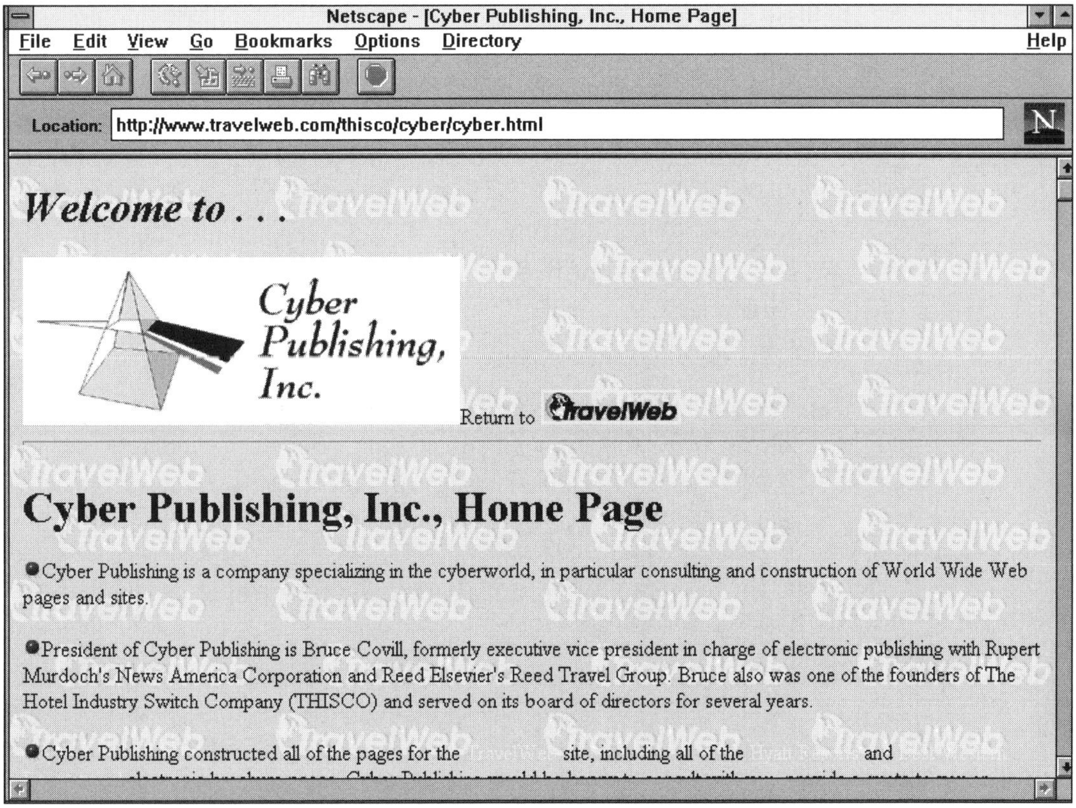

FIGURE 8–1 Cyber Publishing Web Site (Reprinted with permission.)

> Later this year [1995], I expect a tremendous negative reaction in the press based on reaction from many of these companies now shelling out \$25,000-\$100,000 to "pioneer" on the Web, but who will receive no real business or other tangible benefit from their Web investment. I sincerely hope there are enough serious, "industrial strength" Web sites such as TravelWeb in existence by that time to ward off the negative publicity from the thousands of disenchanted companies that have invested in "vanity" sites.

You can contact Cyber Publishing and Bruce Covill by telephone at 602-912-8822 or by e-mail at bcovill@cyberpub.com.

ElNet Corporation

EINet Corporation of Austin, Texas, provides consulting and planning services to help companies use the Internet to achieve their business goals (see Figure 8–2). EINet, known for its Web site, EINet Galaxy, specializes in the integration of Internet technologies with industry-specific applications. The EINet staff provides the technology, services, and labor necessary to meet clients' objectives using Macintosh, IBM PC, or UNIX platforms. Pricing is determined on a client-by-client basis.

Staff members have been working on electronic commerce and security solutions for the Internet since 1992. Their free Internet directory, EINet Galaxy, is one of the leading directory services on the Internet today. They also have an interesting concept, the Virtual

FIGURE 8–2 ElNet Corporation Web Site (Reprinted with permission.)

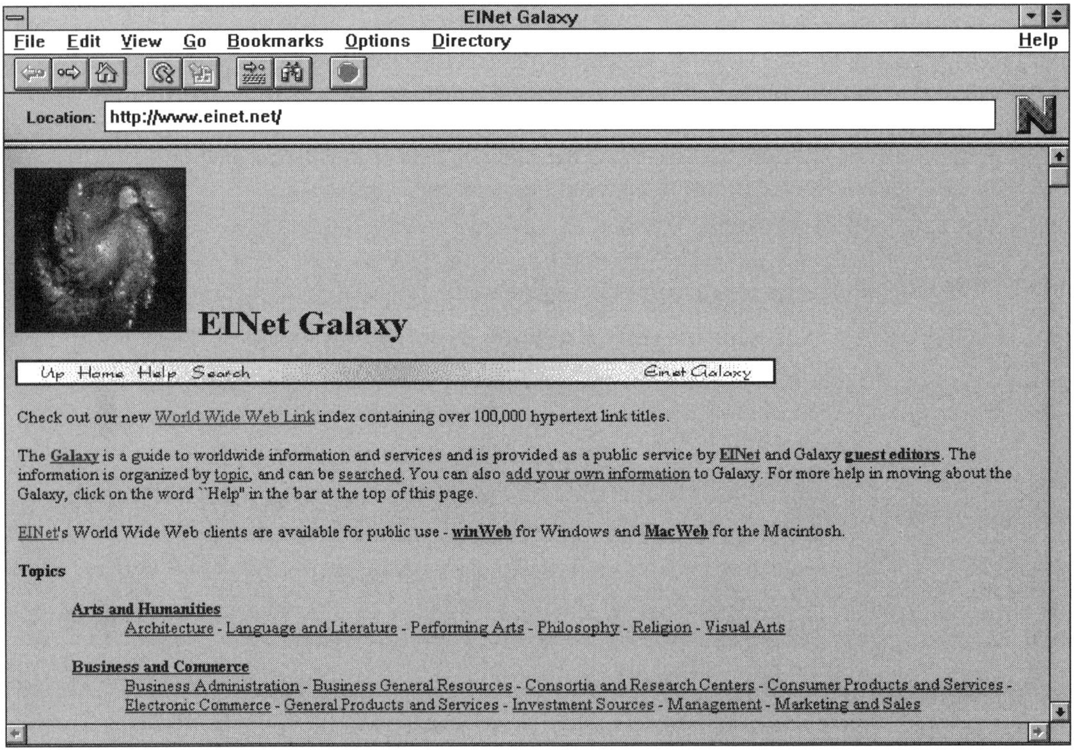

The ElNet Galaxy is copyrighted 1993, 1994, 1995 ElNet Corporation. All rights reserved.

Private Internet, which uses cryptographic techniques and firewalls to allow businesses to create a private set of resources across the Internet.

For information on the EINet's service offerings send e-mail to info@einet.net; voice 800-844-4638 (U.S.), 512-338–3544 (outside the U.S.). EINet's Web site is <*http://www.einet.net/*>.

Innovative Concepts Network

Innovative Concepts Network (ICNet) offers what it calls its Virtual Host Service (see Figure 8–3). You can establish your own FTP, Gopher, or WWW server on Virtual Host Service's machines for $200 per month, including support, plus $200 in set-up fees. You don't have to buy a machine or lease a line. Virtual Host Service means that you get your own URL and IP address, which you do not share with anyone else. Virtual Host Service also offers mailing list services.

FIGURE 8–3 Innovative Concepts Network (ICNet) Web Site
(Reprinted with permission.)

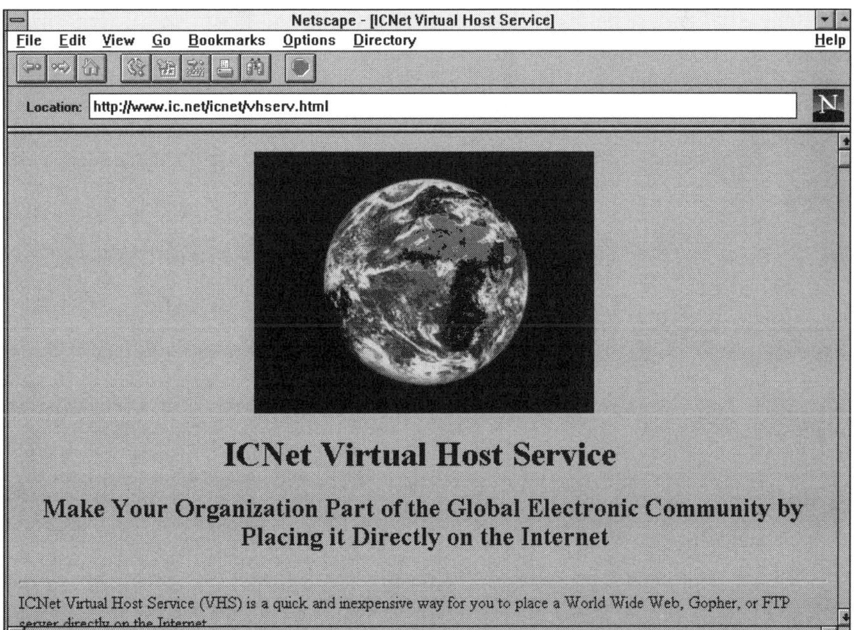

Virtual Host Service's servers are mostly Pentiums running BSDI UNIX with customized NCSA HTTPD for Web services and GN for Gopher services. You can add anything you want, including a back-end database (the server looks up answers to questions in a separate database and sends the results to the user). You have complete control of your server. The company is only the platform provider and does no publishing of its own. <***http://www.ic.net***>

Virtual Host Service is based in Ann Arbor, Michigan; voice 313-998-0090; e-mail support@ic.net.

Internet Distribution Services, Inc.

Internet Distribution Services, Inc., develops and implements electronic storefronts or catalogs for organizations that want to market their products and services on the Internet (see Figure 8–4). Each customer of Internet Distribution's has an independent presence on the Internet. Since January 1994 Internet Distribution Services, <***http://www.service.com/***>, has created more than 40 servers for a variety of large and small organizations, including

Ziff-Davis Expositions	Siemens Rolm Communications, Inc.
Silicon Graphics	Country Fare Restaurant
Palo Alto Weekly	CareerMosaic
Syntex	DIALOG Information Services
Science Television	Center for Software Development
NEC	Infor[illegible]
National Semiconductor	Bay City [illegible]ws (Wire Service)
Shopping 2000	CyberCash

Costs consist of fixed-price set-ups and monthly operation fees if Internet Distribution Services provides space on one of its Internet servers. Set-ups have been running $10,000 to $25,000, including all consulting, design, graphic generation, forms, domain registration, and document translation. Monthly hosting costs have been running $1,000 to $2,500 per month.

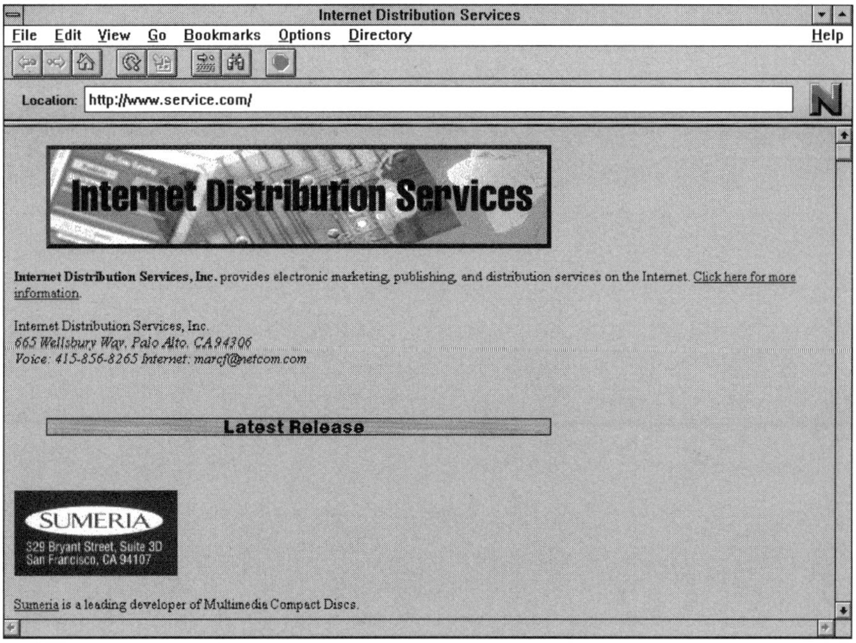

FIGURE 8–4 Internet Distribution Services Web Site
(Reprinted with permission.)

For more information contact Marc Fleischmann at 415-856-8265 (voice) or e-mail marcf@netcom.com.

Liberty Hill Cyberwerks

Liberty Hill Cyberwerks is a one-person shop, based in San Francisco and run by Eric Theise, an academic-turned-Internet-educator, consultant, and writer (see Figure 8–5). A long-time Internet educator (in academia, online forums such as the WELL's Internet conference, public spaces, and in-house settings), Theise began running Internet servers for clients in early 1993 when Gopher was still the information space of choice.

Clients include Circle International (global logistics), digital:// threads (Web strategy and marketing consultants), Hearts of Space Radio/Records, New Albion Records, Project Inform (national AIDS treatment information clearing house), online newsletters such as

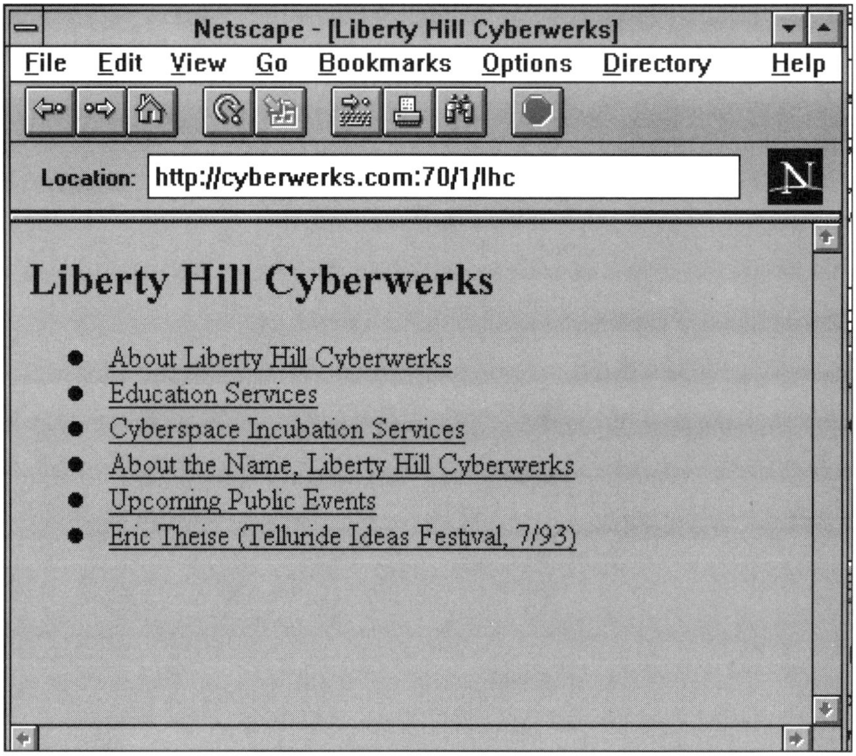

FIGURE 8–5 Liberty Hill Cyberwerks Web Site

Brock N. Meeks's *CyberWire Dispatch* and *DataLine—The Glass Ceiling,* and local organizations such as the Bay Area Internet Users Group, the Virtual Reality Education Foundation, Radio Valencia (a cafe/performance space Theise frequents), and others.

Cyberwerks prices its work on a per-project basis, with server set-ups thus far ranging from $1,000 to $7,000 and monthly maintenance fees ranging from $200 to $800. Theise favors a configuration that dedicates a computer to each client; he finds this offers the greatest flexibility in configuration and the option to simply relocate the computer should the client decide to bring its Internet connection in-house. But he is now offering "virtual host" services as well—a single server masquerades under multiple domain names in a way that is largely invisible to the outside world.

Theise describes Liberty Hill Cyberwerks's mission as twofold:

- To educate people in the possibilities of networking technologies—cyberspace literacy—in forums ranging from corporate boardrooms and trade shows to free or low-cost venues such as bars and book stores, galleries and theaters, museums and community centers
- To form strategic alliances with clients wishing to develop an Internet presence. Cyberwerks puts up servers with significant content—erring in the direction of functionality instead of glitz—and representing clients in online forums while offering them training in ways to begin to do it themselves

Liberty Hill Cyberwerks's connection to the Internet is a T-1 line through a regional provider, the Little Garden at <***http://www.tlg.net***>. Most production servers are Intel-based machines, ranging from 386/16s to 486/66s, and run BSD/OS UNIX <***http://www.bsdi.com***>. Cyberwerks's development machines include Macintosh, Windows, DOS, and NeXT platforms. A color scanner, Apple QuickTake 150 digital camera, and Adobe Photoshop form the core of the in-house design tools.

Because Cybwerks believes in the importance of reaching as many people as possible, it relies heavily on the Web/Gopher capabilities of John Franks's GN server and Brent Chapman's Majordomo mailing list manager. Cyberwerks devotes one machine to virtual Web hosts using Franks's WN server and an experimental server capable of running the NCSA HTTPD and Apache Web servers, University of Minnesota's Gopherd, and Cornell University's audio/videoconferencing reflector software, CU-SeeMe.

Theise says:

> For heaven's sake, if you're thinking of "hiring it out," browse through as many of your potential providers' pages as possible, preferably with a couple of different browsers (such as Netscape and Lynx). Have a friend on the other side of the country do it, too. Can you find the content you're interested in? How fast do the graphics load over a modem connection? Can you navigate

through the site with graphics turned off? How many visible "under construction" areas are there and how long have they been that way? Does the site have consistency, integrity? Does it have quality? A quick scan around the Web at the multitude of typo-laden pages, painful color schemes, and broken links indicates that there's a new self-proclaimed Internet presence expert coming online every hour.

You can reach Eric S. Theise at 415-552-6543 (voice); e-mail verve@cyberwerks.com; <*http://cyberwerks.com*>, <*gopher://cyberwerks.com*>, <*mailto:info@cyberwerks.com*>.

WAIS, Inc.

WAIS, Inc., of San Francisco was founded in 1992 by Internet pioneer Brewster Kahle (who helped design the original version of WAIS while at Thinking Machines Corporation). WAIS, Inc., provides products and services for organizations that want to deliver information over the Internet (see Figure 8–6). Using the WAIS, Inc., product WAISserver™, organizations such as Dow Jones, Novell, CMP Publications, and Encyclopedia Britannica have given Internet users access to books, magazines, news, product data sheets, technical overviews, company information, and more. WAISserver allows content providers to index and publish large databases on the Internet, where they can be searched from around the world.

WAIS Production Services create turnkey, Internet-based services using WAISserver as the core technology. WAISserver automatically creates HTML documents on the fly as it indexes content databases (databases with textual content). WAIS Production Services can integrate custom modules for user registration and feedback, transaction-based and subscription-based billing, personalized invoicing for online shopping, archive searching for back issues, automatic content expiration, and new content alerting.

You can reach WAIS, Inc., at 415-356-5400 (voice); fax 415-356-5444; e-mail frontdesk@wais.com; <*http://www.wais.com/*>.

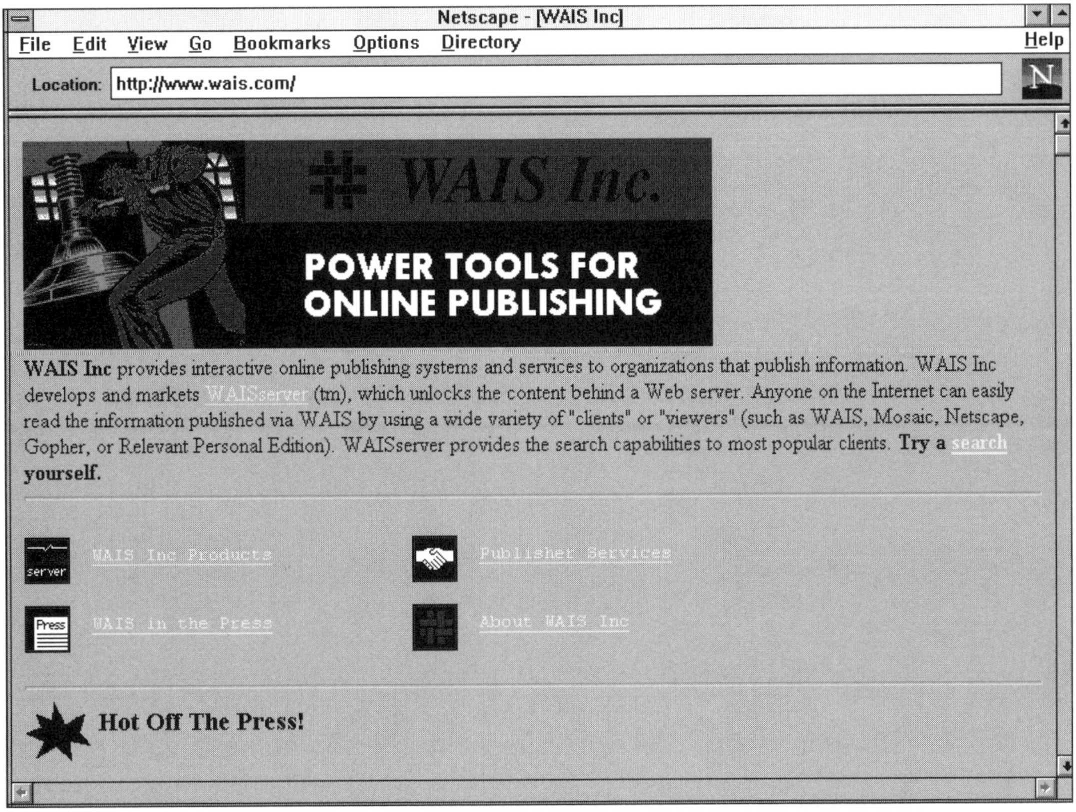

FIGURE 8–6 WAIS Inc. Web Site (Reprinted with permission.)

Web Communications

Web Communications offers both FTP and WWW server privileges at $9.95 (personal), $29.95 (business), and $95 (corporate) per month. (Corporate is for companies with more than 15 employees.) This allows for between 5MB (personal and business) to 10MB (corporate) of disk storage per month. Web Communications also offers discounted rates to nonprofit organizations. There are no update charges or per-link charges.

Although WebCom does not allow you to write your own CGI scripts, the company has made it easy to add online forms. Just write up a form in HTML and leave it in your directory. Any responses to that form will be mailed to you. WebCom has a forms processor with sample set-ups for the following purposes:

- Feedback forms
- Forms for subscribing to an e-mail list
- Guest book registration
- E-mail server
- Selecting a Web page from a list box
- Order forms

WebCom also provides mailing list services that are easily set up by filling out online forms.

Your WWW pages are automatically indexed into an Archie database and can be easily added to the ALIWEB index by placing text markers on each Web page. Full-text indexing of your site's materials is provided via Glimpse. Just check this on a form.

The WebCom server runs on an HP9000/series 800 (which is a mid-range work group server designed to service up to 100 simultaneous connections). WebCom runs a Netscape Communications server but will soon have a Netscape Commerce server that will support secure commercial transations. WebCom has a T-1 connection to the Internet (which means a data rate of 1.5Mbps), and company officials say they will upgrade the link as needed.

WebCom is a self-service Web provider (see Figure 8–7). Content is entirely up to you. You have full access to your account and can update using FTP or via a Web browser. WebCom's 450 customers include the U.S. Coast Guard, the Jimi Hendrix Foundation, and Curtis Matheson Scientific. WebCom can be reached at 408-457-9671 (voice) or <***http://www.webcom.com***>.

Summary

It's possible to hire out all or part of the pieces of the Internet publishing process. It can be done inexpensively or you can spend a lot of money, and many different services offer very different plans.

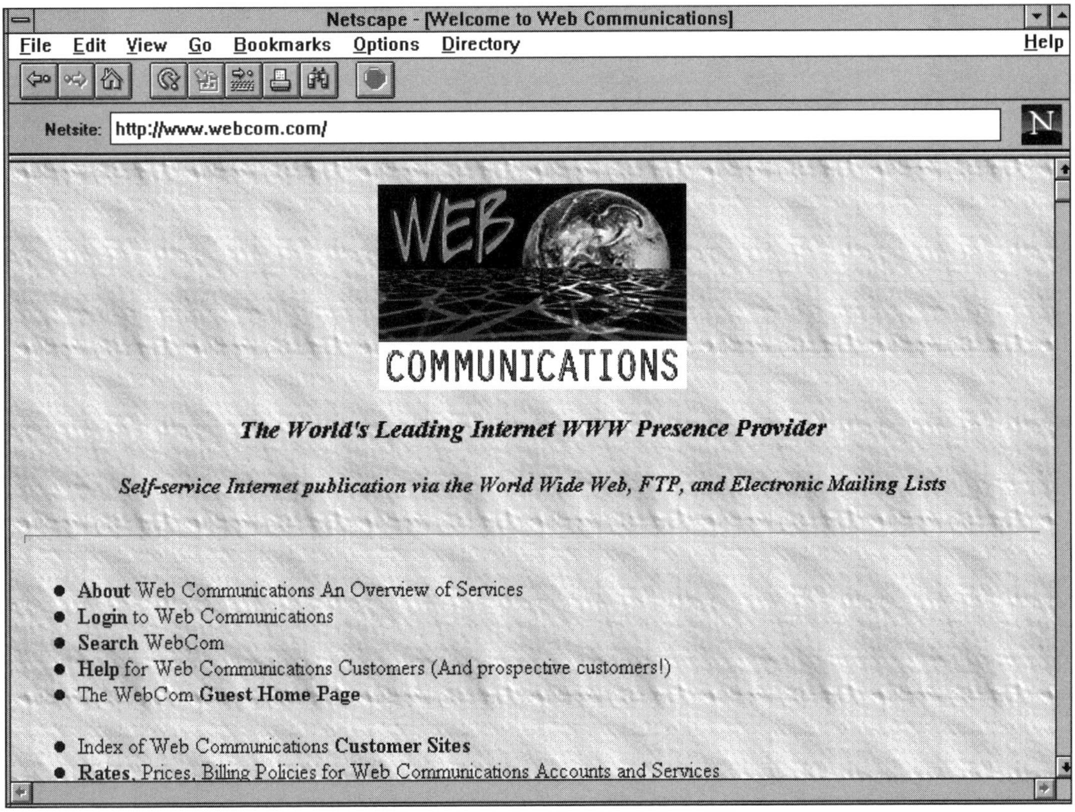

FIGURE 8–7 Web Communications (WebCom) Web Site (Reprinted with permission.)

Be aware of what you are paying for and shop around, because the disparity in prices is huge.

But even if you want to do all the work yourself, you need to make sure that your Internet connection can handle the load. That means dealing with an Internet service provider on issues of bandwidth, dependability, and technical support.

Creating a presence on the Internet can be as simple as giving some files to a Gopher or Web provider. Or it can consist of marketing campaigns using traditional print and broadcast media in conjunction with a Web site. Whatever you decide to do, be sure that you know what your money is buying in graphics, marketing, and programming expertise, as well as hardware and software.

The variety of consulting and service approaches profiled in this chapter give you an idea of what's possible. As you see interesting sites on the Internet, look for who set them up, because you'll often find links to consulting companies and individuals.

CHAPTER 9

Copyright

Publishing on the Internet is not just a matter of hardware and software. This chapter addresses some publishing issues of which you need to be aware. Publishing on the Internet is as much of an advance today as the invention of the encyclopedia was in its day. The encyclopedia brought much of the knowledge of the world to one set of books. The Internet, especially Gopher, WWW, and WAIS, can take you to a new world each day. If your Internet search on a subject one day yields nothing interesting, the same search a day or two later might well bring several new sources. (In fact, searching the Internet through different indexes on the same day will yield different sources, just because no one index covers everything.)

Publishing on the Internet is so simple and inexpensive (relative to traditional publishing techniques) that many who would not previously have considered it will find themselves in the publishing business.

A Different Kind of Publishing

The Internet is a new medium for publishers. That means all the rules aren't set and the full potential isn't known.

Text, Pictures, and More

You can put pictures and text together on the Internet, just as you can in magazines, newspapers, and books, but on the Internet you can publish a lot more. Your files can include sounds and movie clips. Users can run programs from your server to search, calculate interest rates, or make animated figures jump around on the screen. The Internet offers possibilities never before considered in a publishing medium.

You Don't Control the Whole Package

This will be disappointing to the control freaks among us, but the appearance of your documents will vary from browser to browser, and not everyone will start at the beginning of your home page or at the top level of your Gopher server. Because of the open nature of Gopher and WWW, it's possible for a person browsing your server to save the links to the parts of your server that they find most useful. And if they pass those links on, or others get them through index searches, they'll return to your server directly at the point that most interests them, which may not be where you expected at all. Your access logs might show you where this is happening, but they still don't let you control it.

Change

Once a book or a magazine comes off the presses, it's done. There may be revisions, or later editions of a book, but not anytime soon. With the Internet everything is changing all the time. Even your own server. I guarantee it. The constant change is both advantageous and problematic. One advantage is that you can constantly update your material without incurring large reprint expenses. On the other hand, you'll have to spend a significant amount of time maintaining links to other servers and updating your own material.

Technology

Although print technology has advanced quickly in recent years (remember when color pictures first appeared in newspapers?), the speed of change is much greater and much more apparent on the Internet, as with anything having to do with computers. This is an advantage because many more tools are constantly being made available. However, keeping up with the technology can be time-consuming.

Interactivity

More than any other medium, the Internet provides ways to get rapid feedback from your readers. In fact, the real wealth of the Internet is the knowledge and experience that all the participants around the world bring to the table. Usenet News, Internet Relay Chat (see Chapter 6), and Gopher and Web forms give you access to that knowledge and experience. Think about how to take advantage of it.

Geography

Distance simply is not a factor when someone has Internet access. So your words will be available worldwide at no extra cost to you. This international aspect of the Internet is what's most often ignored by those in the United States. Not all servers are in English. But leapfrogging geography leads to one of the great pluses of the Internet: it's possible to build a community where there isn't one geographically. People from all over the world meet via mailing lists, Usenet News, Internet Relay Chat, and HyperNews to discuss their favorite subjects.

Access to Information

More than anything else, the ability to include information from other sites and servers makes the Internet truly a new medium. A footnote in a book or a citation in a magazine take a certain amount of effort and energy to follow up on. But links in Web pages or Gopher sites are so simple to follow that a reader who isn't paying attention may not even notice where all the items are coming from. Thus you could establish a new server about a particular subject, not because you're an expert on that subject but because you've tracked down links to a number of sites that do have experts. And given the Net's interactive nature, you can expand such a site through the contributions of the users. And then you can develop the expertise which you went searching for in the first place.

Copyright

Let me start this section by stating that I am not a lawyer, and the opinions expressed here are no substitute for competent legal counsel. See Table 9–1 for other sources, including the invaluable Copyright FAQ by Terry Carroll.

Copyright is how authors protect themselves from unauthorized copying of their work. There is tremendous concern on all fronts about what copyright means and how it can be enforced in an environment like the Internet, where something has to be copied just to be viewed. And it is difficult if not impossible to ensure that it is not redistributed illicitly by the recipient.

Although legal challenges and changes to existing copyright statutes may help us adapt to the digital age, some facts are not in dispute.

Copyright law does apply to the Internet. The United States and most other countries consider original material copyrighted as soon as it is created and "fixed in a tangible medium." Text on Gopher, WWW, and WAIS servers (as well as e-mail) is considered a tangible medium and thus fulfills that criterion. Copyright protection is granted with or without a copyright notice.

Notice

Nonetheless, you should place a copyright notice on work on the Internet. U.S. law does not require a copyright notice, but giving copyright notice is an announcement of your intention to protect your rights. Clearly marking material as copyrighted makes it harder for someone to claim innocent infringement as a defense. And some countries do require the copyright notice.

TABLE 9–1 Copyright Issues Resources

Documents and Sites	
U.S. Copyright Office *<gopher://marvel.loc.gov:70/11/copyright> <gopher://marvel.loc.gov/>* or telnet to marvel.loc.gov and login as marvel.	This is the U.S. Library of Congress's Gopher site and the section for the U.S. Copyright Office.
Document Marking and Electronic Publishing *<http://www.research.att.com/#docmark>*	This is AT&T Bell Laboratories' Research Site; it contains current research on copyright protection via document marking and encryption techniques.
U.S. Copyright Office—Description of Fair Use *<gopher://marvel.loc.gov:70/00/copyright/fls/fl102>*	Read this then start getting those permissions.
Publication via Electronic Bulletin Board—U.S. Copyright Office *<gopher://marvel.loc.gov:70/00/copyright/other/onlinepub>*	This article discusses whether publishing on an electronic bulletin board is considered publishing under the terms of U.S. copyright law.
International Copyright—U.S. Copyright Office *<gopher://marvel.loc.gov:70/00/copyright/fls/fl100>*	U.S. Copyright Office section on international copyrights.
"Study on Waiver of Visual Artists' Rights"—U.S. Copyright Office *<gopher://marvel.loc.gov:70/00/copyright/news/varastudy>*	This study discusses changes in U.S. copyright law concerning the "moral rights" of visual artists.
Association of Computing Machinery (ACM) Interim Copyright Policies, Author's Guide, and Electronic Publishing Plan *<http://www.acm.org/>*	The ACM is the professional organization for computer scientists. As such, its take on what the future will hold and what copyright will mean may be influential.
"Fair Use in the Electronic Age: Serving the Public Interest" *<http://arl.cni.org/scomm/copyright/uses.html>*	This document from the Association of Research Libraries outlines the lawful uses of copyrighted works by individuals, libraries, and educational institutions in the electronic environment.
"Intellectual Property and the National Information Infrastructure" *<http://www.uspto.gov/niiip.html>*	This is the preliminary draft of the report of the Working Group on Intellectual Property Rights, a subgroup of the Information Infrastructure Task Force (USA).
Legal Information Institute, Cornell Law School *<http://www.law.cornell.edu/lii.table.html> <http://www.law cornell.edu/ topics/copyright.html>*	A very good collection of legal information, including an excellent set of resources on copyright law.

Table 9–1 *(continued)*

Documents and Sites	
WWW Virtual Library—Law *<http://www.law.indiana.edu/law/lawindex.html>*	Subject index for law from the WWW Virtual Library.
The SEAMLESS WEBsite, Law and Legal Resources *<http://seamless.com/>*	A WWW server for lawyers and on legal issues. It includes the Information Law Web with links to documents on copyright and intellectual property.
"Legally Speaking: The NII Intellectual Property Report," by Pamela Samuelson of the University of Pittsburgh *<http://www.eff.org/papers/samuelson.html>*	This is an excellent analysis of proposed changes to U.S. copyright laws to "protect" publishing interests on the Internet.
The Copyright FAQ by Terry Carroll *<http://www.cis.ohio-state.edu/hypertext/faq/usenet/Copyright-FAQ/top.html>*	This extensive 1993 FAQ focuses primarily on U.S. copyright law and includes legal citations. When he wrote it, Terry Carroll was a student in his final year at Santa Clara University School of Law and editor in chief of the *Santa Clara Computer and High Technology Law Journal.*
Copyright Clearance Center Online *<http://www.openmarket.com/copyright/>*	A nonprofit organization providing collective copyright licensing services to help comply with U.S. copyright law.
Usenet Newsgroups	
bit.listserv.vpiej-l	This is a mirror of the VPIEJ-L mailing list below.
Electronic Mailing Lists	
VPIEJ-L To subscribe, send e-mail with the following command to LISTSERV@VTVM1 SUB VPIEJ-L [your_full_name] Archives are available at *<ftp://borg.lib.vt.edu>*	VPIEJ-L is a discussion list on electronic publishing issues (especially relating to scholarly journals) for publishers, editors, technical staff, programmers, librarians, and end users. Topics include software and hardware considerations for creation of, storage of, and access to online journals.
Interactive Publishing Alert *<gopher://marketplace.com/11/ipa>*	Edited by Rosalind Resnick, this monthly electronic newsletter costs $149 per year and tracks trends and developments in the interactive publishing industry.

Table 9–1 *(continued)*

Electronic Mailing Lists	
Information Law Alert *<gopher://marketplace.com/11/ila>*	*Information Law Alert* is a fee-based electronic newsletter on legal disputes involving intellectual property, wireless communications, and telecommunications.
Journal of Electronic Publishing *<http://www.press.umich.edu/jep/JEPsubject.html>*	Check this out.

If you own the copyright to something that you or someone else wishes to publish on the Internet, make sure it is labeled as copyrighted material, with you as the copyright holder. Specify what, if anything, you consider reasonable use of that material. Some of what is available on the Internet is in the public domain. But the presumption that if it's on the Internet, it's free for the taking is false. This is not true, and labeling your material as copyrighted is an important step in changing that presumption and the public perception of the protection of copyright materials.

Proper copyright notice reads simply:

> © John Doe 1995

Given that someone can easily link to just one item in your Gopher, Web, or WAIS server, it would seem appropriate to repeat the copyright notice with each document or file, although U.S. law does not require this. Your copyright protection for original work is the same whether you've given notification or not, but the deterrent effect is greater if each document has its own notice. Using a copyright notice may give you certain advantages in court. In addition, different documents and images will often have different copyright owners, which should be noted. Finally, with the massive indexing by Archie, Veronica, Lycos, the Web Crawler, InfoSeek, Yahoo, and so on, a significant percentage of the browsers reaching your site will not be coming in through your home page. Instead they'll be landing at some document deep in your hierarchy that matched their search criteria. They may never see your home page, so if that's the only place the copyright notice sits, you'll lose whatever deterrent effect such a notice offers.

Permission

Make sure you have written permission for any copyrighted material you put on your server. If it's your own material, put your copyright label on it. Do not copy other people's material into your site without their written permission. This applies to e-mail postings too. If you appropriate copyrighted material for use on your server, you could be infringing on someone's copyright.

Using someone's copyrighted material and giving that person credit does not satisfy copyright law. Copyright is about authors' having *control* of where their work is copied and being compensated for the use of their works. U.S. copyright law states clearly: "Acknowledging the source of the copyrighted material does not substitute for obtaining permission."

A legal exception to copyright law is "fair use" for certain purposes, such as criticism, comment, news reporting, teaching, scholarship, and research. Fair use has definite (although not always clear) limits, however. The U.S. Copyright Office lists four determining factors:

> (1) The purpose and character of the use, including whether such use is of commercial nature or is for nonprofit educational purposes;
> (2) the nature of the copyrighted work;
> (3) the amount and substantiality of the portion used in relation to the copyrighted work as a whole; and
> (4) the effect of the use upon the potential market for or value of the copyrighted work.
>
> The distinction between "fair use" and infringement may be unclear and not easily defined. There is no specific number of

words, lines, or notes that may safely be taken without permission. *<gopher://marvel.loc.gov:70/00/ copyright/fls/fl102>*

If you can't find the copyright owner to get permission, don't use the material. There are limits to what is considered a reasonable effort to locate the copyright owner, but you may have to prove that you made sufficient effort in court, which takes time and money. Consult a copyright lawyer if you cannot find the owner and want to use the material anyway.

Images

With modern graphics tools it is becoming easier to embed a small text copyright notice within an image instead of just placing the notice in text below the image (on Web servers). Gopher and WAIS servers have no provision for sending text alongside an image, so the only way to include a copyright notice is to embed it in the image.

You do face the problem of the need to include the copyright notice on the work and the damage to the image involved in overwriting part of the image with the copyright notice. The aesthetic considerations notwithstanding, embedding the copyright notice in the image would seem to be preferable. Even so, embedding offers limited protection because the notice can be stripped from the image. For additional information about image protection, see Digital Watermarks in Chapter 11.

Public Domain

It is a myth that by not defending a copyright from infringement the material passes into the public domain. The only ways for copyrighted material to pass into the public domain are for the author to explicitly waive all rights to it or for the copyright to expire. The U.S. copyright lasts 50 years past the author's death if the work was created after 1977. However, certain time limits may apply to filing suits for copyright infringement.

International Copyright

International copyright does not exist, but many countries abide by copyright agreements between countries and through international conventions, principally the Berne Convention, to which the United States is a signatory. It is always wise to check the copyright laws of the countries concerned in specific cases and to consult a knowledgeable attorney. The U.S. Copyright Act is available online, thanks to the Legal Information Institute (LII) at Cornell University. LII also provides related materials from the Berne Convention, U.S. Supreme Court copyright decisions since 1990, and links to related online information on copyright law. <***http://www.law.cornell.edu/topics/copyright.html***> Hopefully other nation's copyright laws will soon be available online as well.

Editing for an International Audience

Be aware that the material you put on the Internet is going to be available in more than 60 countries. In addition to determining in which languages you should make your documents and menus available, you'll want to

- Avoid local geographic references that won't make sense to outsiders: the Bay Area, tri-cities, the peninsula.
- Avoid or explain any slang or local references. Many international browsers do read English but will not catch references to, say, certain television programs.
- Avoid large graphics, or offer text alternatives, because many international sites have narrow bandwidth Internet connections, and downloading large images can be extremely slow and painful.
- Avoid making cultural assumptions about your viewers. As you'll see from your logs, your users will come from all over the world.

Summary

The Internet is a different medium, and the rules and potential have not been fully explored. It differs from print media in many ways. For one, the Internet gives you the ability to constantly update or revise what you publish. Unlike print media, revisions involve little extra expense, just the labor to make the changes. The technology is also constantly changing, sometimes within months or weeks. You will find that new tools and capabilities are arriving constantly, so you will need to allocate time to keep abreast of these changes.

Interactivity is one aspect of Internet publishing that is easy to lose sight of. If you provide for it, users can download and view material from your server, upload comments and fill out online surveys or participate in chat sessions, or simply give e-mail feedback. Ignore the interactive nature of the Internet at your peril.

Finally, geography can simply disappear. The Internet makes it possible to build a community around a subject or theme, regardless of geography. If only 20 people in the world are interested in your subject and they all live in different places, you won't be getting together for dinner. But by using a central Web, Gopher, or WAIS server, as well as e-mail mailing lists and Usenet newsgroups, you can unite your efforts. At the same time, there are times when it is appropriate to emphasize geography, such as publishing oral histories from your community, local maps, and tourist information.

Although the Internet is a different publishing medium, copyright laws still apply. Because publishing on the Internet fulfills the legal criterion of being "fixed in a tangible medium," most material is copyrighted automatically as soon as it appears. You should, however, place a copyright notice on your work as an announcement of your intention to protect your rights. This applies to images as well as text. It is probably better to embed your copyright notice in your images so that it cannot be deleted if someone copies the images out of context.

While you should protect your own copyrighted material, you should also respect the copyright rights of others and never use someone else's material without permission. Don't assume that because there's no copyright notice, it's free to use as you want. Acknowledging the source of the material is not enough.

International copyright protection is not guaranteed even though many countries have signed international copyright agreements such as the Berne Convention. Be aware that the material you put on the Internet will be available in more than 60 countries, so you need to avoid local geographic references and slang that won't make sense to others. Also avoid making cultural assumptions about your audience. They will come from all over the world.

CHAPTER 10

Putting It All Together

This chapter profiles and interviews administrators of exemplary and interesting sites from around the world to show you how they've put it all together. The interviews were done by e-mail, telephone, or in person. The profiles are in alphabetical order, but check out Table 10–1 to find summaries for all the sites.

TABLE 10–1 Internet Publishing Profiles

Businesses	Gopher	WWW	WAIS	Charging	Notes
Burlington Coat Factory		√		Not yet	A traditional business experimenting with online technology.
CareerMosaic		√		Free	Jobs and career information online.
Midnight Special Bookstore		√		Orders	A small bookstore that posts events, booklists, and commentary online and also takes book orders.
Palo Alto Real Estate		√		Free	Houses and links to other real estate sites.
Services	**Gopher**	**WWW**	**WAIS**	**Charging**	**Notes**
CICA Shareware	√	√		Free	A huge collection of shareware for Windows.
Project Gutenberg		√		Free	A volunteer effort to put public domain books online for free.
Internet Movie Database		√		Free	A massive international effort to compile film information.
MicroSemanario (U. of Buenos Aires)	√	√		Free	Weekly news from Argentina in Spanish.
Monster Board		√		Mixed	Put your resume on line for free.

Table 10–1 *(continued)*

Services	Gopher	WWW	WAIS	Charging	Notes
OncoLink	√	√		Free	Cancer information for doctors, patients, and families.
On-line Books		√		Free	Index to free online books.
PhoNETic		√		Free	Makes words out of phone numbers.
Virtual Shareware Library		√		Free	An easy way to search for shareware on the major FTP sites.
Print Publishers	**Gopher**	**WWW**	**WAIS**	**Charging**	**Notes**
Britannica Online		√	√	Yes	An online version of the Encyclopaedia Britannica with full text searching and links to related topics, both inside and outside.
CMP TechWeb		√	√	Free	An online archive of 16 technical computer publications.
Playboy		√		Some	*Playboy Magazine* offers magazine excerpts, cartoons, and the Playboy Advisor FAQ.
Art and Music	**Gopher**	**WWW**	**WAIS**	**Charging**	**Notes**
Hearts of Space Radio	√	√		Free	This radio program/record label gives play lists and takes orders.
Kaleidospace	√	√		Orders	An online art gallery, home to all types of art.
L.A. Murals		√		Free	A sampling of some of the 1,500 murals in Los Angeles.
Individuals	**Gopher**	**WWW**	**WAIS**	**Charging**	**Notes**
CyberWire Dispatch	√	√		Free	Via mailing list, Brock Meeks publishes his own column on the machinations of the telecommunications industry.
Travels with Samantha by Philip Greenspun		√		Free	His story of a summer trip across the U.S. is accompanied by more than 250 photographs.
Universities	**Gopher**	**WWW**	**WAIS**	**Charging**	**Notes**
Census Lookup		√		Free	Uses CD-ROMs to let you look up 1990 U.S. Census data online.
InfoUCLA	√	√	v	Free	UCLA library, departmental, and campus information.

Britannica Online
<http://www.eb.com/>

For a company that has been in business for 225 years, Encyclopaedia Britannica certainly got off the mark quickly when it came to publishing on the Internet. According to Doug Paul, executive vice president and general manager of Britannica Publishing Division, and Anne Long, executive director, electronic products, Britannica first started experimenting with multimedia in 1988, with its creation of Compton's Multimedia CD-ROM. Britannica felt strongly then, as now, that you don't experiment with your flagship product. They sold the Compton's New Media Division in 1993 when they saw the CD-ROM business moving toward entertainment instead of education. The initial text-only CD-ROM version of the *Encyclopaedia Britannica* ($995) has enjoyed sales stronger than expected and the recently released illustrated version is also proving to be successful.

The Compton's period was a crucial experience, however, in that it made Britannica aware of the value of electronic publishing and brought the company a joint relationship with an advanced programming group in La Jolla, California. These engineers had close ties to high-level academic computer research, including search-and-retrieval development.

In December 1992 Britannica began exploring the possibility of putting the text of the *Encyclopaedia Britannica* on college and university servers. But they quickly realized that proprietary servers were not the way to go. Their technical advisers then connected them with WAIS, and 18 months later Britannica Online debuted on the Internet. Along the way Britannica garnered the advice of an advisory group of college and university librarians and system administrators.

Britannica is still working out its marketing strategies, adding individual subscriptions and other institutions to what had been only college and university access. It has been using IP address validation

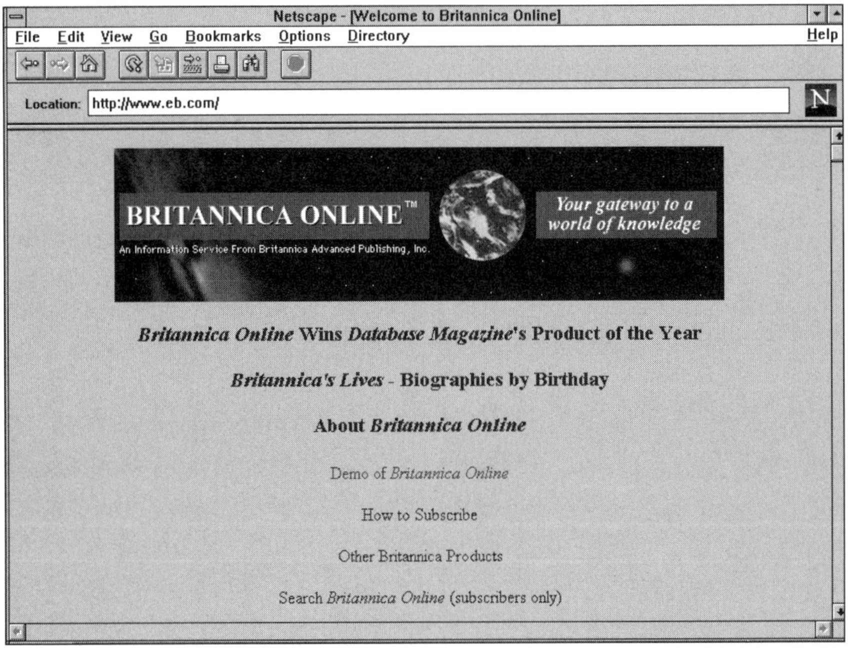

FIGURE 10–1 Britannica Online Web Site (Reprinted with permission.)

but has recently added passwords, which will allow the company to sell individual subscriptions as well as site licenses.

In addition to copyright statements and legal notices scattered here and there, Britannica uses a variety of means to secure its intellectual property rights and those of its third-party providers. Britannica has embedded many of their images with copyright notice instead of putting that information in a line of text beneath the graphic.

Technical Notes

Britannica Online consists of the full range of articles in the print set with a growing number of links (3,000) to outside resources. A section on scuba diving, for example, might link to a scuba-diving home page.

Britannica Online dynamically serves every article. That is, headers and footers are added onto each retrieval, and search terms are bolded in the text. They can also add and suppress links for market and presentation variability without changing the core content.

Britannica has been using a Sun Microsystems Sparc 10 with 64MB of memory as its server behind a firewall. Their server is running Netscape's Secure Server with WAIS, Inc., server software modified to optimize relevance ranking. They enhanced the WAIS engine particularly in searching for phrases, e.g. red herring.

Advice

Harold Kester, vice president and general manager of the Advanced Technology Group of Encyclopedia Britannica North America, urges entrepreneurs to "understand the utility of what you're doing and develop a business plan around that." He notes that brand name identity is almost always a key to success. But for marketing or delivering products on the Internet, it's probably ten times more important.

Burlington Coat Factory
<http://www.coat.com/>

Burlington Coat Factory's Web site offers company information, a map to its stores, and pictures of some of its products. According to Percy S. Young III, director of store systems:

> We had been using the Internet for several years for e-mail and occasional FTP access. When we heard about Mosaic and the Web, we started exploring the Web. In April 1994 I got the idea that Burlington should be able to easily put up a Web presence and should also be able to turn it into a commercial site. In addition, I was interested in the possibilities for internal uses of the Web behind the firewall.

By June I had a functioning server in-house behind the firewall and was creating internal content. By July we had the prototype of the external pages pretty well set up and went to the marketing side to

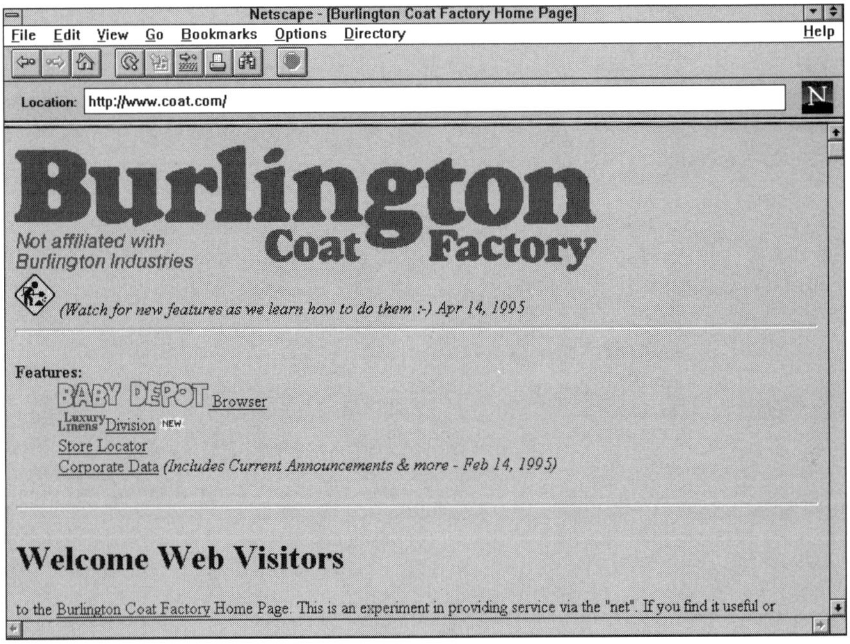

FIGURE 10–2 Burlington Coat Factory Web Site (Reprinted with permission.)

get approval. This was finally set by the end of August, and on September 1, the external server was installed and publicized.

Burlington promoted its site with a coupon good for a $5 discount on a purchase of $50 or more to anyone who filled in an online form commenting on the site. In two and a half months the coupon brought in more than 2,000 responses, which were overwhelmingly positive. At the peak of the offer Burlington was getting more than 100 responses a day and serving an average of 10 documents per visit, Young said.

Burlington plans to use the Net as an active sales site but is waiting for a security protocol to be established. In the meantime the company may use Netscape, "given the wide distribution and acceptance of their browser," Young said.

Actual out-of-pocket costs directly attributable to the Web pages are essentially zero—Burlington's firewall machine and Internet link were already in place and budgeted for other uses, Young said. "We added a one-Gig disk to the machine for the additional storage, so I guess that is extra. The software so far has all been from the Net. We just added a new scanner ($1,000) and are looking at some UNIX-based scanning software ($1,500). In terms of people time, we are looking at about four man months, probably of a senior analyst, about half of the time in learning," Young continued.

Burlington is working on using a Web site to disseminate information to employees; an employee telephone directory and some graphics already are online. Burlington wants to add linked biographies, skill matrices, and weekly status reports and store them as Web documents for easy reference, Young said. The company's long-range goals include integrating its training and documentation on the Web or similar multimedia graphical environments.

Technical Notes

Burlington runs its Web server on a Sun Sparcstation with a firewall and runs the NCSA HTTPD server. The images were scanned on PCs and then moved to UNIX with some hand editing done via simple pixel editors. Burlington is looking at more sophisticated imaging solutions.

All the scripts for forms processing were written in C based on the models provided with the NCSA server. One set of linked entry forms has the first form run a program that creates the next form and so on, passing "session" information along to ensure continuity across four linked entry screens.

Advice

Young thinks that anyone who sees the Net as a pot of gold "is probably dreaming right now, but for those who look to learn from their adventures in Web publishing, and for those who seek to further the culture of the 'Net, the minimal costs are far outweighed by the potential future opportunities. . . . By having started early, we hope to keep ahead of the competition."

CareerMosaic
<http://www.careermosaic.com/>

CareerMosaic, launched by Bernard Hodes Advertising, provides employers with a cost-effective way to tell prospective employees about the company. According to Tim Gibbon, executive vice president, and Bruce Moore, director of systems and planning for the Western region, companies can present as much information as they want, including graphics, annual reports, and the full text of a pension plan. With the aid of Bernard Hodes Advertising, companies can communicate their "corporate personality" in hypermedia, using text files, graphics, audio, photographs, and video.

Companies represented include Bellcore, First USA (financial services), the Good Guys! (electronic retail chain), Intel, Intuit, National Semiconductor, NeXT, Sun Microsystems, Symantec, Union Bank, Wells Fargo Bank, and Cedars-Sinai Medical Center of Los Angeles.

Online job application forms are in the works. CareerMosaic's Web site includes an example of the "ultimate résumé," a multimedia extravaganza by Joe Mack. Moore said the most innovative thing CareerMosaic does is publish so that the material is equally accessible from all types of Web browsers. The challenge has been to keep CareerMosaic's Web designers from using all the experimental HTML features that Netscape and others are devising. CareerMosaic needs to ensure that its business is delivered to the largest audience possible.

Technical Notes

To write HTML pages on the fly CareerMosaic created a custom database application built on the 4th Dimension database package running on PowerPCs. CareerMosaic's Web server is a Sun Sparcstation 5 with 64MB of RAM running NCSA HTTPD and a modified freeWAIS. The server is rarely taxed and has about 3 million connections per month.

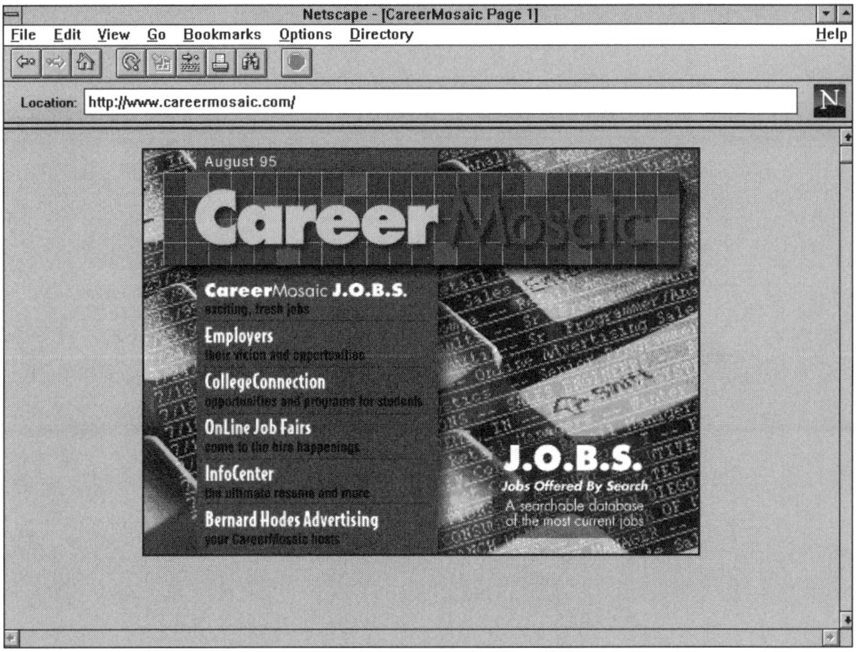

FIGURE 10–3 CareerMosaic Web Site (Reprinted with permission.)

Advice

Moore said that the most important lesson is not to forget what you know about your own area. Consider your objectives, and don't be confused by the technology. People look for the 100 percent solution, but forget the 80 percent solution that can be implemented quickly.

CICA Shareware Repository

<http://www.cica. indiana.edu/>, <gopher://gopher.cica.indiana. edu>*, and *<ftp://ftp.cica.indiana.edu>

The Center for Innovative Computer Applications (CICA) at Indiana University is one of the world's largest collections of Microsoft Windows public domain and shareware applications, tips, utilities, drivers, bitmaps, and such. The center has more than 5,300

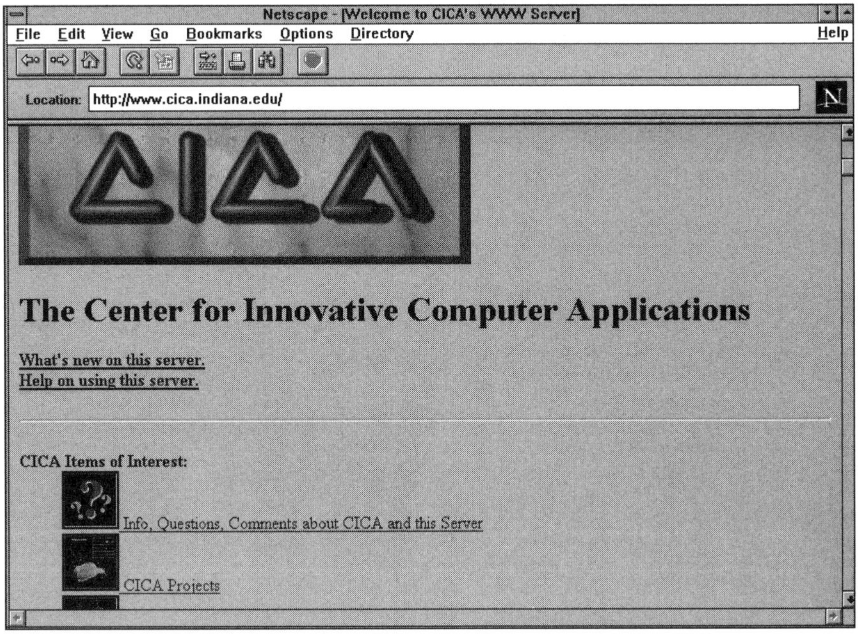

FIGURE 10–4 CICA Web Site (Reprinted with permission.)

files totalling 1.5GB. Its Web site sees approximately 50,000 logins per month requesting more than 70GB of those files, for an average of 2.3GB per day of file transfers. The site is considered so valuable that it is mirrored by at least 15 other sites around the world, including sites in England, Holland, Germany, Finland, Sweden, Switzerland, Israel, Australia, Taiwan, Thailand, Japan, Singapore, and Poland.

According to FTP librarian and administrator Michael Regoli, the site is maintained by volunteers on an old machine. His real job is director of publications for the Organization of American Historians, also at Indiana University. He recounts some problems in running the CICA FTP site:

> On the administrative computing side of things, network bandwidth has been the biggest obstacle. People think we are limited to 45 connections [from the Internet] during the day because we haven't the horsepower on the desktop to service that many users. They couldn't be further from the truth. If left unchecked,

and wide open, the FTP site could easily consume half, if not more, of Indiana's three T-1 links.

Technical Notes

The FTP server is a Sun Sparcstation 1 with 28MB of RAM. It will be moving to a 90Mhz Pentium (PCI bus) with 64MB of RAM and a PCI ethernet card for faster network access. Regoli said that CICA uses Washington University's FTP daemon (FTPD) for FTP services and has been pleased with its performance. CICA's Gopher server uses GN, and Regoli says it is an intelligent, load-aware server. CICA's Web server runs NCSA HTTPD on a Silicon Graphics Challenge M running Irix 5.3, with 64MB of main memory (85 MIPS).

The bandwidth is effectively increased by the more than 15 mirror sites because they provide an entirely new set of lines into the archive. CICA finds they are extremely important in handling demand.

CMP TechWeb
<http://techweb.cmp.com/techweb/>

CMP publishes 16 computer trade magazines; *CMP TechWeb*, which started November 1994, is its platform for interactive publishing, which the company expects will become a big business itself. *TechWeb* offers recent headlines, a resource guide for technical job hunters, links to current issues of its magazines, and an extremely useful full-text search of its issues published since January 1994. Since July 31, 1995, *TechWeb* has required that you register with the company for these services, but all that involves is filling out an online survey. *TechWeb* also has ads and links to its sponsor sites.

The CMP magazine list includes *Communications Week, Comm Week International, Computer Reseller News, Computer Retail Week, Electronic Buyers News, Electronic Engineering Times, Home PC, Information Week, Interactive Age, Internet Business Report,*

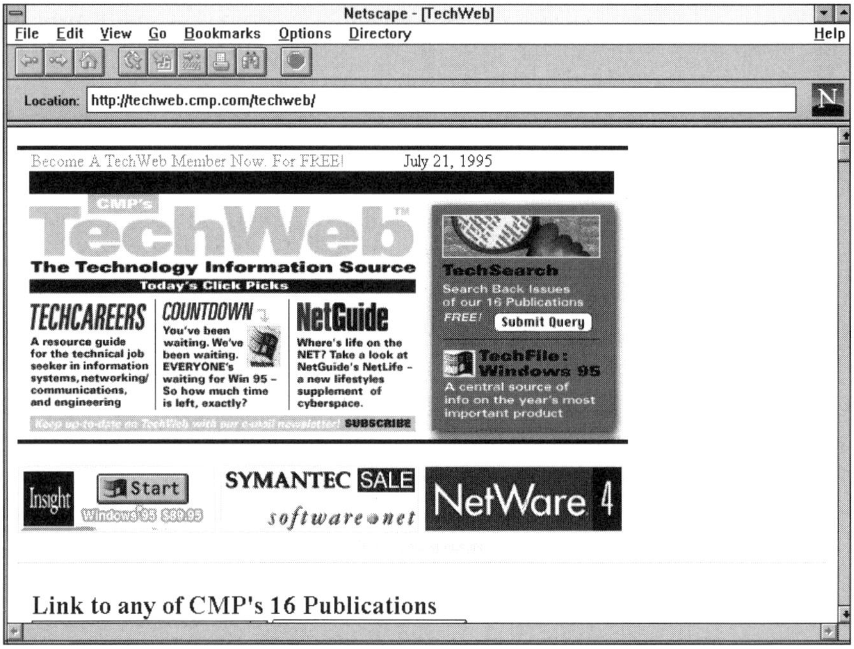

FIGURE 10–5 CMP TechWeb Web Site (Reprinted with permission.)

Max CD-ROM, Netguide, Network Computing, OEM Magazine, VAR Business, and *Windows Magazine.* Most are "controlled subscription" magazines, which means that they are free to people who hold jobs that put them in the target populations the magazines' advertisers want to reach.

Users query *TechWeb*'s WAIS searcher by filling out an online form that permits a user to specify which (or all) of the 16 CMP magazines to search, as well as starting and ending dates, title, author, section, column, and text. The results screen has been formatted nicely—it displays title, source magazine, date, relevance ranking, and file size.

Technical Notes

TechWeb's site runs on UNIX with Netscape and WAIS server software. It has a T-1 connection to the Internet and handles 175,000 connections per week.

Advice

Mitchell York, publishing director of CMP Interactive Media, says:

> It's wonderful that literally anyone can now be a publisher with a potential audience of millions. But the fact is most Web sites don't have staying power—that is, the ability to attract one user more than once or twice. . . . It's quite okay for someone to put up a Web site for personal enjoyment, but if the purpose is to build an audience, you're in a different league. In this arena, the key is to have targeted content aimed at an audience that needs the information you supply, and that the information is refreshed often. (In our business, this means at least daily, if not several times a day.)

CyberWire Dispatch
<http://cyberwerks.com/cyberwire>* and *<gopher://cyberwerks.com/11/cyberwire>

In September 1993 readers of the WELL's Wired conference were greeted with a new topic that audaciously began with:

> This is the place for breaking news from the CyberFront. There's no press card issued; you hammer out the copy, jack in and upload. In some cases, you'll read news "as it happens." In other cases, there could be a string of dispatches running throughout the day as an issue or situation develops.
>
> Quick, off-the-cuff, interactive journalism.
>
> You don't need credentials, a degree or editorial approval.
>
> You do need attitude, desire and nerve.

It was followed by the first issue of what became Brock N. Meeks's *CyberWire Dispatch* with its trademark opening, "Jacking in from . . ." Over subsequent weeks the *Dispatch* quickly developed a reputation on and off the WELL for brash, occasionally off-color, but always accurate reporting on federal telecommunications policy and the antics of those working to change cyberspace for better or worse.

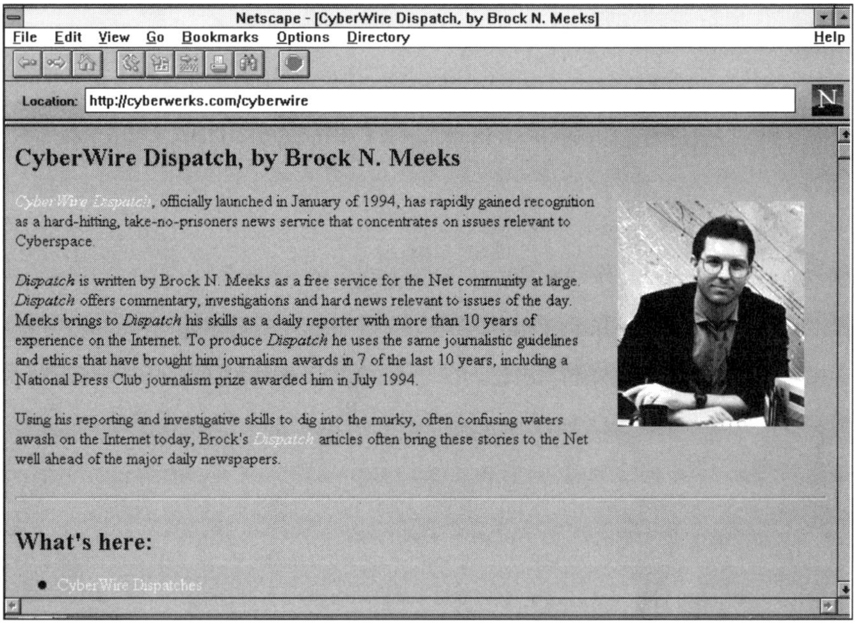

FIGURE 10–6 CyberWire Dispatch Web Site (Reprinted with permission.)

Meeks, an award-winning veteran journalist who is Washington bureau chief for *INTER@CTIVE WEEK*, understands better than anyone the speed, reach, and freedom associated with online publishing. *CyberWire Dispatch* consistently scoops the print media. Although Meeks's early dispatches were used without acknowledgment in the bylined articles of others, the now-copyrighted *Dispatch* has been cited by national news wires and publications like the *Economist.*

Dispatch was originally distributed only on the WELL and over the com-priv mailing list. In mid-1994 Meeks asked Liberty Hill Cyberwerks's Eric Theise what it would take to set up a dedicated *Dispatch* mailing list. Theise, a supporter of Meeks's work, set up a list and searchable Web/Gopher archives of back issues in a matter of days at no charge. The Web site has links to organizations Meeks thinks you should know about, including the Electronic Privacy Information Center, Voters Telecomm Watch, and other organizations working to preserve constitutional freedoms on the Internet.

The e-mail mailing list has about 7,100 subscribers, many of which are local mail exploders (which resend to many other addresses). *Dispatch* is known to circulate on internal U.S. government e-mail networks, including the Pentagon's.

Technical Notes

Combined Web and Gopher traffic through the *Dispatch*'s archives average roughly 1,500 hits per day. Because Meeks uses few graphics, most of those hits are document retrievals.

The *CyberWire Dispatch* archive server runs GN for Gopher/WWW services on Liberty Hill Cyberwerks's main server, an Intel 486/66 with 32MB of RAM, running BSD UNIX.

The mailing list is managed with Majordomo.

Liberty Hill Cyberwerks uses a simple sed script to reformat the mailings into a form usable by the Web and Gopher server. Appropriate links are added by hand to HTML versions of *Dispatch.*

Advice

Theise says:

> Never underestimate the amount of time it's going to take to manage a large mailing list. Despite the fact that Majordomo, LISTSERV, and Listproc [three different e-mail list server programs] automate many of the functions needed to keep a list going, you'll be amazed—you'll despair?—over what can happen with a large list. People abandon their e-mail accounts without unsubscribing. Bounced mail comes back with headers that take minutes to decipher, if they're decipherable at all. People try to spam [send unrelated messages to] your list. And, as anyone who's been on a list for more than two days knows, there's a steady stream of people who don't know how to unsubscribe from the list, even if you've told them repeatedly.

Hearts of Space Radio/Records

<http://www.hos. com/>, <gopher://hos.com>, <mailto:info@hos.com>

Liberty Hill Cyberwerks' Eric Theise tells this story about driving from San Francisco to Minneapolis for the 1993 Gopher Developers' Conference:

> In the middle of Nebraska in the middle of the night, a National Public Radio affiliate began broadcasting the syndicated Hearts of Space program. After a very long day of country and western and classic rock, the HoS mix of space, ambient, electronic, and ethnic music was a welcome change to these tired ears.
>
> At the end of the program, producer/host Stephen Hill announced that program playlists were available in the WELL's radio conference. . . . As soon as I arrived, I sent him e-mail asking if he'd be interested in making his playlists available beyond the WELL's subscription-only doors.

Within weeks, the duo had opened the Hearts of Space section of the GN-based WELL Gopher, offering a searchable archive of play lists from mid-1990 to the present, a list of the nearly 300 stations carrying the program, a catalog of CD and cassette releases on Hearts of Space's record labels, and a simple "About Hearts of Space" file. They uploaded new playlists every week and began to develop a presence on the Usenet newsgroup rec.music.newage, Theise recalled.

A year after they teamed up, the Web was becoming the information space of choice. After some discussion Liberty Hill Cyberwerks was selected to create and maintain the standalone Hearts of Space Internet site, hos.com. The Gopherspace and listener mailing list came online in fall 1994; early 1995 saw the opening of the Web site and the installation of an e-mail gateway between Hearts of Space's office/studio network and the Internet, Theise said.

From a marketing perspective, one of the most valuable features of the Hearts of Space Web site is the ability to link selections in the Hearts of Space Radio playlists to descriptions, cover art, and sound samples from releases on Hearts of Space's own labels. Hearts of

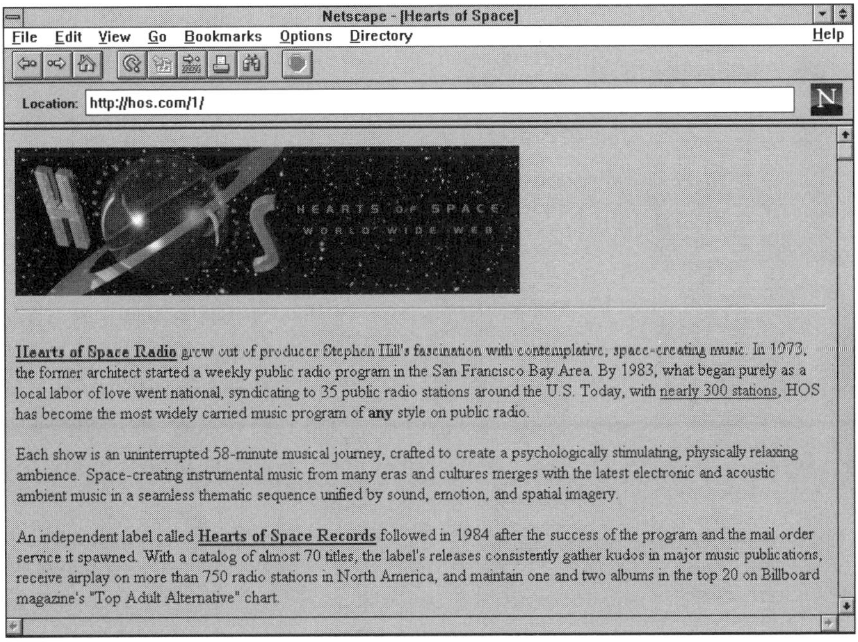

FIGURE 10–7 Hearts of Space Radio/Records Web Site
(Reprinted with permission.)

Space is arguably the most active New Age label on Usenet, monitoring rec.music.newage, rec.music.ambient, alt.radio.networks.npr, and other groups for discussion and questions about its programming and artists.

Technical Notes

Marking up five years' worth of playlists by hand would have been impossible, so Theise created a relatively simple awk (UNIX utility) script to recognize HoS releases by title and insert links in addition to the boilerplate HTML. Simple awk and sed scripts were used extensively in the initial formatting of the release sheets for the approximately 70 releases from Hearts of Space, and they still use sed scripts to facilitate the weekly site updates.

The Hearts of Space Internet server is an Intel 486/66-based computer with 16MB of RAM. It runs the BSD/OS UNIX operating system, uses Majordomo as its mailing list manager and info@hos.com autoresponder, and GN as its Gopher and Web server. It's a textbook example of using GN to deliver materials via Gopher and the Web and makes fairly extensive use of GN's built-in search facilities so that browsers can search the play list archives and the recordings catalog. The server is housed at Liberty Hill Cyberwerks and connected to the Internet at T-1 speeds.

As of July 1995 nearly 2,100 listeners receive the weekly playlist via e-mail, and the autoresponder—mentioned at the end of each radio broadcast—averages dozens of inquiries per day. Combined Web and Gopher traffic averages around 1,100 hits per day. Credit card orders for CDs and cassettes are accepted through Web forms and e-mail; customers concerned with security can fax their orders or send them through regular mail.

Hearts of Space's internal QuickMail system exchanges e-mail with the Internet using the StarNine MailLink Remote UUCP gateway, allowing staff to be in communication with artists, radio stations, distributors, and others worldwide.

InfoUCLA
<http://www.ucla.edu/>

UCLA's Web site is similar to many university Web sites in that it provides central access to campus resources. These include the campus e-mail and phone directory, campus map, library hours and policies, library card catalog access, admissions and records information, administrative policies, central computing, associated students, bookstore, and student newspaper, and a diverse set of departmental Web, Gopher, and FTP servers. Those departmental sites are rich with content and will become more so as faculty, staff, and students learn new tools. Many research centers are putting at least some of their research material up, and several national journals based at UCLA are thinking about turning electronic.

The interesting thing that UCLA is doing, though, is providing virtually free dial-in SLIP/PPP access to the Internet and e-mail for

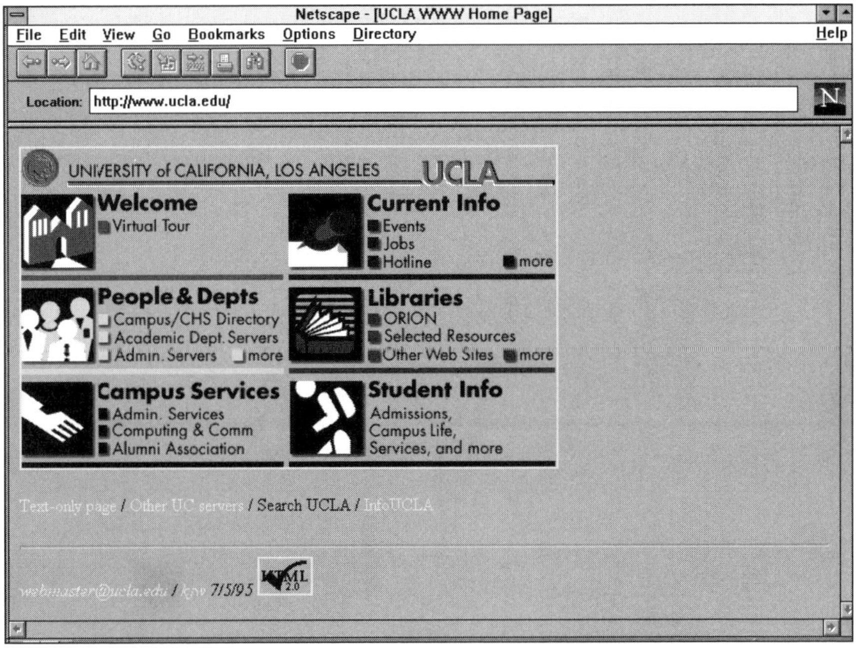

FIGURE 10–8 InfoUCLA Web Site (Reprinted with permission. © Regents University of California.)

all students, staff, and faculty. Called BruinOnline (after the campus mascot), this ambitious project started as a reaction to an increase, from one year to the next, of 10,000 undergraduates who wanted e-mail accounts. At the time those were mainframe e-mail accounts, and that huge increase began to provoke worries of affecting mainframe performance.

The implications of every student's having e-mail access (from campus labs, if a student didn't have a computer at home) are just starting to hit the faculty. The possibilities are fascinating: receiving homework assignments by e-mail, creating local Usenet newsgroups or mailing lists for every class, starting online discussion groups and holding online office hours, building class Web sites, and sending and updating problem sets by e-mail or FTP. Some faculty members are already preparing their lesson plans in HTML, and a Slavic languages professor had his students learn enough HTML to annotate a Russian novel.

Technical Notes

InfoUCLA sits on an IBM RISC system/6000, model 59H, with 256MB of RAM, running NCSA HTTPD, freeWAIS, Gopher, and QI (a campus directory service). This machine also provides Usenet News for the campus.

Internet Movie Database
<http://www.msstate. edu/Movies/>, <http://www.msstate.edu/Movies/alternative_access.html>

The Internet Movie Database WWW server is a repository of movie details, reviews, ratings, and trivia as well as biographies and filmographies of actors and directors. The original Cardiff, Wales, site is mirrored by servers in Australia, the United States, Germany, Japan, Korea, and South Africa.

The Internet Movie Database began in 1989 with periodic postings to the Usenet newsgroup rec.arts.movies. Since then it's grown into an "international volunteer effort whose principal objective is to provide useful and up-to-date movie information freely available on-line, across as many systems and platforms as possible," according to its FAQ. It covers more than 47,000 movies with more 630,000 filmography entries and is expanding continuously. The database is available via FTP, WWW, and e-mail and grows by about 7,000 filmography additions and 500 new titles per week. It includes more types of movie information than you can imagine in an amazing amount of detail.

All data are contributed freely by movie lovers around the world, and the management is all volunteer. The link to rec.arts.movies and other Usenet Newsgroups continues. The author of the Web interface to the Internet Movie Database (Rob Hartill) was inducted into the WWW Hall of Fame in 1994, and the database itself received an honorable mention in the Best Entertainment category. The highly coordinated international volunteer pursuit of a common interest epitomizes what is possible on the Internet.

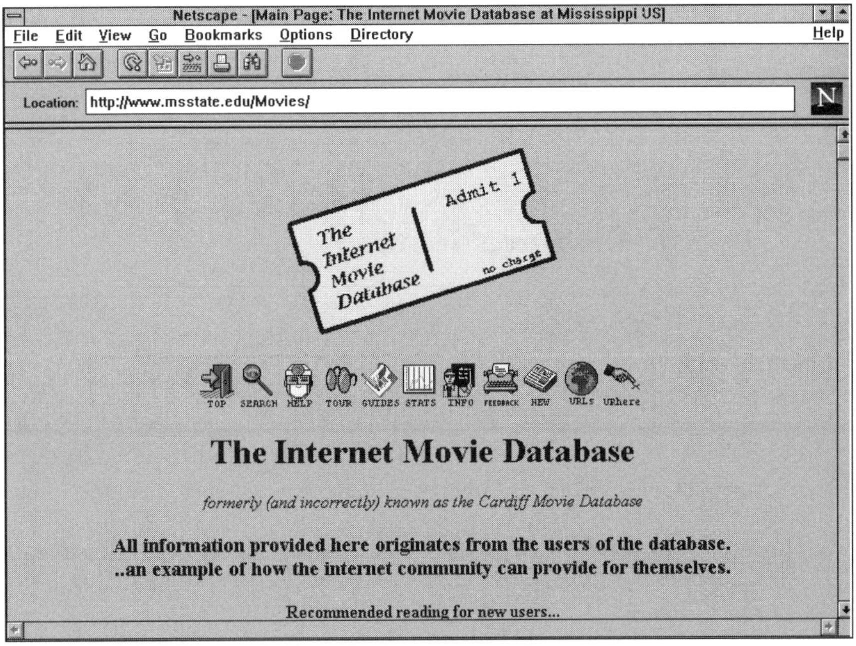

FIGURE 10–9 Internet Movie Database Web Site (Reprinted with permission.)

The users maintain the database and police its accuracy. Anyone who uses the database can fill out an online form or submit corrections or updates by e-mail. Database managers have special scripts to help them update the database and keep them consistent. One script warns managers when updates are being made to database items that they have marked "complete" or "verified complete." This is a method of ensuring that good data don't get corrupted by accident or malice while relying on user-supplied data and input.

Hartill, who manages WWW interface to the database, and Col Needham, overall coordinator and creator of the Internet Movie Database, write:

> The database is maintained by a core team of 15 people at the moment. For most of them, it's a case of giving up a few hours of their spare time each week and being able to quickly respond to a problem that needs fixing. In the first four months of 1995 about 1,500 different people contributed new data to the system—some just a few lines and others tens of thousand additions.

Hartill adds, "A few of the managers spend 10 or more hours a week, just trying to stay up to date with submissions, and then there's Col, who probably spends more time working on the database than the rest of us put together."

Technical Notes

The voting system (users get to vote on the ratings of any movie they look up) is coordinated independent of the different mirror sites because it actually predates them. Votes are e-mailed to a vote collection address, and updates are processed weekly and distributed to the mirror sites. Mirroring between the sites is done by simply FTPing the updates.

The original interface with the movie database was developed in UNIX shell script language and over the years was converted to faster C code. When the WWW interface was added, the data were rearranged for optimal speed for the most common types of query, but that meant losing the wider range of query types possible via the traditional interface. The database was also indexed differently to save space and allow for quicker response by the Web server. Special programs were written in C and Perl for different types of queries.

The mail server runs on a Pentium machine running SCO (Santa Cruz Operation, Inc.) UNIX; the main FTP site is a NeXT machine. Cardiff's WWW server runs a Sparc 5 donated by Sun Microsystems Ltd. Until January 1995 Cardiff's Web server was running from an overused Sparc 10. Serving the Web brought it to its knees at busy periods.

All time, computers, and effort are donated. The mail server and the server that collects contributions to the database are provided courtesy of the PC Users Group in England.

From Cardiff alone the database gets more than 60,000 connections a day. The combined number of requests to the database via WWW exceeds 150,000 a day, and with new U.S.-based mirror sites in the pipeline, these figures are sure to grow dramatically. For current statistics at the Cardiff Web site see <*http://www.cm.cf.ac.uk/htbin/Graphs/todays_stats*>.

Advice

Rob Hartill: Don't be put off by the size of the Internet. It's a friendly place with plenty of people willing to give good advice or offer help. . . . Don't be fooled by the silky smooth duck gliding across the pond—there's a hell of a lot of kicking going on underneath. Things don't always run smoothly.

Col Needham: Start small and keep at it. . . . Be wary of an endless series of e-mail questions from users who can't be bothered to read the FAQ.

Kaleidospace

<http://kspace.com/>, <gopher://gopher.kspace.com>, <ftp://ftp.kspace.com>

This arts-oriented Web, Gopher, and FTP site allows artists in all media to showcase and even sell their work on the Internet. Artists pay a set-up fee of $100 and then either a monthly fee of $25 or a 10 percent commission on their sales. Artists can then announce future exhibits and installations, list their biographies, allow sample downloads of their music, writings, photographs, paintings, or rotating video clips of their sculpture or ceramics. Also, any Kaleidospace artist may set up a time for online meetings using the Kaleidospeak chat room.

Before Kaleidospace had a secure online transaction system running, its procedure was to take orders via online forms or e-mail and then call back to confirm the order and take credit card information. Now Kaleidospace is running Netscape's Commerce Server for all the artists, so it can take secure orders directly over the Internet. The site also supports phone, fax, and e-mail orders and maintains the call-back option for unsecured orders.

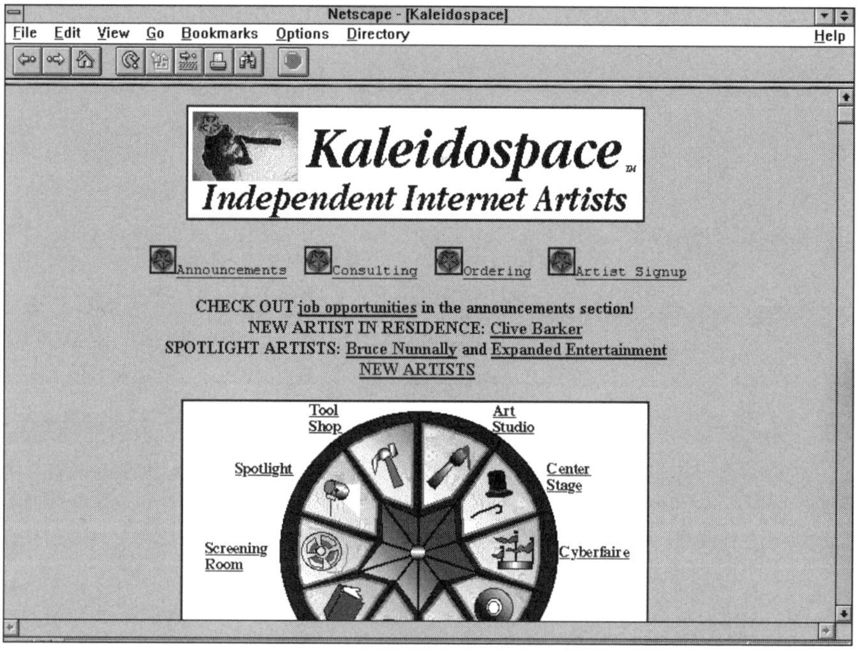

FIGURE 10–10 Kaleidospace Web Site (Reprinted with permission.)

Jeannie Novak, Kaleidospace founder and principal programmer and designer, started the Santa Monica, California–based company in January 1994 because, as an independent musician, she wanted an alternative way to distribute her album of classical and acoustic piano music. The Internet, particularly WWW, seemed ideal and she thought other artists would pay to join her. As of July 1995 Kaleidospace had Web pages for more than 200 artists and had moved into Web consulting with nearly 100 commercial clients.

Novak said, "We do ALL the HTML for the artists. We also do all the scanning/digitization, though some artists provide us with predigitized material. This way we create a consistent interface for the users and are able to support artists who don't have computer access (about 40 percent)." Pete Markiewicz, who does general support at Kaleidospace, adds that Novak writes all the HTML by hand but is working in Perl to create auto-entry forms specifically targeted for Kaleidoscape Web page formats. They are also setting these up so that client companies can add material to their own servers easily.

Technical Notes

The primary Web server runs on an accelerated Sun Sparc 2 with 64MB of RAM running a modified version of NCSA HTTPD. It was modified to enhance security.

The Netscape Commerce Server runs on a Pentium 90 with 64MB of RAM. The combined Gopher-FTP server was run off a Macintosh Quadra with 24MB of RAM for a year, but Kaeidospace is moving it to a UNIX machine. Quadra's performance was fine, but the Macintosh is more useful as a development platform. Novak and Markiewicz claimed that Web site development is easier on Macintoshes, so they build them there and transfer them to UNIX later.

They frequently get several thousand individual users a day (with "hits" in the hundreds of thousands).

The chat room is done with WebChat server software. <***http://www.irsociety.com/wbs.html***>

Kaleidospace runs a virtual host system for its commercial clients to allow each to have its own host name.

Advice

Jeannie Novak advises:

> The main way to cope with high traffic is to increase RAM to 64 or 128 MB. If access becomes higher in the future, we will probably create a single "virtual" server from several machines.
>
> Style and design are much more important than fancy HTML tricks. Make sure you cross-promote and cultivate relationships with other sites on the Internet. And be prepared to work very hard.
>
> Make sure you have focused, real content not available elsewhere. Too many "cybermalls" put up anything they can get money for rather than offering variety within a central theme. The resulting "hodgepoge.coms" are jarring and ultimately irritating to the users. On our own site we work with artists, musicians, writers, CD-ROM authors, performers, filmmakers,

animators, software developers, and artisans—but they're ALL independent [meaning not under contract]. Real content on the Internet is always valuable.

Los Angeles Murals Home Page
<http://latino.sscnet.ucla.edu/murals/>

This Web site is attempting to document and display some of the 1,500 murals in Los Angeles. It is a combined effort of the Social and Public Arts Resource Center, the Mural Conservancy of Los Angeles, UCLA Chicano Studies Research Center, Social Sciences Computing at UCLA, and Robin Dunitz, who is contributing the contents of her book, *Street Gallery: A Guide to 1,000 L.A. Murals* to the Web site.

Plans include providing a clickable map of Los Angeles, with links to murals by location, artists' biographies, and lists of murals by artist, sponsor, neighborhood, and subject. It will also include related documents by artists and art organizations.

Technical Notes

This site is run on a Sun Sparcstation 10, with 36MB of RAM and running NCSA's HTTPD server.

MicroSemanario
<gopher://gopher.uba.ar/11/microsem>, <ftp://ftp.informatik.uni-muenchen.de/local/rec/argentina/micros>, and *<http://www.informatik.uni-muenchen.de/rec/argentina>*

MicroSemanario (*semanario* means weekly in Spanish) was born to serve the many Argentine ex-patriates around the globe. Because of the country's economic woes, many Argentine scholars and scientists left during the last 30 years to continue their careers in the United States and Europe, with smaller numbers in Brazil, Israel, and

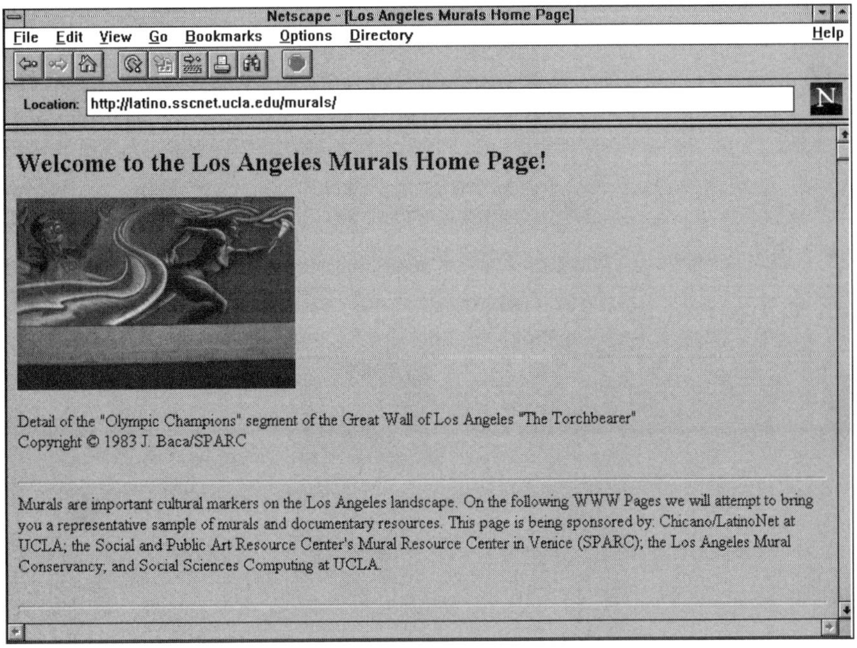

FIGURE 10–11 Los Angeles Murals Web Site (Reprinted with permission.)

Australia. In 1989 and 1990 this situation sharply worsened because of hyperinflation. Because detailed news about Argentina can be difficult to obtain outside of Argentina, especially in Spanish, the School of Sciences (Facultad de Ciencias Exactas) of the University of Buenos Aires decided in November 1990 to start sending out Argentine news by e-mail over the Internet.

This free e-mail newsweekly is divided into sections dealing with politics, economics, society, culture, education, science, and sports. According to Guillermo Gimenez de Castro, originator and director of MicroSemanario, "MicroSemanario is a weekly summary, and as such we take our sources from all the forms of press available: oral, written, and televised. We select the news that seems relevant and write summaries of it. Whenever necessary, we indicate the source. But we DO NOT transcribe the news. We also send news of the academic world and job opportunities, sports scores, and something of the cultural life."

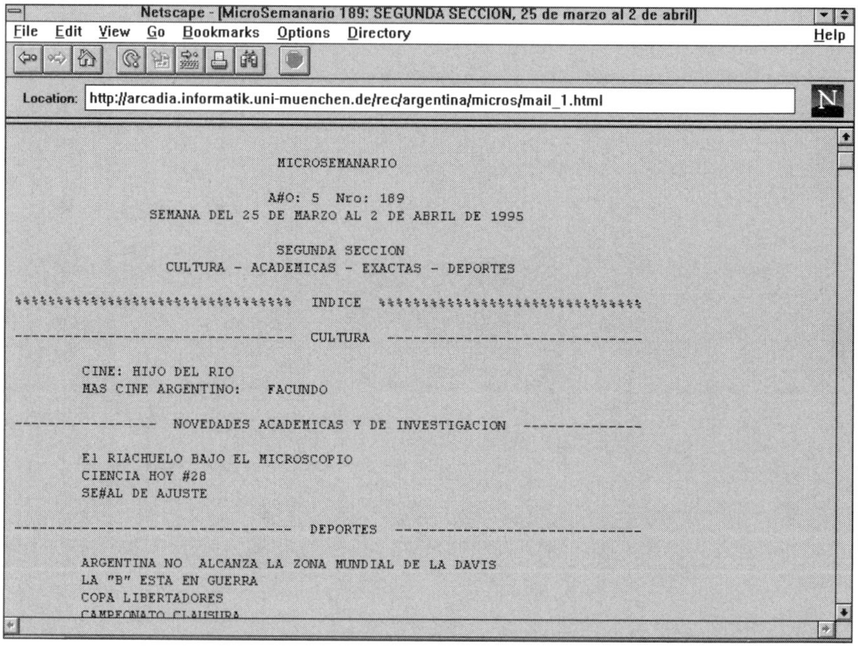

FIGURE 10–12 MicroSemanario Web Site (Reprinted with permission.)

MicroSemanario is distributed through two mailing lists totalling more than 3,000 subscribers and has an estimated readership, including family members and friends of the recipients, of 6,000 to 9,000. Among their subscribers are American and British high schools and Latin American studies departments at universities. MicroSemanario is also read by non-Argentines, who usually have had some relation with Argentina. The size of the weekly edition has grown to roughly 60K so they split it into two parts to avoid e-mail problems.

MicroSemanario gets some support from the university but relies to a large extent on volunteer labor for the writing and editing of the news summaries. The director's job is also unpaid. Current and back issues (more than 200) are archived on the University of Buenos Aires's Gopher site. There are also Web and FTP archives in Germany. (See URLs at beginning of entry.)

According to an article for *Internet News* by Ricardo Bravo (Centro de Comunicacion Cientifica-Universidad de Buenos Aires) and director Gimenez de Castro, "The main aim of MicroSemanario is not that of journalism, but to provide fellow-countrymen something to stay in touch with their society, alleviating in part the feeling of losing links to Argentina. Moreover, Micro usually provides information on living conditions in Argentina, and attends—as far as possible—to questions of readers wishing to come back."

To subscribe to MicroSemanario send e-mail to majordomo@ccc.uba.ar and in the body of the message put *subscribe micro*.

Technical Notes

MicroSemanario is sent out entirely in low-end ASCII (32–127) to avoid e-mail translation problems. Accents are omitted, which they say generally causes little confusion. Special characters are replaced with #, and though it doesn't look good, it does cross e-mail systems consistently.

The University of Buenos Aires's Gopher and WWW server runs on a Sparc Sparcstation.

Midnight Special Bookstore
<http://msbooks.com/msbooks>

Midnight Special is an independent bookstore in Santa Monica, California, that has its own WWW site. The store rents Web space for $75 per month and is busy converting store sections into Web pages with resident experts, e-mail discussions, book reviews, and employee recommendations. Midnight Special is a social and cultural bookstore that presents "books and ideas to change the world." The store's motto is taken from Bertolt Brecht: "Hungry man, reach for the book: it is a weapon."

Midnight Special's Web site advertises its calendar of events and offers weekly lists of best-sellers. It also sells videos of its regularly scheduled readings by, and interviews with, authors. Its inventory is searchable by title, author, and ISBN number for 90,000 titles and

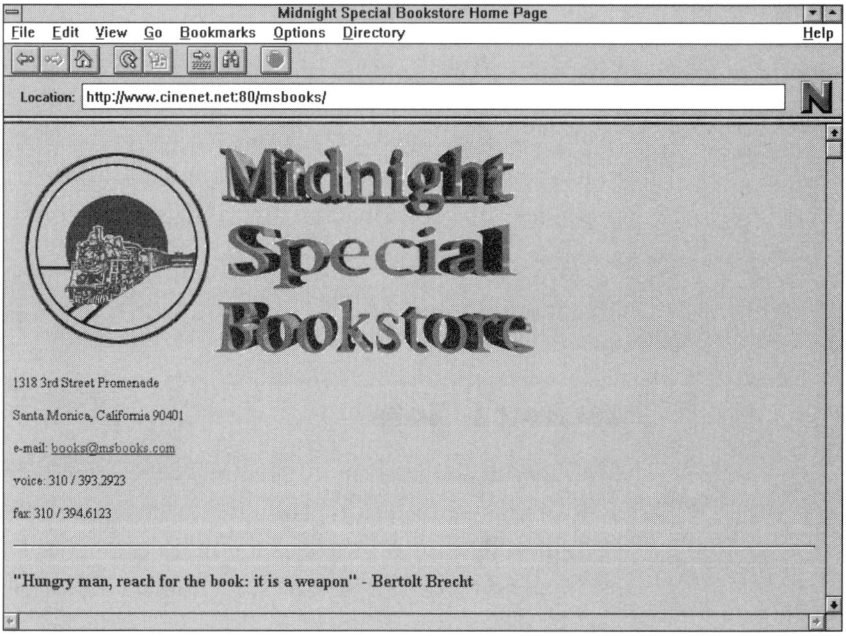

FIGURE 10–13 Midnight Special Bookstore Web Site (Reprinted with permission.)

leads to order forms along with the search results. The bookstore also sells political t-shirts and posters. Midnight Special's Web site also offers opinions and solicits opinions from users (just fill out an online form). And if you can't think of anything to say, check out the list of issues, with links to related books.

Tony Cappelli, the bookstore's Webmaster, has even started a Web column called "Tools of Dissent" in which he comments on the latest Internet technology and how it might be used for social and political action. The bookstore used the Internet to expand its market after several book superstores have moved in down the block from Midnight Special. As Cappelli says, Midnight Special is "using technology in some unbookstore-like ways."

Technical Notes

Midnight Special's WWW server is running NCSA HTTPD on a Pentium computer with 24MB of RAM and BSD UNIX. The Web provider service writes Midnight Special's CGI scripts. Approximately 80 different IP addresses (distinct machines) hit Midnight Special's WWW site, accumulating about 200 hits per day.

Monster Board
<http://www.monster.com>

The Monster Board is a career development site and a center for human resources information on the World-Wide Web. Anyone may post a résumé to the "Resume On-Ramp" for free. In May 1995 the Monster Board had more than 10,000 résumés and expected that number to skyrocket with its increased investment in equipment, advertising, and faster Internet feed.

This combination Web-WAIS site is a branch of ADION Human Resource Communications, a New England recruiting and advertising company. Job searches and browsing human resource information are free. Job listings cost money, and companies can pay more for more elaborate Web spaces. Companies are also charged for the right to review the résumé database. These aren't traditional résumés, however. Posting a résumé is a matter of filling in online forms, with questions that include all the traditional résumé subjects like education, work experience, technical skills, willingness to move, and salary requirements. The data go right into database fields that feed the search programs. There is even room for a brief cover letter message. Once users fill out the form, they receive a password good for updating at any time during the next 12 months. After that their résumés are dropped from the database, which helps to ensure a certain currency. Whenever users update their résumé, the expiration date is extended for another 12 months.

The Monster Board provides companies with two separate résumé-related services:

- A company that posts jobs to the Monster Board may review all résumés posted for that particular job.

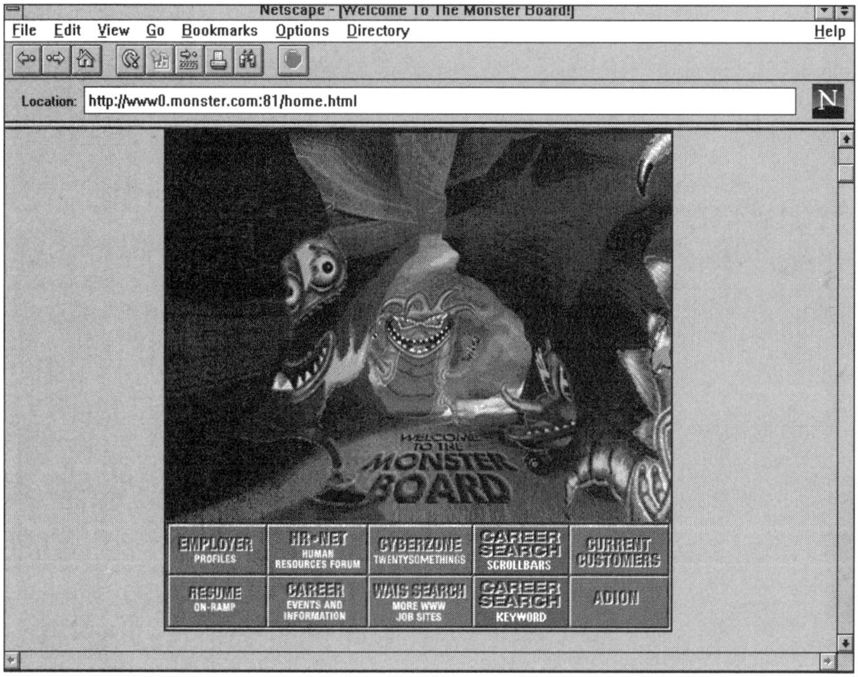

FIGURE 10–14 The Monster Board Web Site (Reprinted with permission.)

- A company can pay to review all the résumés in the database. This service permits companies to search by keyword for certain skills. When companies find résumés they like, they contact ADION for the personal information that goes with them. A company can buy this service in addition to posting jobs or instead of posting specific jobs.

The colorful monster images, meant to symbolize big and unique ideas, were actually in use by ADION in other projects but carried over well to the Web. ADION also claims that the monsters represent the characteristics its subscriber companies want in their employees: creativity, innovation, communication, energy, and positive results.

John Kirby, project manager for the Monster Board, claims, "The Monster Board will literally change the face of human resources because jobs will be posted to the world, and you'll be collecting applicants from all over the world as well. Applicants can take advantage of the searching capabilities to narrow their focus considerably."

Technical Notes

The Monster Board runs on two Sun Sparc 20s (it started with a Sparc 2) running CERN HTTPD and a custom WAIS gateway based on freeware. It sees 10,000 connections per day and has a 10megabit Internet feed, upgraded from 56K.

Advice

Kirby says, "Make sure your site is unique. Make sure your idea is unique. If it's commercial, you should question hard if someone is going to buy it online. If it's a side business, don't rely on the Web to make your business for you unless you have a well-defined niche. It will certainly add to your business, though."

1990 Census Lookup
<*http://cedr.lbl.gov/cdrom/doc/cdrom.html*> and <*http://cedr.lbl.gov/cdrom/lookup*>

The Lawrence Berkeley Laboratory and University of California at Berkeley are working together to create the world's largest online database of federal government statistics. Lookup is an experimental WWW server for retrieving data from 1990 U.S. Census summary tape files. Lookup uses the University of California's CD-ROM Information System. Lookup source code is publicly available, and development of compatible modules is strongly encouraged.

Although not all levels of census data are available, the Web site offers cross-tabulations of answers to various combinations of census questions by national, state, and urbanized metropolitan regions. The lab's goal is to help others set up similar servers with the same or different data. Lookup is receiving 80,000 URL requests (from 7,000 users) each month (as of April 1995). Usage is doubling every month.

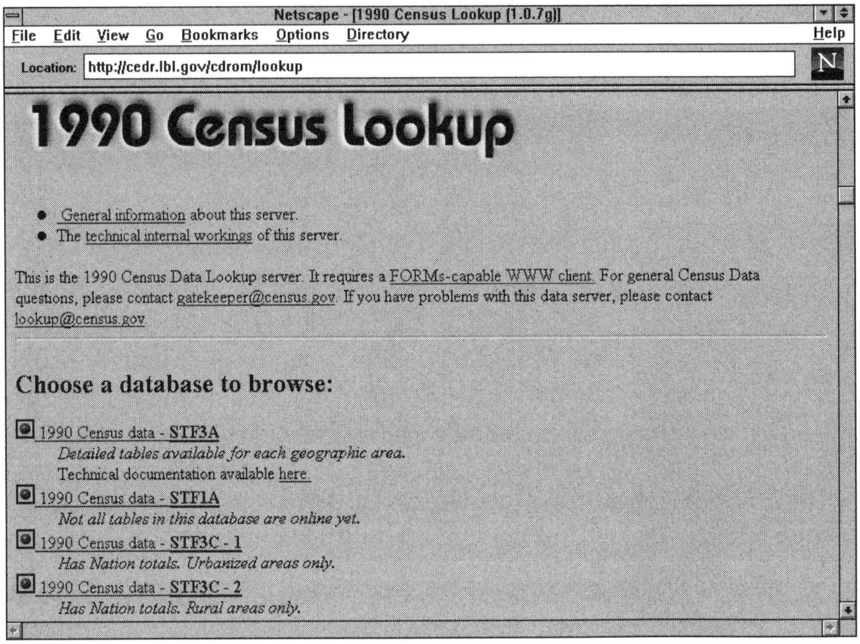

FIGURE 10–15 1990 Census Lookup Web Site (Reprinted with permission.)

OncoLink

<http://cancer.med.upenn.edu>, <gopher://cancer.med.upenn.edu>

OncoLink is a patient-physician cancer information resource sponsored by the University of Pennsylvania Medical Center and available via Gopher, WWW, and telnet. OncoLink attempts to provide one-stop shopping for the patient, family member, health care provider, researcher, or browser searching for cancer-related information. OncoLink was awarded the 1994 International Best of the Web Award for best professional service. Since its inauguration on March 7, 1994, OncoLink has been accessed 350,000 times from more than 75 countries and averages 4,000 accesses a day.

According to a paper presented to the American Medical Informatics Association in the fall of 1994, the OncoLink Web and Gopher sites were originally ordered around the academic specialties of the

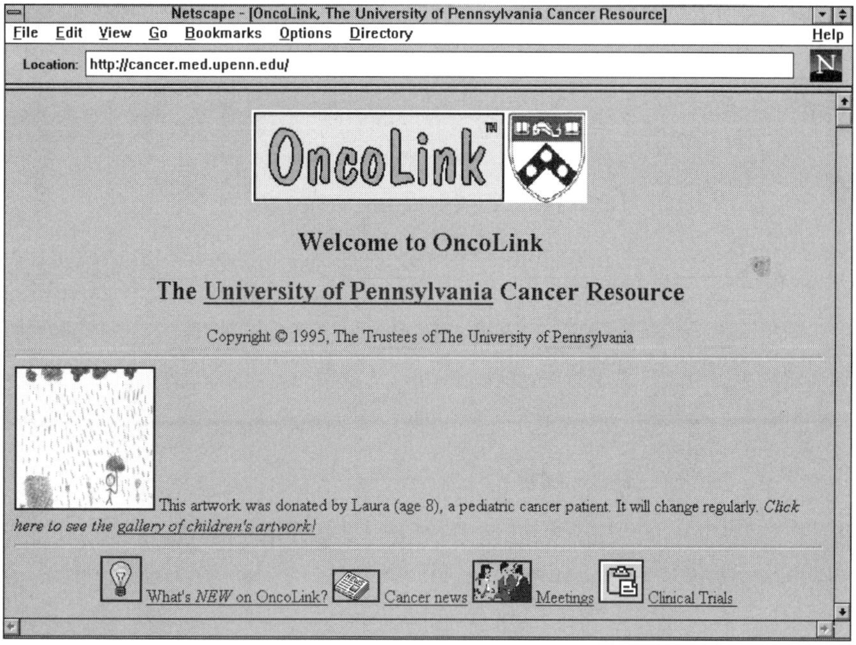

FIGURE 10–16 OncoLink Web Site (Reprinted with permission.)

faculty contributors. This made sense to the faculty, but users (primarily laypeople who either knew someone with cancer or had it themselves) soon e-mailed urging a different arrangement. They requested, and the center quickly added, a menu of various cancer types, so the layperson can easily find all the relevant material for a particular cancer. This is one example of the need to build feedback mechanisms into even the most thoroughly planned servers. The paper also discusses the center's study of server logs, particularly in terms of what links were being followed and what patterns they revealed. The paper is available at <***http://cancer.med.upenn.edu/manuscripts/amia.html***>.

Statistical reports through April 30, 1995, show that 83.4 percent of all transactions are from Wide-World Web clients and 16.6 percent from Gopher clients. Approximately one-third of the WWW clients accessing OncoLink appear to be text-only clients. (This might be surprising to those who think that everyone is using the WWW for the graphics.)

OncoLink also has found that whether a link is text or a small image makes a difference in how often that link is picked. The image links appear to be more popular than text links.

Technical Notes

OncoLink is running a DEC station 5000/25 with 40MB of RAM. The model 25 is roughly a 20 MIPS (millions of instructions per second) machine. OncoLink's Gopher server software is GN, and its WWW server runs NCSA HTTPD.

Advice

According to Dr. Joel W. Goldwein, co-editor in chief of OncoLink, you should be sure to

1. Clarify your mission.
2. Develop a strong infrastructure.
3. Select good people to help.
4. Turn your e-mail off after 6 p.m. and marry a saint.

On-line Books Page
<http://www.cs.cmu.edu/Web/books.html>

The On-line Books Page Web site, based at Carnegie Mellon University in Pittsburgh, is an index of hundreds of online books. It also points to some common repositories of online books and other documents, including the Project Gutenberg texts, as well as specialty or foreign-language repositories and book catalogs and retailers.

According to site administrator John Ockerbloom,

> The On-Line Books Page started in 1993, when the Web was still a novelty in most places. . . . [A staff member] had made up some nice HTML versions of some Project Gutenberg texts, and as part of our initial departmental Web, I made up a page that

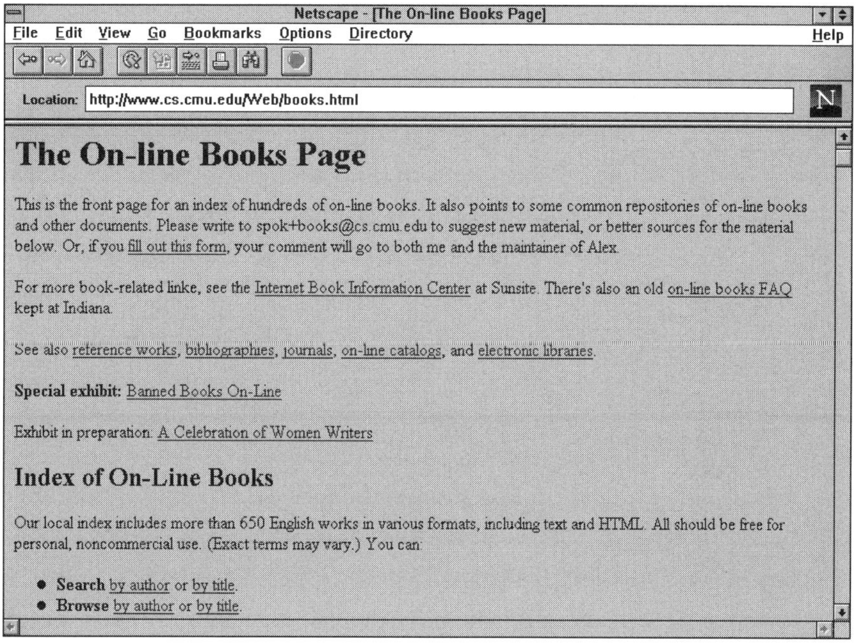

FIGURE 10–17 On-line Books Page Web Site (Reprinted with permission from Carnegie Mellon University.)

> pointed to his texts and included pointers to a few major book repositories like Gutenberg. Later I noticed that there was no overall list of titles and that this would be useful to avoid having to check each archive individually. So I expanded the listings and eventually added other features like a search capability.

Special exhibits include Banned Books On-line and Celebration of Women Writers.

Technical Notes

The Web servers are Sparcstations running NCSA HTTPD 1.3 (with local modifications). The pages are served from AFS (Andrew File System), which Carnegie Mellon uses as its campuswide filing system.

The On-Line Books Page only indexes the books; all texts are stored elsewhere, so it uses relatively little space.

Advice

Ockerbloom lists the following steps for publishing information:

1. See what's already out there on the topic. Decide whether you should work on putting up new material, work on indexing or explaining existing material, move into a different or more specialized niche, or some combination of these things.
2. Find a place to publish your pages. If you can't do it through your school or workplace, many public access providers now give people the opportunity to publish Web pages. Find one that is reasonable (in price and in administration), seems to have an easily reachable Web server, and can provide you the space you need. Note that if you're indexing information, like us, rather than supplying a lot of new material yourself, you don't necessarily need a lot of space.
3. Construct your pages. Make them well organized and easy for people to find the content they want. You don't need fancy graphics or markup; those often get in the way more than they help.
4. Tell people and indexes like Yahoo about your pages and commit to maintaining your pages. Respond to e-mail in a timely fashion, and leave some indicator on your pages as to how often they're updated. Word of mouth will do much of the rest; once word gets around people will add their own links to you and suggest additional information you can put on your page.

Palo Alto Real Estate
<http://none.coolware.com/real/realestate.html>

This Web site offers some real estate listings in the Palo Alto area of northern California as well as a map and information about the community. Agents and their telephone numbers are listed; users are asked to tell agents they saw their listings on the Internet. Each house gets its own page with color photos.

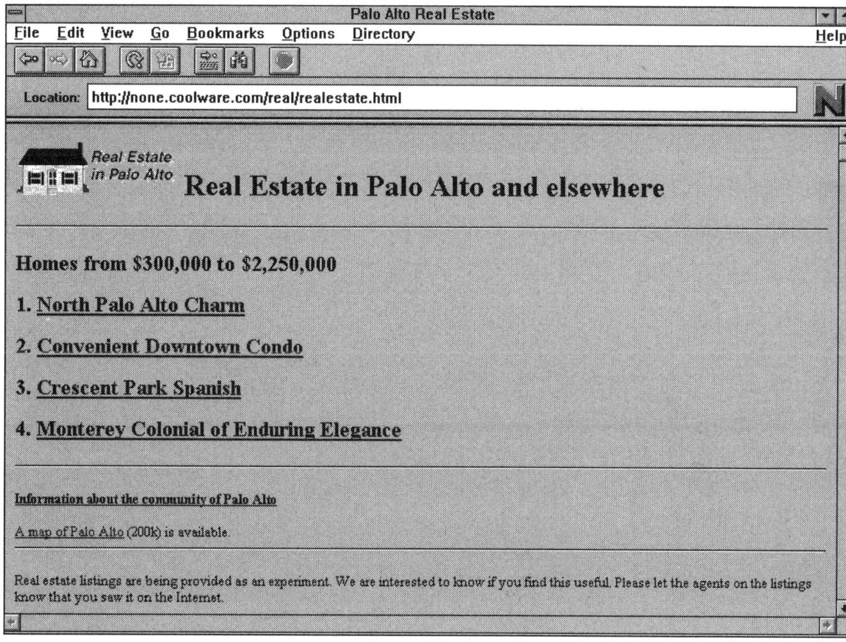

FIGURE 10–18 Real Estate in Palo Alto Web Site (Reprinted with permission.)

Technical Notes

Palo Alto Real Estate runs its Web site from a Sun Sparcstation. The site is accessed about 70,000 times a week.

Advice

Keith Cooley of Coolware, the sponsor of the Palo Alto site, says, “Spend two hours learning HTML and then do it—break the mold and do what feels right.”

PhoNETic
<http://www.soc.qc.edu/phonetic/>

PhoNETic is a Web service that converts phone numbers to letters and vice versa. That’s all it does, but it gets 3,000 to 6,000 hits per day. Either people just have to see it to believe it, or converting

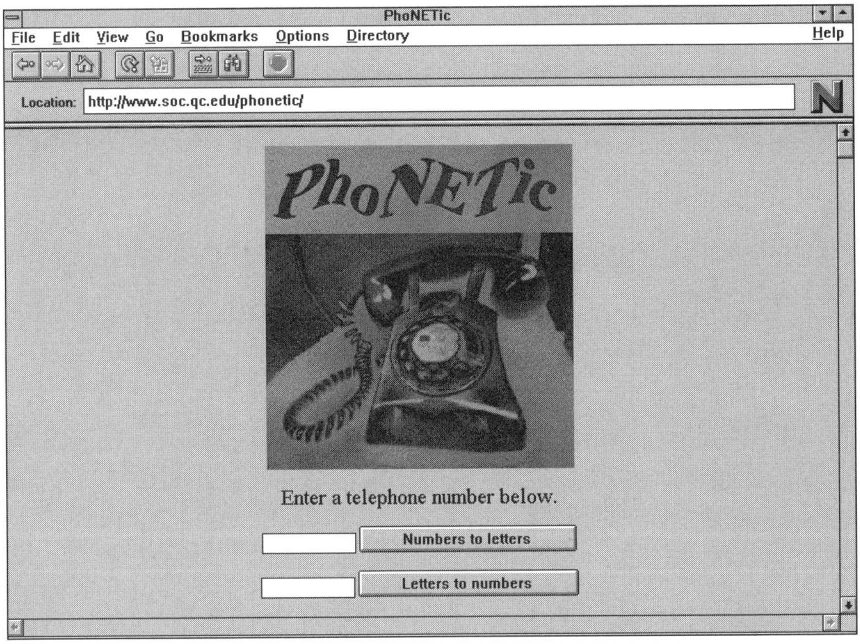

FIGURE 10–19 PhoNETic Web Site (Reprinted with permission from Queens College, CUNY.)

phone numbers to letters is more useful than you might think. This is a textbook case of using CGI scripts (or programs) behind a Web server to perform a task for whoever wants it.

PhoNETic was designed by Nick Sklavounakis and Nikolay Uglov, LAN/UNIX system administrators of the Department of Sociology at Queens College of the City University of New York. Sklavounakis recounts the origin of PhoNETic: “It was a rare (very rare) day when my assistant and I didn’t have much to do. I thought it would be a good idea to experiment with writing CGI scripts and implementing interactive forms on our Web pages. Our little experiment turned out to be quite popular! I am still amazed at the type of attention it has gained.”

Technical Notes

PhoNETic runs NCSA HTTPD from a DEC Alpha 3000/300X (175mhz) with 96MB of RAM. It shares Queens College’s partial T-1 link to the Internet. The CGI scripts were written in DEC OSF/1-C (standard UNIX C). The graphics for the page were created on a Macintosh Centris 650 using Photoshop 3.0 and a Connectix QuickCam. The day PhoNETic was "Cool Site of the Day" (awarded by Glen Davis at InfiNet), it had more than 70,000 hits. Its server handled the traffic with no trouble.

Advice

Nikolay Uglov: Make sure your server can handle the load in case of a huge success; be friends with your network administrator. Write the CGI script first [and the] HTML script second.

Nick Sklavounakis: I think most important is to determine how much activity you think your server must deal with on a daily basis. Based on that, the appropriate hardware and software can be determined, as well as the type of link to the Internet you will have. At this stage, I wouldn't go any less than a T-1 if you plan to have an active server.

The users will enjoy quick response time, and the server will have a less overall load (people can connect and disconnect quicker when data is transferred faster). As for hardware, there are many options available now, and for newcomers I would probably recommend looking at the alternatives to operating in a UNIX environment, like using a Macintosh Internet Server, Windows NT, or OS/2.

Playboy
<http://www.playboy.com/>

Playboy Magazine's Web site home page, with its faint background pattern of the *Playboy* bunny logo, includes excerpts from the magazine, cartoons, and Playmate images, links to Playboy news and announcements, the full text of some interviews from *Playboy* archives as well as the *Playboy* Advisor FAQ file. In addition, the Web

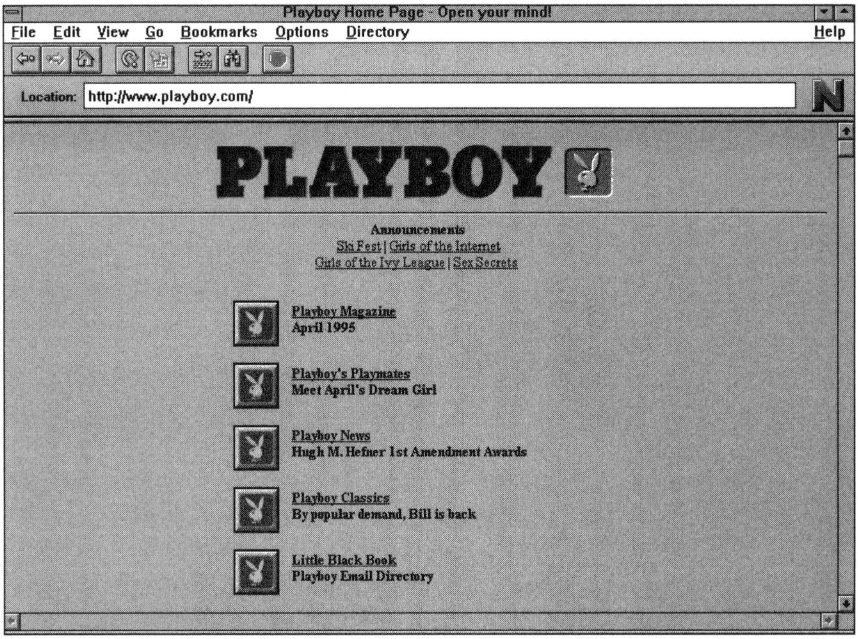

FIGURE 10–20 Playboy Web Site (Reprinted with permission.)

site accepts online questions to the *Playboy* Advisor and is conducting an online search for a photo feature of the "Girls of the Internet."

According to Eileen Kent, who started and runs *Playboy*'s Web site, the magazine originally got an Internet connection in order to see what was being said about it on the *Playboy* newsgroup and mailing list (alt.mag.playboy and playboy-request@lovesexy.com). She says that as soon as she saw WWW she knew it was a natural for *Playboy.* But just doing an electronic version of the magazine never appealed to her, although *Playboy* updates the Web site simultaneously with the newsstand version. *Playboy* has had a "phenomenal response with a great deal of positive feedback from users," Kent says. When Hugh Hefner, founder of *Playboy,* saw a collection of e-mail that came in from the Web site, he said it reminded him of the letters readers sent when the magazine first started.

Kent says that to her, "The best, the really good stuff [on the Internet] is the homegrown stuff." Mirsky's Worst of the Net <***http://turnpike.net/mirsky/Worst.html***> is one site she finds particularly hilarious. "WWW is the greatest thing since Gutenberg. As a bottom-up publishing phenomenon it's excellent," says Kent. "This is a shot at getting your stuff out there to the world without having a million dollars."

One concern she has is that Net users accord copyrighted material insufficient respect. She's convinced that "every year a new crop of freshmen come in with Internet accounts, and they aren't getting educated about copyright issues as they should be. They don't seem to be aware that there are laws (in the U.S.) that make application software infringement a felony." *Playboy* often finds illegal archives of *Playboy* images and contacts site administrators about these copyright infringements, Kent said.

Playboy has been using Netscape Server and is moving to Netscape Commerce Server. *Playboy* created its HTML files in-house and gets more than 800,000 hits per day—"and not just downloading the Playmate images," Kent says.

Advice

According to Kent, "Nobody should limit the Net to just thinking of it as a marketing phenomenon. The clutter is terrible. There is too much stuff happening on most Web pages. You need a purity of design that makes it comfortable for the user. There's lots of publications and Web sites [that] aren't used to having to listen. They should be smart enough to listen to their users. The users will tell you what they want."

Project Gutenberg
<http://jg.cso.uiuc.edu/pg/pg_home.html>, *<ftp://uiarchive.cso.uiuc.edu/pub/etext/gutenberg>*, and *<ftp://ftp.etext.org>*

The philosophy of Project Gutenberg is to make information, books, and other materials available to the general public in forms that most computers, programs, and people can easily read, use, quote, and search. That means plain vanilla ASCII text, and the folks at

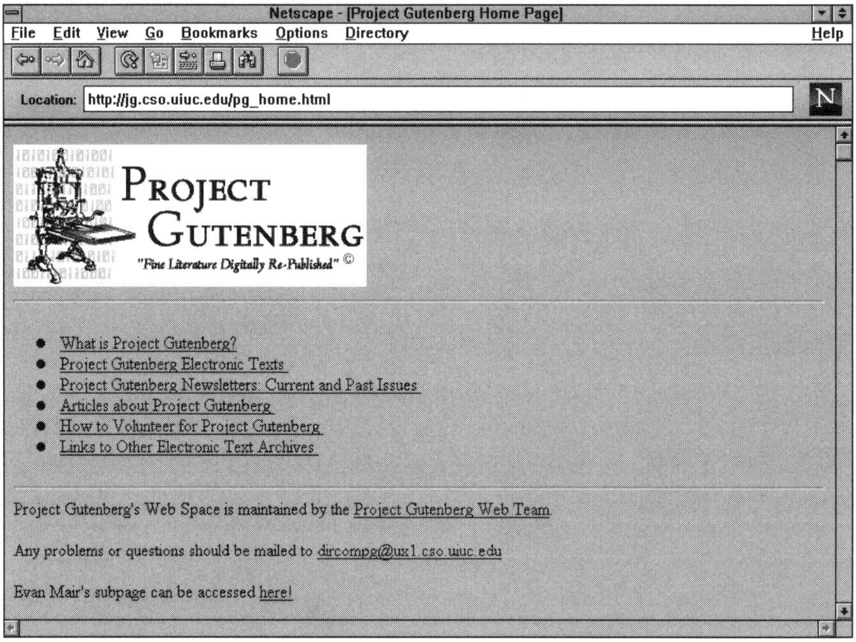

FIGURE 10–21 Project Gutenburg Web Site (Reprinted with permission.)

Gutenberg are proud of it. They reason that years from now, when programs and systems have changed, plain old ASCII, readable on Macintoshes, PCs, and UNIX systems, will still be usable, if not any prettier than it is today.

Project Gutenberg has been publishing works in the public domain with the help of volunteers since 1971 when Michael Hart, professor of electronic text and executive director of Project Gutenberg at Illinois Benedictine College in Lisle, Illinois, decided to "earn" the equivalent of $100 million–worth of computer time he had been given on a mainframe at the University of Illinois. (See the University of Illinois's Web site above for the full-story.) Hart figured there was no "normal computing" he could do that would be worth that amount of money. So he looked for something that computers could do that would have an equivalent value. His answer was the storage, retrieval, and searching of what is on library shelves.

Starting with the U.S. Declaration of Independence, Project Gutenberg has compiled 250 online books entirely through volunteer labor. The goal is 10,000 books by the year 2000. Project Gutenberg selects public domain books in the categories of light literature, heavy literature, and references.

Technical Notes

Project Gutenberg runs a modified version of the NCSA HTTPD server, which runs Mach NextStep v3.0 on an original 68000 NeXT cube. The modifications were designed to provide a firewall that has serving capability similar to what is available in the CERN HTTPD.

The Web site enjoys about 13,000 hits a week, well distributed among all its pages, which is considered a good sign that people are actually reading them and not just browsing. Statistics about machine load are available at <***http://jg.cso.uiuc.edu/jg.cso***>.

Advice

John M. Koontz (aka Kahn), the system administrator, advises:

> *Provide good content.* Contribute something to the Net soup, don't just add more water.
>
> *Courtesy.* Consider people who use text browsers or have slow Net connections. Are all those large images REALLY necessary? Also keep in mind that Netscape, although neat, is still nonstandard.
>
> *Fresh links.* If you provide links to other sites, be sure that they are current and operational. A link to a closed site is no fun. . . . Keep them [the links] to a minimum and keep them good.

Travels with Samantha by Philip Greenspun

http://www-swiss.ai.mit.edu/samantha/>

Philip Greenspun is a graduate student in computer science at MIT who has a background in advertising photography and a knack for putting words together. In late 1993 he found the World-Wide Web and decided to put the story of his summer travels around the United States on the Internet as a "Web book."

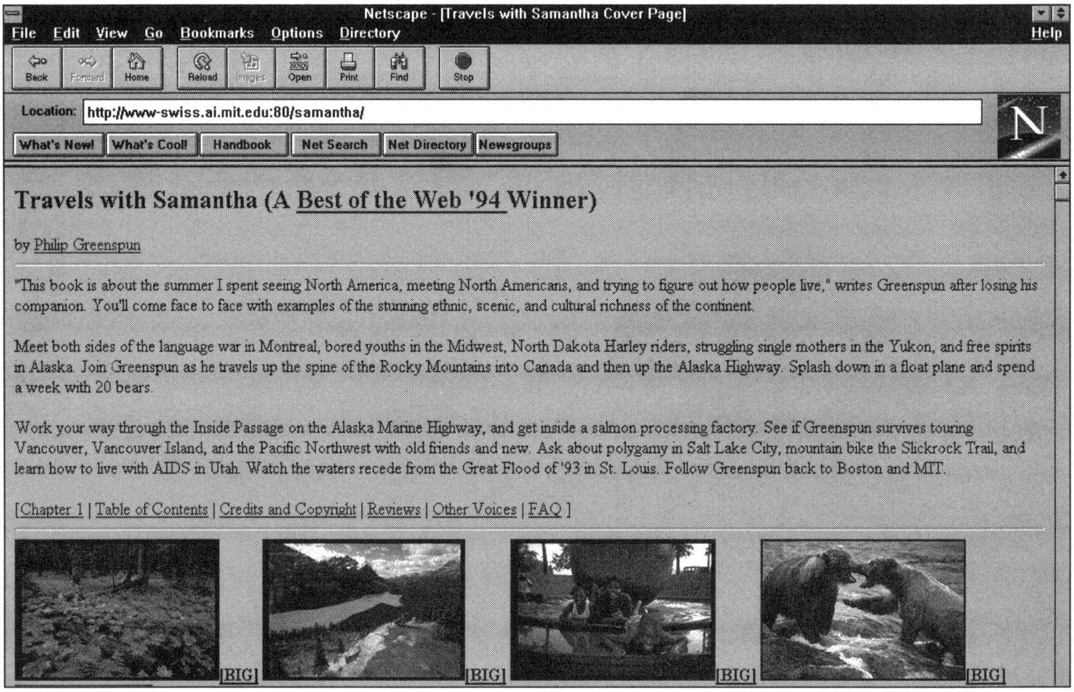

FIGURE 10–22 Travels with Samantha Web Site (Reprinted with permission from Philip Greenspan–philg@mit.edu.)

In the literary tradition of John Steinbeck's *Travels with Charlie, Travels with Samantha* is a highly readable chronicle of the places he saw and the people he met, as well as his moving reason for taking the trip. *Travels with Samantha* includes 250 excellently digitized photographs to go with the stories written on his Macintosh PowerBook (Samantha) while on the road. *Travels with Samantha* won a 1994 Best of the Web Award and attracts more than 1,000 readers a day.

Since *Samantha* Greenspun has written of his travels to Berlin, Prague, and New Zealand and put up earlier writings on photography and computer science. He even started a legal defense fund for a friend's brother. Because there is no charge to read *Travels with Samantha,* he was surprised when he started making money. With 2,000 photos scattered among his online stories, he'd inadvertently become a stock photo agency. After several months he'd received five photo requests and one assignment and was about $5,000 richer. Now he's working on software to automate the maintenance of indexed photo archives.

Technical Notes

Greenspun also edits two online journals, *Web Tools Review* <***http://webtools.com/wtr***> and *Photo Journal* <***http://photo.net/photo***>. He uses the PBMTOOLS graphics package to do his graphic manipulation. His Web server runs on a HP 9000 series UNIX machine with a T3 connection to the backbone. His Web server ships out 1.5GB per day answering user requests.

Advice

Greenspun finds that "Web publishers with desktop scanners and 8-bit video boards are the biggest source of ugly images on the Internet today." He recommends using a 24-bit video card for any image work, Kodak PhotoCD as the minimum acceptable quality scan, and a T-1 connection as the minimum speed necessary for serving popular pages with many photographs.

Virtual Shareware Library
<http://www.fagg.uni-lj.si/SHASE/>

Descriptions of more than 100,000 pieces of software are available on the Internet, archived at FTP sites like SimTel, CICA, Hobbes, and SunSite. Typically, these archives are mirrored to reduce the load on the original site. The Virtual Shareware Library (VSL) acts as a catalog by using a search-and-retrieval mechanism (SHASE) behind a WWW server to provide a user-friendly way to select particular sites and then search those software descriptions.

Dr. Ziga Turk (pronounced *Zheegah Toork*), a member of the faculty of civil engineering at the University of Ljubljana, Slovenia, developed the service out of personal frustration, "The Internet opened

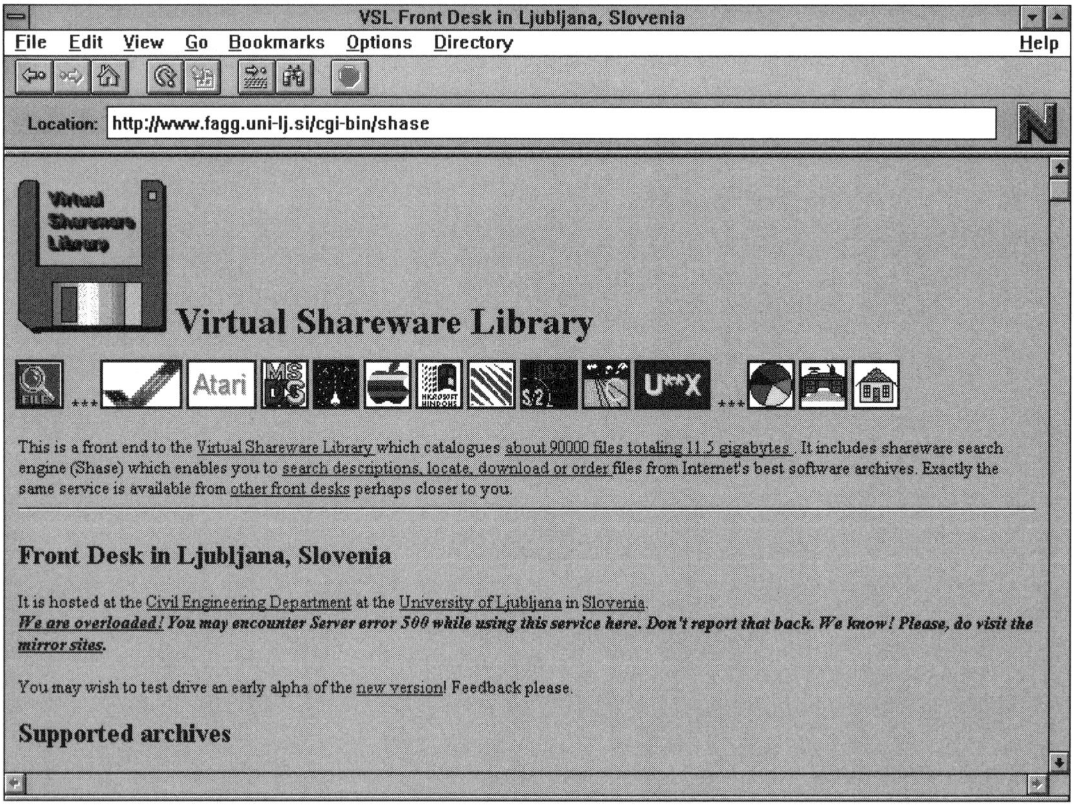

FIGURE 10–23 Virtual Shareware Library Web Site (Reprinted with permission.)

up tons of shareware and related software," but he could not tell what was available and what wasn't. "Indexes of CICA and SimTel provided the most vital information," he recalls. "At about the same time I started the WWW server, I found out that Perl is a language everyone uses for CGI scripts. As an exercise in Perl and for my own use I wrote the search engine pointing to CICA and SimTel only."

It was rudimentary but proved popular. "I started to receive mail from all over the world, the great majority of which praised the service. The feedback, 5 to 20 thank you notes a day, was the greatest motivation for developing the service," Turk says. "Heavy usage was the motivation for more improvements. One remaining problem is to verify that the sites storing the files are really there."

Another, more serious problem was a legal matter that arose when some FTP site managers claimed their indexes should not be used in Turk's service without their explicit permission. That forced Turk to close his service for a week or so, until he and the site managers were able to reach a friendly agreement. "The lesson I learned was to ask for permission from the managers of all the other archives (most had been contacted before)," Turk said.

Technical Notes

In Ljubljana the VSL runs on an HP710 workstation running NCSA's HTTPD server. Mirrors run on other, usually better, machines.

When the VSL-related load on the server in Ljubljana approached 50,000 hits a day, users at the university found they had difficulty gaining access to other services run from the same server and to mirrors pumping the database each day, so now the server in Ljubljana does not allow access for the commercial and "unresolved" domains. A growing number of mirror servers are offering exactly the same service (three in North America and two in Europe).

Advice

Turk offers the following advice: "First impressions are important. When you announce [your server] make sure it works perfectly. Users will not come the second time if you disappoint them. If you write forms, test them with UNIX Mosaic. It's the most picky about the case of keywords."

CHAPTER 11

The Future of Internet Publishing

It's difficult to write about the future of Internet publishing when it's changing literally day by day. But in the year that I've been thinking about and working on this book I've seen some trends that I think will continue. To state it simply, publishing on the Internet is becoming easier and more widespread much faster than I think anyone anticipated. Graphics are important, more so than people would like to think, but text and useful content are even more important. Fee-charging techniques are here and working, although much more is coming.

Computers do not solve problems, but people do, and computers are linking people together in ways never before imagined. Books and magazines won't go away. Computers, even the tiny ones, are not nearly as portable and inexpensive as books and magazines. If the theory that online versions will stimulate interest in buying print versions proves true, perhaps Project Gutenberg and others like it will stimulate a renewed interest in the classics as well as less well-known literary works.

This chapter is loosely divided into several sections, but it's important to read the sections you're not interested in. Although you might not think so at first, changes in protocols, software advancements, and more sophisticated encryption techniques are interrelated. Something that doesn't interest you may very well affect something that does. A new protocol for search and retrieval can open up commercial and business opportunities. Encryption techniques have social and political implications and vice versa. Software advancements can lead to new publishing techniques. In short, the implications are in the interconnections. Pay attention.

Internet Hardware and Services

A natural and realistic concern is how well the Internet will hold up under all the attention and massive growth. U.S. government support for large sections of the U.S. Internet is already being phased out in favor of commercial support. Although loss of federal support may lead to higher access charges, it's not clear how much that will affect end users.

Whether the Internet is ready or not, the influx of new users and new hosts is tremendous. These users will affect all services currently available, and publicity can provoke wild distortions in the load on any given server. Consistently popular servers will often be unavailable or require constant retries to get in. Only faster hardware and greater bandwidth will solve this part of the problem.

Whether the growth comes from integrating the cable TV system and the Internet, from ATM (Asynchronous Transmission Mode), or from ISDN (Integrated Services Digital Network) access to home and office, the Internet pipeline is likely to get bigger and faster in the next few years—probably not big enough or fast enough to accommodate everyone and their multimedia dreams but considerably improved over today.

Archie, Lycos, and Veronica, among other centralized indexing services, are becoming overloaded. One alternative that's arising is commercial versions of these services, assuming that people will be willing to pay to get immediate service. However, Internet habitués hope that free alternatives will continue to multiply too. Multiple mirrors of the popular servers will help, a phenomenon already evident in Australia. Programmers already are trying to redesign the way indexes collect their information to spread the load across the system. Corporations looking to contribute to the Internet should consider investing in a few key services such as Veronica and Lycos.

We're now on the second generation of WWW indexing approaches, which are becoming more sophisticated. Developers are learning from their mistakes. One approach, I think, will be for user input to become an important element in adding to the depth and accuracy of the Internet indexes and subject directories. Lycos, for example, makes a strong step in that direction by allowing users to fill out an online form to remove a URL from the Lycos index.

InfoSeek <*http://www.infoseek.com/*> and Architext <*http://www.atext.com/*> both offer new searching technology. InfoSeek is a commercial Internet indexing service that indexes the Internet (WWW, Usenet News) as well as commercial databases. Architext was designed to do conceptual searches. The service uses statistical and analytical methods to turn up documents related to the words you used in your search, even if those words don't actually appear in the documents. These and other searching systems will accomplish Architext's primary goal, raising users' expectations for information retrieval.

Software, Data Formats, and Protocols

When you think about how much has happened because a few people at different universities and institutes decided to write some software (Gopher at the University of Minnesota, Veronica at the University of Nevada at Reno, WWW at CERN, and Mosaic at NCSA at the University of Illinois), trying to predict what might happen in the next few years is foolish. But some interesting developments may give us an inkling.

But first let me deal with the competition between Gopher and WWW.

Even if everyone had a fast computer and speedy Internet link, Gopher would have a future. Gopher server software may not be that much easier to administer than a Web (HTTPD) server, but it is definitely simpler to put Gopher documents on the Internet than it is to write HTML and maintain links for Web documents. The irony here—and WWW zealots will loudly proclaim this—is that nothing prevents you from putting plain text documents on a Web server, just as you do on Gopher servers. But the killer is the expectation for WWW servers. WWW with HTML formatting can make online documents look so much nicer (to those with the right equipment) that it would be a waste to ignore that capability—and few do.

But that's just my opinion. Here are some others.

Michael Regoli, administrator of the CICA Windows FTP site, says:

> I think that in terms of "bleeding edge" Internet technology, Gopher has indeed seen its day; this was predicted when I first saw the Web in action, some 12 to 18 months ago [as of April 1995]. Gopher, though, still has its users. It doesn't take big hardware to run it (on the client side), and I think it will continue to have a following, especially [among] those using limited computing resources (low-end 386s, 286s, etc.) and limited net access. Gopher is useful, don't get me wrong. Its beauty and usefulness lie in its simplicity. It'll be here for a while.

Paul Hoffman, president of Proper Publishing, an Internet consulting company <***http://www.proper.com/***>, believes that

> Gopher will never go away, in the same sense that FTP hasn't gone away. They are not as 'good' as WWW for some, but they are much better for others. Gopher is inherently better for character-based browsers than WWW and will thus live on well into the next century.
>
> Anyone who thinks that the whole world is going to graphical browsers doesn't understand the large corporate and the academic markets. Look at radio in the U.S.: it is far from dead 30 years after television reached a 90% penetration in the home.
>
> There are no technical advantages to Gopher versus the Web, but that is irrelevant. What will keep Gopher alive is that it is easier to install and support Gopher clients on character-based systems than it is Web clients.

The University of Minnesota Gopher Development Team is also working on the interaction of Gopher and WWW. Paul Lindner presented a paper about their work at GopherCon95. <***gopher://boombox.micro.umn.edu:70/00/gopher/Gopher_Conference_95/Papers/WebbedGopher***>

Both Gopher and WWW browsers will be enhanced by the development of plug-in viewers that handle documents with special formatting. Some already exist and others are coming. Commercial organizations are sponsoring some, and others are technical improvements that may or may not be adopted as browser standards.

One essential element of software is the formatting of the data that are being manipulated. In this case the data are, for the most part, a combination of textual and graphic information. The following are some entrants in the competition to become the standard data format for the Internet:

- *PDF*—Adobe's Portable Document Format provides the graphic control that many Internet publishers want, but file sizes are rather large. Adobe made the right move by offering its Acrobat viewer for free across Windows, Macintosh, and UNIX.

    PDF is starting to get its own add-on products, which increases the probability that it will be seen as a real graphical alternative, and perhaps a new standard, for publishing on the Internet. One add-on is RE:MARK for Windows from Software Partners, Inc., which allows members of a work group to share and co-edit documents in PDF. Readers can send their comments (including voice annotations, pictures, bit maps, sound files, spreadsheets, and so on) back to the author, who can then incorporate comments from several different readers in a revised version of the original document. Available first for Windows and Macintosh, this product will be more significant if it becomes available for UNIX as well.
- *SGML*—Companies like SoftQuad are starting to make Standard Generalized Markup Language viewers become available.
- *IIF*—Interactive Image Format (used in Blue Skies Gopher) is one alternative to WWW's clickable image maps; it offers immediate feedback to users as their mouse moves over hot

or warm areas of the map. Developed under a National Science Foundation grant at the University of Michigan, its viewers are available embedded in Macintosh and Windows Gopher clients and will be added as a viewer for Web clients. <***http://cirrus.sprl.umich.edu/IIF/***>

- *Microsoft Word for Windows Format*—This program has some advantages if you think of how many people use Word for Windows. Microsoft has offered its Word for Windows viewer for free and promises a Macintosh version. If Microsoft does not provide a UNIX version, it will ignore a huge segment of the Internet browser population.
- *HTML*—HyperText Markup Language is fighting to maintain its place as the document format of choice for WWW servers. It has a huge advantage because it is easily portable between platforms and WWW was built on it. HTML 3.0 adds significant features for greater flexibility in document formatting and control. See <***http://www.ics.uci.edu/pub/ietf/html/***> and <***http://www.w3.org/hypertext/WWW/MarkUp/MarkUp.html***> for more information on where HTML is going. But the drive for a powerful formatting language still wages war with the drive for a language that clearly defines the structure of a document. HTML will have to satisfy both camps and that is hard to do.
- *ASCII*—ASCII text has been the underlying text format in Internet protocols like Gopher, WAIS, and WWW (HTML is written in ASCII), but it has some basic flaws. The main one is that it doesn't work well for languages other than English, especially ideographic languages like Chinese, Japanese, and Korean. ASCII may eventually be replaced by Unicode.
- *Unicode*—Unicode is a superset of ASCII that was designed to solve the problem of representing all of the world's modern written languages (including ideographic languages), but it has not been widely adopted. Microsoft has said that Unicode is part of its long-term strategy and in fact adopted it with Windows NT and Windows 95. The growing trend toward internationalization will make solutions like Unicode even

more important. See <*http://www.unicode.org/*> for more information on Unicode.

Password Validation and Secure Systems

The combination of two different and formerly competing security systems (SSL and S-HTTP) in Terisa's cooperative venture should go a long way toward establishing a system of secure communication across the Internet. Once a secure system is developed and becomes available for other companies to use, browsers with these new features will become available. At that point Internet commerce will become widespread, a development I expect by early 1996.

3-D Virtual Gopherspace

The Gopher team at the University of Minnesota is working on a three-dimensional virtual Gopherspace system that will offer a new way to browse Gopherspace. Unfortunately, it will require the browser to have a powerful machine, which runs contrary to Gopher's strength in being friendly to low-end PCs. <*gopher://boombox.micro.umn.edu:70/00/gopher/Gopher_Conference_95/Papers/3DUnixServer*>

3-D Web and VRML

The April 1995 WWW Conference in Darmstadt, Germany, saw the announcement of the availability of VRML, or Virtual Reality Markup Language for WWW. VRML apparently allows users of different Web browsers to interactively and cooperatively build a common virtual reality environment. The educational, social, and commercial applications (and implications) of this are just starting to be explored. One commercial example might be an auto company that simulates its new car in VRML and puts the simulation on the Internet for online suggestions and improvements. For more information on VRML, see <*http://www.ncsa.uiuc.edu/General/VRML/VRMLHome.html*>,<*http://www.sdsc.edu/vrml*>, and <*http://vrml.wired.com/*>.

Better HTML Editors

One clear trend is toward improvement in number and quality of such WWW publishing tools as HTML editors and converters. Microsoft and Novell have already brought out free HTML authoring add-on packages for their word processors, Microsoft Word for Windows 6.0, and Novell's WordPerfect. These make it simple to save word-processing files in HTML format. Quarterdeck is planning a product that will work with those word processors as well. The efforts should quickly improve the functionality and ease of use of HTML editors. And as authoring tools become more prevalent and easy to use, the number of sites and amount of content will increase exponentially, especially if quality is maintained.

PDAs and Web Browsers

PDAs, or Personal Digital Assistants such Apple's Newton, are computers and therefore candidates for Internet browsers. One version of Mosaic already runs (in demonstration mode) on the Newton. That means it can display HTML files it has stored in memory but has no facility for easily browsing the Internet. With improvements in communications and wireless technology, it might be possible to look at the Southern California Real-Time Traffic Reporter Web site while you are driving in that traffic <*http://www.scubed.com/caltrans/*>.

New Schemes for Resource Naming

URLs (or Uniform Resource Locators) should be familiar to you by now. They simplified life on the Net immeasurably, but a significant drawback to the URL is that moving a file or changing a host name can invalidate documents around the world that link to it. If the host specified in a URL is not available, or too busy, or has changed its name, that link won't work. Many people have thought hard and long about improving the URL scheme. The results include an alphabet soup of acronyms—URI (Uniform Resource Identifier), URN (Uniform Resource Name), URC (Uniform Resource Characteristic), and URA (Uniform Resource Agent).

URI (Uniform Resource Identifier). URI is a generic term for different methods of describing addresses on the Internet, including URL, URN, and URC. The original term, URL (Uniform Resource Locator), combines the name of a resource with its location. The URI working group of the Internet Engineering Task Force (IETF) is attempting to move WWW and other Internet services to a system by which a name (URN) is assigned to a resource that is described (by author, title, keyword) in a URC and can be found at various locations (URLs).

The IETF draft proposals on URIs are located at <*http://www.ietf.cnri.reston.va.us/ids.by.wg/uri.html*>. The archive site for the e-mail discussion of URIs is <*http://www.acl.lanl.gov/URI/archive/uri-archive.index.html*>.

URN (Uniform Resource Name). URNs provide a way to specify a resource without specifying the computer host (site) on which it resides. A URN server would take a given URN and look up the closest site that has that resource. That is, if a document proves extremely popular, many sites around the world might maintain a copy, and the URN server would list all of them.

URC (Uniform Resource Characteristic). URCs provide meta-information about documents and resources specified by using URLs and URNs. This meta-information might include owner, encoding, access restrictions, cost, language, and location. Having a clearly defined way to store information about a document can be crucial to being able to retrieve documents that match your search criteria. See <*http://www.acl.lanl.gov/URI/urc_draft.txt*> for the URC draft specification.

URA (Uniform Resource Agent). URAs refer to agents that would be programmed to work within our computers to do certain types of searches on the Internet. For example, a URA might be defined to do a "person search" using existing (free) Internet search services, such as Netfind <*http://www.rpi.edu/Internet/Guides/decemj/itools/nir-utilities-netfind.html*> and Whois <*http://www.rpi.edu/Internet/Guides/decemj/itools/nir-utilities-whois.html*> to find a long-lost friend who might be online. The user needs to know nothing more than that this URA is designed to find people. If in the future another type of person-searching service develops, scripts that interact with it could be added to the person-search URA. Bunyip Information Systems is developing a proof-of-concept (or demonstration) model of this, called the Internet Resource Discovery Client <*http://services.bunyip.com:8000/products/client/client.html*>, to show that it works. The link to the IETF working group's draft description of URAs is <*http://services.bunyip.com:8000/products/client/draft-ietf-uri-ura-00.txt*>.

Developing the URA is important because it could become a building block for more sophisticated tools that could make finding information on the Internet less of a hit-or-miss process. This area of software development would enhance the abilities of Internet clients like Netscape and Mosaic browsers.

Common Client Interface

Common Client Interface (CCI) is the converse of the already-established Common Gateway Interface (CGI) that provides for scripting or programming links behind the scenes on WWW (and now Gopher) servers. CCI would lead to programs that control Web clients. For example, you might have a program that starts your WWW browser 30 minutes before you get to work each morning and does a standard set of searches for news and information pertinent to your interests. The program would control the Web browser through the CCI. When you arrived at work, your computer would have a list of pertinent documents waiting for you.

WWW Client-Pull and Server-Push

Two new innovations from Netscape include Client-Pull and Server-Push scripting in HTML. Client-Pull allows WWW browsers to download an HTML document and then go back repeatedly (with no command from the user) to download a particular document, image, or resource from that same server. The inverse of this is Server-Push, which requires the HTTP server to keep the connection open and to send updates at certain intervals to the Web client. One application might be a stock market service that constantly updates stock prices and downloads them to the Web browser, with no action on the user's part.

Hot Java from Sun

Java is a new programming language developed over the last several years by Sun Microsystems as an improvement on the C++ language. Hot Java takes this language and puts it into a Web browser so that it understands (or interprets) programs written in the Java language. Once you have the two together (Hot Java in the browser and Java programs on the server), a Web publisher could create a special program (or "applet," as Sun calls them) in the Java language that would be *immediately available* to all Hot Java–compatible Web browsers. Hot Java is significant because it opens the door to an amazing amount of innovation and flexibility. For example, if someone wants to develop a utility for users of her Web site, she can write it in Java; users with a Hot Java–compliant browser could automatically download the program and run it on their machine. The obvious concern of controlling against viruses and other destructive software is said to be handled through extensive safeguards. Sun has released a beta version for X-Windows and is porting it to Macintosh and Windows. Hot Java is adding quite a bit of excitement to the WWW development world because of the opportunities it offers. Find out more about Hot Java at <***http://www.sun.com***>.

WebForce

Silicon Graphics, Inc. (SGI), is starting to bundle Netscape's Commerce Server, WebMagic Author WYSIWYG HTML Editor, and an enhanced Netscape Web browser with a new line of SGI workstations. The bundle provides turnkey, or right off the shelf, entry to Web publishing. Makers of other platforms are likely to do the same almost immediately. This development could mean that publishing on the Web is as easy as browsing it, if you buy one of these new machines.

Bundling HTTP and other Internet server software with some workstations and PCs is a trend that signals that Internet publishing has arrived. As bundles become a standard feature, administering a Web site will only get easier.

Oracle World-Wide Web Interface Kit

Oracle, the leading database server company (for UNIX, Netware, Windows NT, and OS/2), is offering the World-Wide Web Interface Kit—at no charge. Oracle has a clear fix on the relationship between information stored in databases and publishing on the Internet. Its whole approach is to show how you can easily put your Oracle database on the Internet.

Web Mail

The goal of the Web Mail project, partially sponsored by the Open Software Foundation Research Institute, <***http://www.osf.org/RI/***>, is to seamlessly integrate mail processing and the Web browsing environment. The idea is to be able to access e-mail with all the normal e-mail functions—reply, delete, forward, and so on—while browsing the Web. In addition, the project also wants to devise a way to give you Web access to your store of archived e-mail without forcing you to convert it to HTML. One exciting result of this project might be to make it possible to control your e-mail archives through Web browsers, which are usually able only to read (or browse) archives. For more information on Web Mail see <***http://riwww.osf.org:8001/www/webmail/***>.

Speeding Up the HTTP Protocol

Latency refers to the interval between a request for a document and when you can retrieve it. Latency is a problem on the Web, and how to solve it is being researched. Simon Spero, a WWW researcher and developer, presented a paper on latency at the second International WWW Conference in Chicago. The basic complaint seems to be that because each document usually contains inline images, all of which are retrieved separately, telephone costs mount because of the delays resulting from the numerous reopenings of new connections to the server. If the images and documents all were sent together, those extra connections wouldn't be necessary. Spero's paper is located at <*http://www.spyglass.com/techreport/six/developers_tech_doc6.html*>.

Another paper, by Venkata N. Padmanabhan, of the University of California at Berkeley, and Jeffrey C. Mogul, of Digital Equipment Corporation's Western Research Laboratory, describes these problems, methods they devised for resolving them, and statistics showing how their methods improve speed. They suggest including in HTTP a GETALL function that would retrieve a document and all its inline images in one connection. If it works as billed, we can look forward to improvements in speed and access, even without improvements in Internet bandwidth. Their paper can be found at <*http://www.spyglass.com/six/developers_tech_doc5.html*>.

WAIS and Z39.50

According to a company representative, WAIS, Inc., is considering making a free version of its $15,000 commercial WAIS server product available for downloading from its Web site <*http://www.wais.com/*> sometime in mid- to late 1995. It probably would be limited to indexing files of 10MB or less, but otherwise it would have all the features of the commercial WAIS server 2.1, which is Z39.50-V2 compliant. This would be a big improvement for the low-end Internet publisher who wants to do full-text searching.

Z39.50-1995 (version 3) was approved at the end of 1994 and should become final in 1995, hence the name. This means that an international protocol has been established for highly sophisticated information retrieval systems. Internet publishers who want to do really powerful search and retrieval should plan to become Z39.50-1995 compliant. For more information on Z39.50 applications and WWW to Z39.50 Gateways, see Table 5–1. The U.S. Library of Congress, AT&T, the British Library, Chemical Abstracts Service, European Space Agency, Knight-Ridder Information, Inc.,

LEXIS/NEXIS, and MIT Information Systems are developing or using Z39.50 in their applications.

Commerce

Commerce on the Internet is alternately seen as its salvation and its destruction. Some have expressed the viewpoint that until commercial services and content arrive on the Internet, "nothing of value" will be available. That point of view ignores the cooperative work that's being done and the real virtue of the Internet, access to millions of people all over the world.

I think that commercial activity on the Internet will take two major forms. One form involves items or information being bought and sold, and the other involves items or information exchanged at no cost in indirect support of a company's business. Given the public relations, advertising, focus group, and customer support aspects of modern business, the Internet provides an excellent medium in which to conduct these activities.

Recent developments in the areas of digital signatures, digital watermarks, document coding, and digital cash are going to make it easier to do business on the Internet.

In March 1995 Utah passed a law making digital signatures legally binding, and the states of California and Washington are said to be considering similar legislation. This movement removes one hurdle for commerce on the Internet. The law in Utah is based on public key encryption and requires certification authorities to register with the state. The law is designed to allow the transmission of court documents.

Digital watermarks consist of an image or piece of text married to a graphic file in such a way that it can be used to identify the owner of the image. If the image is visible, it might deter unauthorized reproduction. If it is invisible until processed in a specific way, it could be used to detect unauthorized reproduction. Systems Research and Applications Corporation (SRA) of Arlington, Virginia, has applied for a patent on a technique it developed and calls Imprint™ that is being used by large online publishers of digital photos.

Imprint runs on a Macintosh and marries a company logo or other image file in PICT format to a TIFF image file. The TIFF image file can later be converted to other formats without losing the watermark. The intensity, or "strength," of the watermark can be varied from blatantly obvious to almost invisible. The watermark becomes apparent during color separation. Placement and the color of the watermark are two other variables in the Imprint software (see Figure 11–1). The technique can also be used on black and white images. For further information contact Anirudh Kulkarni, director, Media Systems Initiative, SRA, via e-mail at anirudh_kulkarni @sra.com or at 703-803-1883 (voice).

AT&T has been researching the encoding of small amounts of information (four binary digits) in formatted text. *Formatted* in this case

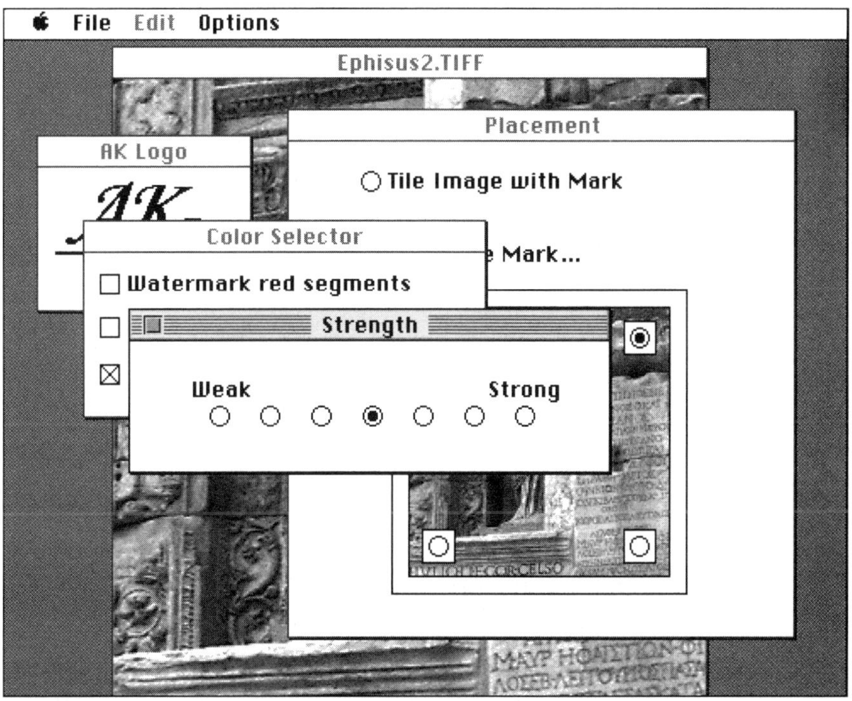

FIGURE 11–1 Imprint™ Watermark Software (Reprinted with permission from SRA Corp., Arlington, Virginia.)

means that the text is in either an image file or in a format description language such as PostScript, TeX, or troff. The encoding techniques include shifting lines of text, shifting the position of words, and altering the features of certain letters or fonts. AT&T's goal is to ensure that the encoded information is retrievable even after it has been photocopied several times. <***http://www.research.att.com/#docmark***>

Popularization and trust of digital cash and other electronic payment systems are essential for large-scale purchasing over the Internet. These payment systems are becoming available, and trust is starting to build. It's quite likely that 1996 will see the arrival of many more sites with something to sell and that they will accept electronic payment of some sort.

Publishing Issues

Subscribing to academic journals is becoming increasingly expensive, and many university libraries are unable to maintain the wide variety of subscriptions their faculty demands. As the financial stability of these journals weakens, online publishing will become increasingly attractive, as it has in the last few years in some disciplines. The desktop publishing technology many of these publications use is easily transferable to Internet publishing techniques. Many have small circulations, and they often can reach their audience more easily and less expensively through the Internet. The delay caused by peer review has led to extensive publishing of preprints in some academic disciplines. High energy physics is one field that has come to rely on Internet distribution of research papers. Other disciplines have taken note. The *Journal of Medical Imaging* is a demonstration of this concept. <***http://www.umds.ac.uk/JMI/ejourn.html***>

Seals of APproval (SOAP) is a system under discussion that online academic journals might use to give their "seal of approval" to particular journal articles or documents to show that they have passed a peer-review process. The actual seal would be some sort of digital signature using public key encryption.

Academic journals are not the only ones going online. 'Zines (short for electronic magazines) have exploded. Many are free, and some will experiment with charging for part or all of their issues.

Sometime in 1996 or shortly thereafter you will find it possible to move documents directly from your word processor to an Internet server format such as HTML, PDF, ASCII, or PostScript. Organizing the content and maintaining links will continue to be labor intensive, but that load will increasingly be spread among the actual producers of the documents as well as increasingly sophisticated data librarians.

Several U.S. newspapers, including the *Los Angeles Times,* the *New York Times* <***http://nytmesFax.com/***>, and the *San Jose Mercury News* <***http://www.sjmercury.com/***>, have begun to offer online editions of some sort. The *Los Angeles Times* puts its version on Prodigy. The *New York Times* offers an Internet version of the paper in Acrobat PDF. And the *San Jose Mercury News* offers news summaries and updates throughout the day as well as all its classified ads. Full news stories and archives are available for a $5 monthly fee. All offer hypertext links of some sort that can make reading a newspaper online a very different experience. Journalists already have access to a wealth of online information, and newspapers may link their online stories to related stories in their archives. The problem of rising newsprint prices also will affect what newspapers do. Because online publication means that stories could include video and sound, editors will have more options in stories they put online, although newspapers are still trying to learn how to make money this way. The *New York Times* online is free but carries advertising and requires that you register.

Political and Social Issues

The rise of a completely new, extremely powerful, and far-reaching communication tool is bound to raise political and social issues. The international scope of the Internet adds to the implications.

Many parents, educators, and politicians are concerned about the lack of safeguards to what children may encounter on the Internet. Pornography, enticement by pedophiles, and bomb-making instructions are listed among the potential dangers to children using the Internet. Federal legislation that would make distribution of such material a crime was approved by the U.S. Senate in 1995 as an addendum to the telecommunications deregulation bill. The bill as written was so broad that enforcement would be difficult and threatened a huge censoring effect on Internet publishing. Yet it would have little effect on what comes to the United States over the Internet from other countries. Another problem inherent in such legislation is the application of moral standards from one area to another as the Internet makes geography less of a factor.

Another approach to safeguarding children is to develop restricted access systems that can reach only certain limited (pre-approved) sites or newsgroups. Although commercial servers will almost certainly take this approach, it requires a body that would approve sites for the rest of the Internet. The sites would be left with the problem of checking all their material—wading through an unimaginable amount of material and then filtering all new material the same way. The sheer volume of Usenet News prohibits this unless it's done with some sort of computerized filter. Even so, a site approved for children could add something unseemly later.

Someone may be able to develop a set of Internet tools for limiting access to a certain range of "approved" servers and refuse to link to servers that are not on the list. (This might work as the inverse of the security scheme common on servers that already restrict access to certain servers or Internet subdomains. A restricting mechanism might be built into clients.)

Some critics of these solutions reason that free speech brings with it risks and responsibilities. They argue that parents are the rightful monitors of what their children have access to. Part of the problem is what children might find accidentally; another concern is that children will actively search out forbidden material.

If limiting software is developed, organizations might offer a highly controlled (censored) subset of Internet resources to their users. This has its own risks, even if the censors are monitored.

The next few years will see many and varied solutions to these problems. One can only hope that the solutions allow access to all that is useful and educational on the Internet.

Another problem is who defines what is appropriate? Because almost anyone with Internet access and a computer can publish on the Internet, I think everyone will have to define his own standard. What people post and the items on other servers to which they link will reflect their standards and values and may or may not be appropriate for their audience. Perhaps it will become commonplace to state somewhere on a server exactly who the server is designed for.

The other immediate political problem on the Internet is encryption and who has access to it. Encryption technology is the key to many of the fee-charging systems in use or under development. However, a huge impediment is the U.S. government's ban on the exportation of this technology. The United States considers encryption technology a matter of national security. Although some efforts are being made to change this policy, other countries have even stricter laws concerning the use of encryption techniques. France has made use of unapproved encryption techniques illegal. Other governments are apt to have similar, if not more severe, restrictions.

The movement to make the Internet and its resources available to all is strong. In many cases that requires that a country first acquire sufficient technology and infrastructure to gain access and take advantage of the Internet. In the United States the debate centers on whether the government should license commercial Internet and telecommunications providers, requiring them to connect and provide a certain minimum level of service to all schools and libraries in their communities in exchange for licenses. None of these issues is easily resolved, and you should expect to hear a great deal of discussion about subsidized access.

Even as some people argue about censorship and whether to license commercial gateways to the Internet, others are worrying that the

Internet, like television before it, will lead to the "dumbing down" of society. These critics point out that because abstracts are much easier to distribute and archive on the Internet than full text of articles and books, reading the abstract of an article will begin to replace the reading of the full text. But the popularity of Project Gutenberg and its massive effort to publish the full text of works of literature (described in Chapter 10) is eloquent testimony that the Internet is unlikely to carry television's baggage.

I think the Internet will increase the level of exposure to high culture, the cultures of other countries, and different points of view. My hope is that the profusion of varied points of view on the Internet will be greeted enthusiastically by the majority.

Conclusion

No one book can cover all the technical, philosophical, social, and legal aspects of publishing on the Internet. As I review what I have written, I find many more issues and techniques that I would like to discuss. But as my seven-year old daughter Riley said, "Just stop writing and tell them, 'And that's how it ends.'" Given the amazing rate at which Internet publishing techniques are evolving, and that your next step should be to explore these resources on the Internet, I'd have to paraphrase her. That's how it begins.

Resources

Aronson, Larry. *HTML Manual of Style*. Emeryville, Calif.: Ziff-Davis Press, 1994.

Berners-Lee, Tim, Robert Cailliau, Ari Luotonen, Henrik Frystyk Nielsen, and Arthur Secret. "The World-Wide Web." *Communications of the ACM (Association for Computing Machinery)* 37, 8 (August 1994): 76–82.

Cavazos, Edward A., and Gavino Morin. *Cyberspace and the Law: Your Rights and Duties in the On-Line World.* Cambridge, Mass.: MIT Press, 1994.

Chandler, David M., with Bill Kirkner, and Jim Minatel. *Running a Perfect Web Site.* Indianapolis: Que, 1995.

Cheswick, William R., and Steven M. Bellovin. *Firewalls and Internet Security: Repelling the Wily Hacker.* Reading, Mass.: Addison-Wesley, 1994.

December, John, and Neil Randall. *The World-Wide Web Unleashed.* Indianapolis, Ind.: Sams Publishing, 1994.

Ellsworth, Jill H., and Matthew V. Ellsworth. *The Internet Business Book.* New York: Wiley, 1994.

Ford, Andrew. *Spinning the Web: How to Provide Information on the Internet.* London: International Thomson Publishing, 1995.

Harris, Lesley Ellen. *Canadian Copyright Law,* Second Edition. Ontario, Canada: McGraw-Hill Ryerson Limited, 1995.

Krol, Ed. *The Whole Internet User's Guide and Catalog,* 2d ed. Sebastopol, Calif.: O'Reilly and Associates, 1994.

Lemay, Laura. *Teach Yourself Web Publishing with HTML in a Week.* Indianapolis, Ind.: Sams Publishing, 1995.

Liu, Cricket, Jerry Peek, Russ Jones, Bryan Buus, and Adrian Nye. *Managing Internet Information Services.* Sebastopol, Calif.: O'Reilly and Associates, 1994.

Net. Genesis, and Devra Hall. *Build a Web Site: The Programmer's Guide to Creating, Building, and Maintaining a Web Presence.* Rocklin, Calif.: Prima Publishing, 1995.

Quinn, Christine A. "From Grass Roots to Corporate Image—The Maturation of the Web" (1994). Available from *<http://www.ncsa.uiuc.edu/SDG/IT94/Proceedings/Campus.Infosys/quinn/quinn.html>;* Internet.

Sams Publishing. *The Internet Unleashed.* Indianapolis, Ind.: Sams Publishing, 1994.

Strangelove, Michael, and Aneurin Bosley. *Advertising on the Internet.* Ottawa: Strangelove Internet Enterprises, 1994. Available from *<http://www.phoenix.ca/sie/howto.html>;* Internet.

Wiggins, Richard W. *The Internet for Everyone: A Guide for Users and Providers.* New York: McGraw-Hill, 1995.

Glossary

Administrator The person responsible for a system or server. This person usually has special rights and privileges in order to make system changes and improvements. WWW, Gopher, and WAIS servers all need some sort of administrator. UNIX administrators are known to talk to God.

Anonymous FTP An agreed-upon method of letting anyone on the Internet download files from an FTP server by using a login ID of *anonymous* and a password of the user's e-mail address. See FTP.

Archie A program that collects and indexes information on the contents of anonymous FTP servers across the Internet.

ASK block Online forms capability of Gopher+; users can fill in blanks on a form on their computer screen and then submit that information for processing by the Gopher+ server.

Authentication The process by which one computer system confirms that the user is exactly who she claims to be, with all the rights to the bank accounts and computer accounts that go with that identification. The authentication process might be a lightweight one, which is susceptible to sophisticated attacks, or a heavyweight one, such as Kerberos. Authentication is seen as one of the main areas necessary for development of commerce on the Internet and Gopher and WWW servers.

Boolean searching Refers to the use of the logic of Boolean algebra for searching, or the ability to search for one item AND another item OR one item AND NOT another, and so on. As you can imagine, without this feature only the most limited types of word searching are possible.

Browser A software program that assists in exploring the Internet by following links between documents on the same or different computers. The most common browsers are for Gopher and WWW. WWW browsers can look at Gopher servers, but Gopher browsers can't read WWW servers yet. NCSA Mosaic is one of the most famous WWW browsers, credited with being the "killer app" of the Internet.

Cache Gopher, WWW, and other types of servers temporarily store frequently accessed files in cache, a place in memory (which is faster than the hard disk), so that the next time those files are requested, they'll be sent out faster.

Cache time The amount of time a Gopher or WWW server will trust that the cached version of a document is current and hasn't been changed. *See* cache.

CGI (Common Gateway Interface) Allows programming or scripting languages to be used with Gopher and WWW servers to perform such special functions as searches, calculations, and adding user information to a database.

Clickable image A WWW feature that allows users to click (using their mouse) on different locations in an image (such as a map) downloaded to their Web browser. Then the x-y coordinates of that point are sent back to the WWW server, which can then be programmed to respond with specific information depending on the location.

Client Half of the client/server combination, a client solicits information from a server according to some agreed-upon method or protocol. Internet browsing programs such as TurboGopher, NCSA Mosaic, Netscape Navigator, Cello, and Lynx are also called clients.

Client/servers Tools such as Gopher, WWW, and WAIS, used for accessing the Internet through one computer.

Common Gateway Interface *See* CGI.

Computer Services Office *See* CSO.

Copyright The legal protection of an author or creator to control the copying of their work. A copyright notice does not need to be given. Contrary to popular opinion most of what is found on the Internet has copyright protection unless explicitly stated otherwise.

CSO (Computer Services Office) Computer-resident telephone book.

Cyberspace An informal term for the online computer world in all its forms, from WWW and Gopher servers to the circuitry inside a computer.

Daemon (pronounced *demon*) An independent program or process that runs on UNIX machines with the specific goal of accomplishing a certain task. Because UNIX is a multitasking operating system, many daemons can run at the same time. For example, a Gopher server can be run as a separate program, or daemon, giving it responsibility for answering any Gopher requests sent to that machine.

Data librarian The person responsible for the content (or data) on a Gopher, WWW, or WAIS server. This does not have to be the system administrator and in fact often requires different skills, notably an extensive familiarity with the information presented on the server.

Dithering Creating the effect of additional colors in a digital image by mixing dots of existing colors in various patterns and densities. In black and white images different shades of gray are achieved by placing dots in different patterns and densities.

Domain Short for Internet domain, or domain name, a specified set of Internet addresses or computer host names. Domains are used to break the Internet into manageable parts, either in groups of computer hosts or in IP addresses. Your computer doesn't have to know exactly where the other computer is, it just has to get your computer to that domain, where a "domain name server" will know where to go next. Top-level U.S. Internet domains include com (commercial), gov (governmental), edu (educational), mil (military), and org (organizational). Also, other countries use a two-letter country code as a top-level domain: .fr (France), .tw (Taiwan), and .br (Brazil).

E-mail list server A computer program that performs the functions of an electronic mailing list. E-mail messages sent to a listserver address are automatically forwarded to all members of the list. These lists can be open (anyone with an e-mail account on the Internet can submit messages), closed (only the members of the list can submit messages), and moderated (all messages are checked by a moderator before they are sent on to everyone on the list).

External indexer A program from a site on the Internet that collects and indexes Internet information, usually Gopher, WWW, WAIS, and FTP sites. Users can then check with these indexing programs for items of interest by doing word searches.

FAQ (Frequently Asked Questions) file An Internet custom; the answers to common questions about a given subject are collected and stored in a file or files. These FAQ files are then made prominently available on the Internet so that newcomers won't repeatedly flood newsgroups and mailing lists with the same questions.

Fielded searching A type of searching that specifies that the search term can be found in a certain area, or field, of the source material. For example, if you search for a particular title or author in an electronic card catalog, you are doing a fielded search.

File Transfer Protocol *See* FTP.

Filter A program that lets certain information pass and stops or alters other information. For example, filters could be used to convert all the word-processing codes in a document into HTML codes.

Finger A program that provides simple information (such as a person's full name and last login time) for a user on a UNIX system.

Finger daemon The program that runs independently on a UNIX system to return user information on request.

Firewall A computer that acts as gatekeeper between an internal network's computers and the rest of the Internet. Firewall machines prevent direct connection to the internal computers and instead relay messages and services, thereby providing an extremely high measure of security. For more detail see William R. Cheswick and Steven M. Bellovin, *Firewalls and Internet Security: Repelling the Wily Hacker* (Addison-Wesley, 1994).

freeWAIS The unsupported free version of WAIS software.

freeWAIS-sf An extension of the freeWAIS software that allows searchable fields. It was developed in Germany at the University of Dortmund.

Frequently Asked Questions file *See* FAQ.

FTP (File Transfer Protocol) An Internet protocol (or method) for transferring files from one computer system to another, usually with simple put and get commands.

FTP server A program that runs on a computer to allow it to answer FTP requests and transfer files between computers. See File Transfer Protocol.

Full-text indexing Uses every word in a file when creating a searchable index for that file. In that way, those searching for information in that file will not be limited to certain key words but will be able to call up the file by matching any of the words used in the file.

GN A combination Gopher and HTTP (WWW) server that allows you to serve data to both Gopher and WWW browsers from one source.

GNU Stands for "GNU's Not UNIX" and is a free version of UNIX developed by the Free Software Foundation.

Gopher The menu-oriented data transfer protocol invented at the University of Minnesota. It has since spread to more than 7,000 sites worldwide. See Chapter 3.

Gopher data directory The area on a Gopher server that holds the information being stored on that server.

Gopher+ An elaboration of the Gopher protocol that allows for such features as presenting different views of the same file and forms for asking questions and recording the answers on a Gopher server. See Chapter 3.

Gopherspace Term used to denote either the entirety of all Gopher servers in the world or one Gopher server's section of it.

Harvester A program designed to go out and retrieve information or files from Internet servers, usually for indexing in a central database such as Archie, Veronica, or Lycos.

Home page A spot on a WWW server that is specific to a person, business, or subject. It's usually the starting point for more information in that area. An individual's home page might include a photo of that person, a short biography, some favorite quotes, and links to favorite Internet sites.

Host name The name for a computer, or host, on the Internet. The name is supposed to be easier to remember than that computer's IP address. The host name is always a member of a large domain, or collection of hosts. For example, the domain edu stands for educational hosts (computers) in the United States.

HTML (HyperText Markup Language) The set of codes and structure that defines documents served up on the World-Wide Web. See Chapter 4.

HTTP (HyperText Transfer Protocol) The method used to transfer information between World-Wide Web clients and servers across the Internet. Clients are also called browsers, which are programs such as Mosaic, Netscape, and Lynx.

HTTPD (HyperText Transfer Protocol Daemon) Server software for WWW or Web servers. Technically, WWW servers should be called HTTP servers.

Hyper-G A program from Austria designed to improve on the WWW. See Chapter 6 or *<http://hgiicm.tu-graz.ac.at/>*.

Hypertext Text that contains links to other text, programs, sound, picture, or movie files. You don't read the text straight through; instead, you read along and follow the links that most interest you.

HyperText Markup Language *See* HTML.

HyperText Transfer Protocol *See* HTTP.

HyperText Transfer Protocol Daemon *See* HTTPD.

IIF (Interactive Image Format) This is a system similar to WWW clickable images, (see clickable images) that gives immediate feedback to the user as they move their mouse across an image. It was originally designed as for Gopher browsers by the Weather Underground project at the University of Michigan. Now it is being adapted for WWW browsers as well. See *<http://cirrus.sprl.umich.edu/>*.

Inetd (Internet daemon) A special UNIX facility that listens for Internet requests and starts up designated programs in response.

Inline images A feature of WWW servers that allows images to be embedded in text and transferred whenever that document is requested. The embedded images are called inline images.

Interactive Image Format *See* IIF.

Internet daemon *See* Inetd.

Kerberos A security system developed at MIT that authenticates or verifies the user's identity. Once the ID is authenticated, it is used throughout the session.

Latency The delay between a request for data and the response, in other words, the waiting time.

Link A link is an address pointing to information on the Internet. Usually, links are in the form of URLs (Uniform Resource Locators), which were created along with WWW as a means of codifying all the pertinent information needed to locate something on the Internet.

List server or listserv A program that runs an e-mail mailing list. A message sent to the mailing list is relayed to everyone else on the list, whether they know each other or not. See e-mail listserv.

Meta-information Information about an object, such as its date, author, or language. The ability to store meta-information on a Gopher, WWW, or WAIS server might allow searching for items in a certain language or for items more recent than a certain date.

Metaphor Use of some commonly understood object or process to explain the workings or organization of another. For example, Usenet News is often described in terms of a river of information that you fish in to find what you want. The messages will be gone in a few days, replaced by new messages, flowing by as constantly as the water in a river.

MIME (Multipurpose Internet Mail Extensions) Extensions that add the capability of sending mixed media (audio, video, and binary files) in Internet mail. Mail systems that can handle these extensions are called *MIME enabled*.

Mirror Usually used in the sense of duplicating another site's service or archives in order to lessen the load on that server and widen the accessibility of the information.

MOO (Multiple User System, Object Oriented) Designates a space on the Internet where people can come together to create and manipulate an imaginary environment. The objects one person creates can be used and shared by other people.

MUD (Multiple User Dungeon [or Dimension or Dialog]) Artificial worlds often with role-playing games attached; individuals login through the Internet and join in an online game or activity.

Multiple User Dungeon (or Dimension or Dialog) *See* MUD.

Multiple User System, Object Oriented *See* MOO.

Multipurpose Internet Mail Extensions *See* MIME.

Natural language query A request for information (or query) that can be written in human languages such as English or French. An example of a natural language query would be, Why is the sky blue? Generally, it is difficult for the computer to understand the full semantic meaning of natural language, but it is the goal of many search systems.

Network Information Center *See* NIC.

Newsgroup A subject area in the Usenet News system.

NIC (Network Information Center) A site that maintains information about a particular network. This might include host and domain names only, or cabling, service charges, technical and administrative support staff, and other data.

Parser A program that breaks a statement into its syntactical elements. This might be a natural language parser, or a special purpose parser to deal with specific computer languages or instructions.

PDF (Portable Document Format) A formatting language from Adobe Systems, Inc., that allows documents to be displayed identically on completely different types of computers. PDF viewers are available for Windows and Macintosh.

Perl A free programming language often used in UNIX but available for Macintosh and DOS as well. Many Gopher and WWW CGI scripts are written in Perl because it is particularly good at text manipulation.

Port *(noun)* Ports of call, a feature of the UNIX operating system, that give a machine different access points (ports) that can be designated for specific purposes. The standard ports for Gopher, WWW, and WAIS, for example, are Gopher–port 70, WWW–port 80, and Z39.50 port 210 for WAIS.

Port *(verb)* To port a program to another operating system or machine means to convert the program so that it will run on a completely different type of machine. *Port* in this usage descends from *transport.*

Portable Document Format *See* PDF.

Private key encryption Refers to a message encoded with a special code number called a private key, which is given to whoever needs to decode the message. It is much faster than public key cryptography but requires absolute security in the transport of the private key to the recipient. Private key encryption is often used with public key encryption to solve this problem.

Process On UNIX systems, a process is a program that once started keeps running until either it is killed or it finishes its job.

Prospero A special type of file system developed at University of Southern California's Institute for Scientific Information. It is the basis for some large Gopher servers, including America Online's.

Protocol A specific language that has been developed to coordinate a certain task between different machines or programs. The language is usually limited and only concerns itself with the task it wants to accomplish. It specifies all the parts of the "conversation" that will take place. For example, a mail transfer protocol might start out with machine A contacting machine B by saying HELLO, I HAVE A MESSAGE FOR YOU. Machine B might then reply either, GO AHEAD AND SEND THE MESSAGE, or COME BACK LATER, I'M BUSY. The protocol would specify exactly how the conversation should go, and programmers would later be responsible for writing programs that comply with the protocol. This permits exchanges between machines of different types.

Proxy server A server that stands in (acts as a proxy) for another server so as to protect it from unwanted intrusion via the Internet. Requests for information by the hidden machine are sent out as if they came from the proxy server.

Public key encryption Refers to a message that has been encoded in such a way that it has both a public and a private key. Messages encrypted with the private key can only be decrypted with the public key, and messages encrypted with the public key can only be decrypted with the private key. The private key is kept hidden by the owner. The public key is distributed widely and registered with certifying authorities. These are used in different combinations as well as with private key encryption to keep messages private and to transmit digital signatures, which identify the sender.

Redirection A method of sending the output from one program to some place other than where it would normally go. It could apply to printer output, which might go to a network printer instead of the printer attached directly to a computer. Some Gopher and WWW servers allow requests for information in one directory or area to be redirected to a different area.

Regular expression A standard UNIX method for specifying a pattern of text. It is a flexible pattern-matching system that is used by many UNIX commands.

Relevance feedback A term used in WAIS searching to describe using the first batch of information it returns to refine your search.

Request for Comment *See* RFC.

RFC (Request for Comment) An agreed-upon method of formalizing new protocols, programs, or services (or ideas for same) on the Internet. The information is put in a plain-text document that is made available across the Internet. Interested parties then provide feedback or test out the concepts in the RFC. Software programs are designed to conform to the protocols as expressed in particular RFCs. In this way computer programs from different companies can work interchangeably because they all conform to the same RFC standard.

Scale *(as in "doesn't scale well")* A term that refers to numbers of users and how well a computer tool performs as more and more people use it. Something that works for 100 users may not work as well if expanded (or scaled up) to 1,000 or 1 million users. Scalability is a common concern, given the extremely rapid growth of the Internet.

Script A collection of commands saved in a file for later execution.

Server Half of the client-server combination, a server provides information on request from client programs or computers. Setting up Internet servers is what Internet publishing is all about.

SGML (Standard Generalized Markup Language) A text markup system for both print and online publication. HTML is an application of SGML for the special purpose of hypertext publishing on the World-Wide Web.

Shell scripts A series of UNIX commands saved into a file. Executing the file is the same as running each command in order. UNIX shell scripts are similar to DOS batch files but much more powerful.

Simple Mail Transfer Protocol *See* SMTP.

Site A computer offering a Gopher, WWW, WAIS, or some other Internet service.

SMTP (Simple Mail Transfer Protocol) is a method of exchanging e-mail on the Internet.

SQL (Structured Query Language) database Database designed so that requests for information from the database can be made in a common language.

Standalone A program that runs on its own once it has been started. On UNIX systems WWW, Gopher, and WAIS servers run in standalone mode always there and waiting for requests to come in.

Standard Generalized Markup Language *See* SGML.

Stemming Shortening of every word in a search or query to its stem. For example, the stem *airplane* would retrieve both *airplane* and *airplanes,* and *socio* would find both *sociology* and *sociologist.*

Structured field Containers for certain types of information, such as title, author, date, and other data.

Structured field searching *See* fielded searching.

Structured Query Language database *See* SQL database.

System administrator *See* administrator.

Tagged Image File Format *See* TIFF.

Tar a UNIX program that combines files and subdirectories in one file for easy transport. The encoding .tar is added to the filename.

TCP/IP (Transport Control Protocol and Internet Protocol) Two protocols that form the basis or building blocks for Internet communication as we know it. There are other low-level protocols, but TCP/IP is considered a reliable transport protocol because it guarantees that all the packets (parts) in a message will get through.

TIFF (Tagged Image File Format) A method for storing images in digital form. It's widely used but not supported for inline images by WWW browsers. Add-on viewer programs are usually used in combination to view TIFF files.

Time zone A geographic area that measures its time as a certain number of hours behind or ahead of Greenwich Mean Time, the time in Greenwich, England.

Transport Control Protocol and Internet Protocol *See* TCP/IP.

Uniform Resource Locator *See* URL.

UNIX An operating system originally developed by AT&T and then released to the academic community for use in the public domain. Student programmers then added many options and tools, creating an extremely flexible, powerful, and cryptic operating system. Among other features, UNIX is multitasking many programs can be run at the same time, even by the same user. UNIX is the preferred operating system for development of Gopher, WWW, and WAIS server software.

URL (Uniform Resource Locator) A system for identifying where a particular resource (document, data, image, sound) is located on the Internet. URLs specify the host computer as well as the type of protocol and the directory and file name to be retrieved.

Usenet News An Internet system or protocol for exchanging messages on particular subjects. It is similar to e-mail except that the messages do not pile up in your mailbox.

Veronica A program designed at the University of Nevada at Reno to collect and index the menus and contents of Gopher servers all across the Internet. Users searching Veronica servers will receive a Gopher menu made up of links to the pertinent Gopher servers and files that match the request.

Virtual An adjective used in the computer world to refer to something simulated. For example, virtual memory uses a hard drive to simulate RAM or regular memory.

W3O (World-Wide Web Organization) A joint effort of MIT in Boston and CERN in Switzerland that addresses the editing of standards and the writing of reference code. It will define conformance levels for WWW-related protocols.

WAIS (Wide Area Information Server) An indexing and search and retrieval protocol that has both commercial and freeware versions. It is commonly used as the "back end," or indexing engine, for Gopher and WWW servers.

Wide Area Information Server *See* WAIS.

World-Wide Web *See* WWW.

World-Wide Web Organization *See* W3O.

WWW (World-Wide Web) Also known as W3 and the Web and originally created by Tim Berners-Lee at CERN in Switzerland as a hypertext method for physicists to share research documents. See Chapter 4.

Z39.50 An international protocol for information retrieval. In other words, it describes methods for exchanging information between separate computers. See Chapter 5.

ZDist A free program developed to query Z39.50 databases. See Chapter 5.

Index

G

I

J

K

L

V

W

X

Y

Z